JOURNEYMEN IN MURDER

JOURNEYMEN IN MURDER

*The Assassin
in English
Renaissance Drama*

MARTIN WIGGINS

CLARENDON PRESS · OXFORD
1991

Oxford University Press, Walton Street, Oxford OX2 6DP

Oxford New York Toronto
Delhi Bombay Calcutta Madras Karachi
Petaling Jaya Singapore Hong Kong Tokyo
Nairobi Dar es Salaam Cape Town
Melbourne Auckland

and associated companies in
Berlin Ibadan

Oxford is a trade mark of Oxford University Press

Published in the United States
by Oxford University Press, New York

British Library Cataloguing in Publication Data
Data available

Library of Congress Cataloging in Publication Data
Wiggins, Martin.
Journeymen in murder: the assassin in English Renaissance drama/
Martin Wiggins.
Includes bibliographical references and index.
1. English drama—Early modern and Elizabethan, 1500–1600—History
and criticism. 2. English drama—17th century—History and
criticism. 3. Assassins in literature. 4. Murder in literature.
I. Title.
PR658.A77W5 1991
822'.3093520692—dc20 91–3679
ISBN 0–19–811228–9   C C

Typeset by Butler & Tanner Ltd
Printed and bound in
Great Britain by Biddles Ltd,
Guildford and King's Lynn

6003 82314

PREFACE AND ACKNOWLEDGEMENTS

ENGLISH drama had assassins before the English language had the word
'assassin'. Imported, probably from French, at the end of the sixteenth
century, the word came with attendant complications that I had better banish
at the outset. From the seventeenth century to the twentieth, it has had
several interrelated meanings, contaminating one another and usually not
distinguished in dictionaries: it can refer to a suborned murderer, a political
murderer, and, particularly in French usage, simply an especially opprobrious
murderer. Except where obvious from the context, throughout this book I
use 'assassin' in the first sense: the other types of assassin are, in themselves,
only peripherally relevant to my subject, the suborned murderer.

Another possible misapprehension is that this is a book about the henchman or 'tool-villain'. There is certainly some overlap with my subject: several
of the more important characters I shall be discussing are sometimes classified
as 'tool-villains', and some of my points could also be made apropos of
henchmen. However, there is a difference between a villain's using a man as
an assassin, to take the dirty work off his hands, and his using him as an
accomplice, to act as an extra pair of hands. The former relationship not
only offers more dramatic possibilities, but also was of particular interest to
the English Renaissance mind, for a variety of reasons that I shall discuss.
This study accordingly has different bounds from those that critical tradition
might prescribe.

Since I am concerned with the development of a character type across a
long period, the dating and chronology of plays is obviously important. My
assumptions are set out in Appendix A. In general, these have been guided,
though not dictated, by the second edition of the *Annals of English Drama*,
by Alfred Harbage and Samuel Schoenbaum (1964). However, the dates
assigned there are sometimes no more than rough estimates, and those
estimates can be open to question. In the study of English Renaissance
drama, supposition is apt to resolve itself into fact: the unsupported guesses
of scholars such as Fleay and Chambers have passed into tradition, and that
tradition has often influenced the editors of the *Annals*. I have reconsidered
the evidence in several cases, and assigned new dates to some plays.
Regrettably, in a work like this there can be no room to set out my reasoning
in detail; but it is hoped that the case I make in Chapter 7 for dating *The
Malcontent* 1603 rather than 1604, may stand as a representative sample.

In quotations I have silently corrected obvious misprints, expanded
common abbreviations and speech prefixes, and modernized typographical
archaisms (i/j, u/v/w, y/th). I have given translations of foreign-language

quotations, which are, wherever possible, based on those offered in the source quoted. Plays are quoted from the editions listed in the Bibliography; where no individual edition is given, the text used is that in the author's collected works; and where more than one edition is listed, reference is to the most recent, unless otherwise stated. In using The Oxford Shakespeare, I have taken the liberty of conservatism over the names Falstaff and Imogen. Regrettably, Robert Carl Johnson's critical edition of *Cambises* (Salzburg, 1975) came to my attention too late for me to be able to make use of it.

The ancestor of this book is a doctoral thesis written under the supervision of Emrys Jones; my greatest debts of gratitude are to him and to John Creaser, with whom I first studied English Renaissance drama. David Norbrook and Andrew Gurr examined the thesis and brought to my attention areas of vagueness and incoherence that have, I hope, been ironed out here. The least of Denys Potts's many kindnesses was to check my French; Christopher Smith did the same for my Latin. I am grateful to Nigel Smith and Stanley Wells, who both commented helpfully on draft versions of the text, and to the other friends and colleagues who have given me information, advice, and encouragement: Anne Barton, Susan Brock, Mark Burnett, Martin Davie, Mary Dicken, Martin Dzelzainis, Barbara Everett, Vivienne Larminie, Malcolm Parkes, Holly Snapp, the Revd F. J. Turner, SJ, and John Wilders.

Several of these people are members of Keble College, Oxford, and thanks are due to the Warden and Fellows collectively for electing me to a Junior Research Fellowship, which enabled me to undertake the last stages of the work.

I could not have written the book without the use of the Bodleian Library; and it would have been the poorer without access to the British Library, the Public Record Office, and the libraries of Mansfield College, Keble College, the Shakespeare Institute, the Oxford English and History Faculties, the Taylor Institution, and Lambeth Palace. I am obliged to the librarians and staff of them all.

Of course, though many of the people mentioned here have saved me from blunders and misjudgements, none of them is responsible for any that remain: these things of darkness I acknowledge mine.

The last word (without wrong last to be named) is for the kindness and forbearance of those of my friends who are not specialists in the period: they have had to put up with some pretty eccentric preoccupations during the gestation of this study. I owe particular debts of gratitude to Robert Fairclough and B. A. Shollock (they know what for). Jackie Marshall, especially, has helped in more ways than she realizes. The book is dedicated to them.   M.W.

Oxford,
August 1990

CONTENTS

LIST OF ABBREVIATIONS

Bentley   Gerald Eades Bentley, *The Jacobean and Caroline Stage*, 7 vols.
                 (Oxford, 1941–68)
Bullough   Geoffrey Bullough (ed.), *Narrative and Dramatic Sources of Shake-*
                 speare, 8 vols. (1957–75)
Jones, *Origins*   Emrys Jones, *The Origins of Shakespeare* (Oxford, 1977)
McElwee   William McElwee, *The Murder of Sir Thomas Overbury* (1952)
MLN   *Modern Language Notes*
N&Q   *Notes and Queries*
Nashe   *The Works of Thomas Nashe*, ed. R. B. McKerrow, 5 vols., 2nd edn.,
                 rev. F. P. Wilson (Oxford, 1958)
OED   *Oxford English Dictionary*
PMLA   *Proceedings of the Modern Language Association*
RenD   *Renaissance Drama*
RES   *Review of English Studies*
SEL   *Studies in English Literature*
Tilley   Morris Palmer Tilley, *A Dictionary of The Proverbs in England in the*
                 Sixteenth and Seventeenth Centuries (Ann Arbor, Mich., 1950)

Throughout the notes and Bibliography, the place of publication is omitted when it
is, or includes, London. Titles of articles from periodicals or books are omitted from
the notes, but appear in the Bibliography.

INTRODUCTION

THE assassin, suborned to do another villain's murders, is one of the most recurrent minor figures in plays written during the reigns of Elizabeth I, James I, and Charles I. Some are professional contractors working for money, some have been bribed with offers of preferment or sex, and some are simply obeying orders; some cannot bring themselves to kill at all. The basic situation recurred again and again, in plays by most of the major dramatists of the time. Evidently murder plots of this type remained useful to play-wrights and interesting to playgoers throughout a long period.

To write a book of this length on such a character might be thought to be overworking the subject. Figures like Pedringano in *The Spanish Tragedy* (1587) and Lightborn in *Edward II* (1592) may be arresting cameo roles, but most of their relatives in lesser plays are stock characters whose appearances usually come to no more than a scene or two. Most writers on the drama of the sixteenth and seventeenth centuries have accordingly let them lie in the peripheries of critical attention. It is the aim of this book to remedy that neglect, of this Introduction to question some of the assumptions that lie behind it.

The assassin belongs to a side of English Renaissance drama that we do not now find congenial: its violence and intrigue. The Victorians used to patronize such things as 'childish', and in the twentieth century disdain has deepened into disgust. The popular reputation of Jacobean tragedy today places it alongside Grand Guignol and 'splatter' movies, unpleasant enter-tainments catering for abnormal tastes. Even specialist literary critics some-times treat the plays' stratagems and brutalities as things to be discreetly ignored, or apologized for: they are the things that make the playwrights' art impure. The assassin has been written off as rather an artless device serving these embarrassments: 'The motives of Bosola, Flamineo, Pedringano are of peripheral interest only; in the last resort they kill because they are told to,' remarks Margot Heinemann.[1]

It is not hard to understand Heinemann's assessment. Assassins are more often doers than talkers: they execute action, rather than initiating it. This means that their contribution to a storyline will be narrow; and the assump-tion follows that their claim on our attention will be correspondingly narrow. Most murders in fiction are predicated on the relationship between instigator and victim. The assassin is a third party brought into this relationship: he has no personal reason for wanting his victim dead, so we marginalize any character or motive of his own. It is symptomatic that the most individually famous stage assassin, the Third Murderer in *Macbeth* (1606), should be best

---

[1] M. Heinemann, *Puritanism and Theatre* (Cambridge, 1980), 179.

known for the attempts at the crackpot end of critical speculation to turn him into someone else, usually Macbeth himself.[2]

If we dismiss the assassin like this, though, we have failed to engage with the nature of the dramatic medium. Seeing a play is not like reading a work of prose fiction: we cannot skim over parts of it if we find them trivial or irrelevant. If we can make the scene of Banquo's murder a meaningful or interesting one only by importing a major character to stand in for one of the three anonymous assassins who hold the stage, then there is something wrong with the original scene, and with the play as a whole. A hired murderer (or any other minor character, for that matter) must be of interest in himself, or the playwright need not have introduced him in the first place—for there is rarely any strict narrative reason why the instigator of the crime should not carry it out himself. Of course, no sane critic would ever grant the Third Murderer more interest and importance than Macbeth himself; but we should not, so to speak, allow the light of the sun to blind us to that of the candle.

What I have said so far is founded on New Critical assumptions about the integrity of single works. In this I am reacting against the naïve disintegration of plays into the elements that we find to our taste, and call Great Art, and those we do not, and attribute to commercial pressures—the price we have to pay, so to speak, to the groundlings who financed Shakespeare in the first place. But there was no thought of pleasing us when the plays were written, and if the people whose pleasure mattered, the original playgoers, were the vulgar boors this view supposes, would they not have complained about the Great Art as vigorously as later critics have about the violence and intrigue? It is better to see the plays as wholes, and this means that we cannot ignore elements that seem to us distasteful or unimportant: we must begin with the assumption that everything in a play, from Macbeth to the Third Murderer, has its own significance as a part of the overall structure and effect.

One of my contentions in this study is that most stage assassins do not, *pace* Heinemann, kill simply because they are told to, and that their motives are often the centre of their appeal and interest. In part, this interest is akin to that claimed for stage violence by recent critics who have attempted to rehabilitate that aspect of English Renaissance drama. The impact of violence, they argue, was essentially moral. On the one hand, the grisly realism of violent scenes has a 'persuasiveness' that allows a dramatist to muster pity for the victim, and condemnation for the killer: the audience is left in no doubt about the actuality of evil.[3] On the other, acts of violence have also

[2] The theory was first proposed by A. P. Paton, *N&Q* 4th ser., 4 (1869), 211. If any refutation is required, see G. W. Williams, *Shakespeare Quarterly*, 23 (1972), 261.
[3] M. Charney, *RenD* NS 2 (1969), 59–70.

been shown to have symbolic, iconographical, and thematic dimensions which address moral issues directly.[4] In some cases, the two approaches can be at odds, to powerful effect. An obvious example is the murder of the homosexual King in Marlowe's *Edward II*, done by thrusting a red-hot spit up his anus: the audience has to decide which is more important, the fact that the punishment fits the crime, or pity for the man's unspeakable agony.[5] With the assassin, however, we shall see that the abstract and the literal work together: what he does serves to emphasize the immorality of why he does it.

The other side of the assassin's appeal was more direct: the Elizabethans and Jacobeans were fascinated by murder itself. This was not the sadistic taste for crude sensationalism that detractors of Jacobean tragedy would attribute to its audience. (It has become a commonplace to point out that such tastes were better served by bear-baitings and public executions.) Rather the social phenomenon of murder was one that people had become increasingly aware of as the urban metropolis grew: in the popular consciousness, it was coming to eclipse treason as the most heinous of crimes. The result was a serious interest in the subject, reflected in a considerable body of pamphlet literature.[6] The vogue for killings, intrigues, and assassins in the drama was another aspect of this interest. Plays showed the human experience of murder: the need for secrecy, the obsessive mistrust, and later the social and psychological forces which could make a man a homicide. Again the assassin's motives were of central importance.

So far I have paid insufficient attention to the phenomenology of literary and dramatic experience, a factor which will complicate my argument about the relation of the stage assassin to the contemporary reality of murder. In our every act of perception, we make a compromise between the individuality of the experiences, people, or things we perceive, and our preconceived notion of what they would be like. No matter how absorbing a play may be, an audience can never dissociate itself fully from its context and past experience: anything it sees on the stage will be understood in relation to its knowledge of other plays and of real life. A discussion of a recurring figure like the assassin, then, must be extrinsic and historicist as well as intrinsic and textual: we must talk not only of minor characters, but also of a character type.

Obviously, the assassin type differed in one respect from most others to be found in plays of the period: it had less basis in the audience's extra-dramatic experience than (for instance) the stage soldier, or scholar, or

[4] H. Diehl, *RenD* NS 11 (1980), 27–44; A. C. Dessen, *Elizabethan Stage Conventions and Modern Interpreters* (Cambridge, 1984), ch. 6.
[5] N. Brooke, in J. R. Brown and B. Harris (eds.), *Elizabethan Theatre* (1966), 103–4.
[6] I hope to write elsewhere in detail on the cultural history of murder in this period.

tapster. This is not to say that hired murderers did not exist in Renaissance England. In 1615, for example, the most notorious of Jacobean society scandals broke when it was revealed that the Countess of Somerset, the wife of the King's current favourite, had two years earlier paved the way for her divorce from her previous husband, the Earl of Essex, by having one of its principal opponents, Sir Thomas Overbury, murdered while a prisoner in the Tower of London. The manner of Overbury's death, poisoned by mercury sublimate pumped into his body in an enema, was as lurid as anything to be seen in the tragedies of the time, and to effect it the Countess had to put a small army of poisoners, procurers, and prison officials on her payroll. These men and women are only the best-known examples of paid killers from the period. But though such people were known to exist, few would knowingly have met them: the profession of murder is not one to boast about.

Of course, it would be naïve to suppose that all our preconceptions and representations have their origins in direct experience: there will always be gaps for hearsay, imagination, and ideology to piece out. This process operates even in cases like that of the assassin where the experiential basis for a concept is very narrow: we do not habitually practise agnosticism. For instance, when Iago compares the experience of sexual jealousy with that of poison eating away his innards, no-one supposes that he has ever actually been poisoned and somehow lived to tell the tale.[7] Rather he is drawing on the folk reality that poisons had for the Renaissance mind, much as does, say, space travel for the late twentieth century. It is a dimension of understanding that bears only a tenuous relation to actuality: our 'knowledge' of what it is like to travel in space owes more to science fiction than to the contemporary Apollo and space-shuttle missions; and the pain of a stab wound is quite unlike what we call 'stabbing' pains. These fantasies are collective not only because we pass them to one another in art and conversation, but also because the imaginative processes that produce them are culturally conditioned. This means that a character type such as the assassin will be constituted of a number of recurring conventional elements. In this lies another reason for neglect.

Whereas we tend to overlook minor characters, we usually look down on conventional ones. Because our canons of taste teach us to value works of art for, among other things, the direct representation of reality, we expect of fictional characters, if not the complexity, then at least the individuality of real people. The very word 'stereotype' is a denial of that individuality: in English Renaissance drama, we are told, stock characters were 'hard, isolated units of character which were all of a piece', and which 'could neither interact upon each other, nor develop, for the type was sharply defined and

[7] W. Shakespeare, *Othello*, ii. i. 294–6.

could not be modified'.[8] *Ipso facto*, we assume, stereotypes cannot be of interest: they are uncomplicated, repetitive figures, whose appearance in plays betrays a dramatist's lack of attention to minor characterization; art is imitating art, where we would prefer it to imitate life.

This dismissive attitude to conventional elements in drama was first challenged by Muriel Bradbrook in her pioneering study, *Themes and Conventions of Elizabethan Tragedy* (1935). She defined a convention as 'an agreement between writers and readers, whereby the artist is allowed to limit and simplify his material in order to secure greater concentration through a control of the distribution of emphasis'.[9] Conventions, that is, serve a positive artistic function in so far as they free the dramatist from the limitations of mimesis: to use stock characters is not laziness but shorthand. Moreover, she argued, we must understand the conventions if we are to understand the plays: the things that earlier critics such as Shaw and William Archer found absurd only seemed so because they were not party to the agreement between dramatist and audience, and so tried to read the plays according to their own conventions and expectations of drama.

Bradbrook's approach has been rightly influential, but it carries with it a danger that is pinpointed, facetiously, in the spoof literary history, *The Eng. Lit. Kit* (1982), when it says that in Jacobean tragedy, 'Particularly ludicrous bits are known as "conventions".'[10] It is all too easy to turn off our critical faculties and suppose that the plays' peculiarities may all be explained away with reference to convention. That characters and situations which appear repeatedly were in some sense 'conventional' is not an unreasonable deduction; but it is more contentious to proceed to the conclusion that these characters and situations were therefore unremarkable. Robert Ornstein has argued that this merely collapses qualitative distinctions between plays: the underlying assumption can be that a convention is unsurprising in a good play because it has already appeared in a multitude of bad plays. If we accept this, then we must conclude that audiences responded in the same register to good and bad plays alike—or, more bluntly, could not tell one from the other. Ornstein cannot accept this: 'I suspect that sophisticated Jacobeans accepted implausibility in bad plays much as we today accept it in bad movies—not because it is conventional but because one does not demand from casual entertainment the kind of truth which one expects from great art.'[11]

The implication of Ornstein's argument is that we should not bother studying conventional characters and situations at all: at best, we are confining our attention to a backwater of literary history irrelevant to our

---

[8] M. C. Bradbrook, *Themes and Conventions of Elizabethan Tragedy*, 2nd edn. (Cambridge, 1952), 68, 61.   [9] Ibid. 4.

[10] D. Tweedcroft, *The Eng. Lit. Kit* (Hampton, 1982), 81.

[11] R. Ornstein, *The Moral Vision of Jacobean Tragedy* (Madison and Milwaukee, 1960), 21.

understanding of major texts. A recent book on conventional characters by
G. M. Pinciss, *Literary Creations* (1988), seems to accept this stricture and
look for other justification. He argues that stereotypes can focus ideas and
issues that were of interest to the culture that produced them, so studying
them 'can reveal the distinctive qualities of an age, in particular the consequences of growing religious and ethical pressures on public attitudes'.[12] But
this is to duck the issue: to extract and analyse the ideological 'content' of
conventions is valid, but not in itself fundamentally literary; it illuminates
the history of ideas more than it does drama.

Ornstein's is too summary a dismissal of dramatic convention from the
pale of literary studies. Bradbrook's approach, it is true, can be applied
naïvely: with such emphasis on the original playgoers as the key to understanding the plays, it is easy to slip into the assumption that 'even the
greatest dramatists were enslaved by the memories and expectations of their
audiences'.[13] But his riposte is equally extreme: he prefers to study individual
plays as discrete works of genius, uninfluenced by the dramatic tradition
that (as he sees it) fettered the popular entertainment of the time. One critic
gives primacy to the audience, the other to the artist; but it would be truer
to see a dialogue between the two.

Ornstein's basic error is to emphasize qualitative distinctions between
plays at the expense of generic similarities. It may be that (say) *Hamlet* (1600)
is a far better play than *Hoffman* (1602), and that audiences would have
recognized that. It would be equally obvious, however, that they are both
the same type of play, revenge tragedies. If a playgoer is familiar with that
genre, he will know more or less what to expect. It may be that he will get
it; but it may also be that a great play will exploit to its own ends his
understanding of genre conventions. The study of these or other conventions
can indeed help us to understand major plays, then: any audience that is at
all engaged with the play it is watching will respond, as it responds to any
perception, from its prior experience of literature and of life; and any
dramatist who seeks to create a play that is communicable in the theatre will
take those responses into account.

The danger is that we may misrepresent the nature of the response. Again,
Ornstein's views can be watered down into a useful caveat: 'Seated in our
studies, surrounded by the texts of Elizabethan and Jacobean plays, we may
be far more burdened by the weight of dramatic tradition than were the
Jacobean playwrights or their audiences, whose memories of performances
were no doubt dimmed by time.'[14] When we attempt to reconstruct elements
of the dramatic tradition of the time, we do it perforce with precise docu-

[12] G. M. Pinciss, *Literary Creations* (Wolfeboro and Woodbridge, 1988), 1.
[13] Ornstein, *Moral Vision*, 20.
[14] Ibid. 20–1.

mentation and detailed reference to specific plays. The result is highly explicit, and, in that respect, bears no resemblance to what Emrys Jones has called the 'unthinking effortless familiarity' that characterizes our awareness of the conventions of popular narrative.[15] No matter how alert the playgoers were, we must allow for an element of the subliminal in their expectations and responses.

With all this in mind, we can question the assumption that stock characters were fixed and unalterable. If that is the case, then it follows that a playwright who chose to use a conventional character was bound by its existing limitations in the way that Ornstein denies. However, we have acknowledged the contrary, that dramatists were free to use, adapt, and react against stereotypes as it suited their artistic purposes; so we cannot cling to the notion that stock types and situations were fixed. Rather the audience's conception of the basic archetype must have changed, probably subtly and unconsciously, as new plays presented their own versions—much as, for T. S. Eliot, the literary tradition is constantly altering to accommodate new works.[16]

The analysis of conventionality falls in the hinterland where literary criticism shades into cultural history and the study of *mentalité*, then; but these areas feed back into 'pure' literary criticism in that they help us to understand individual works from the point of view of their reception. Accordingly, this study traces the development of the assassin type from its beginnings in early Elizabethan drama to its decline in Caroline times and afterwards; but it also seeks to elucidate the plays in which such characters appear. It falls broadly into three sections, which might be said to deal with pre-conventional, conventional, and unconventional treatments of the character. The first three chapters are concerned with the origins of the type, up to the point when the assassin had become an established conventional figure, recognizable to audiences: evidence in plays indicates that this was the case by 1592. Much of this discussion deals empirically with the process of creation—the playwright's technical problems of transforming narrative sources, disposing material, and exploiting dramatic tradition. Some readers may prefer to skip directly to Chapters 4, 5, and 6, where I turn to the reasons for the popularity of the assassin: the type's dramatic function, the appeal of the basic scenario, and the issues that were addressed through it. The last four chapters of the book then consider the ways in which dramatists after 1600 exploited playgoers' knowledge of the type, adapted and expanded it, and finally began to lose interest.

[15] Jones, *Origins*, 51.
[16] T. S. Eliot, *Selected Essays*, 3rd edn. (1951), 15.

1

ASSASSINS OUTSIDE DRAMA

I

Since time immemorial, the rich and powerful have used others to do their killing. Sixteenth-century Europe was no exception. It was in Spain and Italy that the hiring of assassins, also known as *bravi* in Italy, was most established. Of course, official culture condemned the practice: according to Angelo Carletti in the *Summa Angelica* (1486), those who kill men for money could be declared by the courts to be assassins (apparently a term of some legal specificity), and then killed by any private person, provided this was done purely out of zeal for justice; Venice in particular passed numerous edicts against *bravi* in the late sixteenth century.[1] Even so, the existence of special legal controls only indicates the extent of the problem. Murder was virtually a profession for some men: for example, Ambroglio Tremazzi, a hireling of Francesco de Medici, was involved in a total of six killings during the 1570s, only falling foul of the law on an assignment in Paris which also led to the arrest of Francesco's secretary.[2]

In Italy and Spain, such men were able to escape justice because even without the sanction of law there was still the sanction of tradition, evident in the almost blasé tones in which the hiring of murderers was sometimes discussed: for instance, when employing a man for the murder of Juan de Escobedo in 1578, Antonio Pérez, the agent of Philip II of Spain, was said to have made the assassin 'the offers *which are usually made in such cases'* — 'A terrible phrase that portrays a whole period', comments Pérez's biographer.[3] In consequence, when public opinion in a case was on the side of the murderers, toleration was assured: in 1513, the assassins of Antonio Bologna escaped simply because no one could be bothered to bring them to justice; Bologna had committed the unpardonable sin of marrying above himself.[4]

French eyes saw these matters very differently. Life had grown cheaper in the 1560s: plague and the wars of religion had seen to that, and to some

---

[1] A. Carletti, *Summa Angelica* (Chivasso, 1486), b8ᵛ; P. Molmenti, *Venice*, tr. H. F. Brown, Part III: *The Decadence* (1908), ii. 65 n. 1.

[2] C. Bax, *The Life of the White Devil* (1940), 36–7; V. von Klarwill (ed.), *The Fugger News-Letters*, tr. P. de Chary (1924), 29–30.

[3] G. Marañon, *Antonio Pérez, 'Spanish Traitor'*, tr. C. D. Ley (1954), 173 (his italics).

[4] M. Bandello, *The Novels*, tr. J. Payne (1890), ii. 55.

'it seemed more criminal and more dangerous to kill a sheep than a man'.[5] The profession of murder began to flourish: 'people have begun to bargain with assassins ... to go and cut the throat of such and such persons as one might bargain for some work with a mason or carpenter', commented Henri Estienne in 1566.[6] During plague conditions, such work was all too easy: a man would simply spread the rumour that his intended victim had the plague, and hire murderers to carry him off, like Death's press-gang, to a hospital; if he was not already infected, he soon would be.[7]

Even so, many found the hiring of assassins morally shocking and, importantly, un-French. In a century which began with French incursions into Italy but continued with an Italian, Catherine de Medici, holding the reins of power as Queen and later Queen Mother of France, it is unsurprising that French nationalism as it developed should have taken an anti-Italian slant. The profession of murderer was held to be among the villainies newly imported from across the Alps.[8] Even the hirers themselves accepted the cultural connection: while a hostage in England in January 1563, the Provost of Paris employed one Claude Andrea to murder Captain Mazin, who had threatened his life; he was, he wrote, dealing with his enemy 'in the Italian fashion'.[9] Small wonder then that Tremazzi came to grief when he brought his trade to France.

Whether or not this view of the provenance of the French assassin is correct, the word itself probably entered the French language from the Italian. It began life in the Middle East as a rendering by Western tongues of *hashishiyyin* (hashish-eaters), the Arabic name of a fanatical Shiah Muslim sect founded in the eleventh century. This group, described by Marco Polo, was thought to deceive its chosen killers with a drug-induced imitation of Paradise, and persuade them that they could return only by committing murders as directed by their leader, known as the Old Man of the Mountain.[10] This was legend; but the murders were fact. Used initially against religious enemies and later let out to hire, the Assassins were best known in the sixteenth century for killing European Crusaders.[11]

Besides being known in their own right, the group entered European

[5] 'gravius & capitalius esset pecudem jugulare, quam civem': A. Turnèbe, *Adversariorvm libri triginta* (Paris, 1580), i. a2ʳ.

[6] 'on a commencé à marchander avec les assasins ... d'aller couper la gorge à tels & tels, comm' on feroit marché de quelque besongne avec un maçon ou un charpentier': H. Estienne, *L'Introdvction av traité de la conformité des merueilles anciennes auec les modernes* (Geneva, 1566), o8ʳ.

[7] J. Nohl, *The Black Death*, tr. C. H. Clarke (1926), 167.

[8] e.g. Estienne, *L'Introdvction*, p1ᵛ.

[9] *Calendar of State Papers, Foreign Series, 1563*, ed. J. Stevenson (1869), 92.

[10] M. Polo, *The Travels*, tr. R. Latham (Harmondsworth, 1958), 70–3; see also E. Burman, *The Assassins* (Wellingborough, 1987).

[11] J. Foxe, *Acts and Monuments*, 4th edn., ed. J. Pratt (1877), ii. 467.

vocabularies as the vehicle of a metaphor. Italian had acquired the word *assassinare* and its cognates by the early fourteenth century, although the *Summa Angelica*'s extraordinary Latin rendering, *ascisinus*, suggests that Carletti at least knew it only in spoken form.[12] A number of editions of the *Summa* that were published outside Italy render the term *ascismus*, a corruption by minim confusion whose persistence provides some scant evidence that the word was not yet known further north.[13] *Assassiner* is first recorded in French in the 1540s, and in the 1560s it was still regarded as a new word, because 'it has been necessary to find new terms for new wickedness'.[14]

Not only new terms but new laws were required. In 1576 the Estates General began to press for special measures against hired murderers.[15] Three years later Henry III decreed that both assassins and hirers were to be subject to the death penalty for 'the mere planning and attempt'.[16] The contract itself was heinous, irrespective of whether the murder was actually committed. France was not alone in Northern Europe in taking measures such as these. The United Provinces, another state with cause to fear incursions from the Mediterranean, punished murder more or less severely 'according to the circumstances of the person killed, or of the more or lesse wicked manner of the act'; accordingly, whereas ordinary murderers were beheaded, assassins and their employers were broken on the wheel, a more painful and protracted fate.[17]

II

There were significant legal and cultural differences between English and Continental attitudes to the assassin. Such men were not regarded as a peculiarly un-English type of criminal; England was a violent society, and there was no need to invoke foreign influence to account for paid assassinations. Some members of the aristocracy maintained gangs of armed bullies for the purpose of physically imposing their will in quarrels: for example, in 1599 John Stanhope, heir to a noble estate, set upon Sir Charles Cavendish

[12] The spelling reflects a false etymology from the Latin verb *scindere* (to cleave): see Carletti, *Summa Angelica*, b8ᵛ.

[13] I have seen six editions containing this error; the earliest was published in Nuremberg in 1488.

[14] 'il a falu trouver des termes nouveaux pour la nouvelle meschanceté': Estienne, *L'Introdvction*, o8ʳ; see also P. Imbs (ed.), *Trésor de la langue Française* (Paris, 1971-), iii. 667–70; L. Lindvall, *Studia Neophilologica* 46 (1974), 32–52.

[15] G. Picot, *Histoire des États Généraux* (Paris, 1872), ii. 552.

[16] 'la seule machination et attentat': A. J. L. Jourdan, Decrusy, and F. A. Isambert (eds.), *Recueil général des anciennes lois Françaises*, (Paris, 1822–33), xiv. 427.

[17] F. Moryson, *An Itinerary* (Glasgow, 1907–8), iv. 471; S. van Leeuwen, *Commentaries on Roman-Dutch Law*, ed. C. W. Decker, tr. J. G. Kotzé, 2nd edn. (1921–3), ii. 267.

with a retinue of twenty hirelings, at least two of whom were killed in the bloody fray that ensued.[18] In some cases such retainers were used specifically as assassins.

A case in point occurred in 1557 when a nine-year feud between Lord Stourton and the Hartgill family over certain provisions in the will of Stourton's father culminated with the forcible abduction of William Hartgill and his son John. After being held in various of Stourton's properties, they were battered senseless in a close by five of his men, and then taken to Stourton House nearby, where one of the attackers, William Farre, cut their throats while Stourton lighted the proceedings with a candle. Allegedly Farre at once regretted the murder, saying, 'Ah my Lorde! this is a pytiouse sight: hadde I thought that I now thincke, before the thing was doon, your hole land could not have woon me to consent to soch an acte.' Stourton's response was, 'What, fainte harted knave! ys yt anny more then the rydding of two knaves that lyving were trooblesome bothe to Goddes lawe and man's? There is no more accoumpt to bee made of them then the kylling of ii sheepe.'[19] Stourton was a Catholic in Marian England, and the Hartgills were Protestants, but his hopes of escaping justice on that score were ill-founded: he was hanged at Salisbury less than two months later. The retainers subsequently suffered the same fate at Bath. The case was well remembered thereafter: the crime-writer Thomas Harman referred to it familiarly in 1566, and the jurist Sir Edward Coke cited it for its 'exemplary justice' in 1613.[20]

It was not only the upper classes who employed other men to kill for them: a number of middle-class property disputes and sexual disagreements escalated to murder by a hired third party. These individuals were not professional murderers on the model of the Italian *bravo*, but men with other occupations picking up a little extra income; frequently they were already employed more innocently by their hirers. For example, there is the case of one Lincolne, a widower of Warehorne in Kent, who found his four children an impediment in his pursuit of a rich widow, and hired an unnamed labourer of his to kill them off.[21] Ulalia Padge, a Devonshire woman forced into an unhappy and unproductive marriage, suborned her household servant Robert Priddis to murder her husband.[22] Elizabeth Caldwell, an adulteress, hired her own brother, George Fernley, for a similar task.[23] The fees paid in this type of case were extremely variable: Priddis was offered £140, Fernley only £5. Sometimes an element of barter crept in: Lincolne offered his labourer forty

[18] L. Stone, *The Crisis of the Aristocracy* (Oxford, 1965), 225–7; J. Chamberlain, *Letters*, ed. S. Williams (1861), 54–5.

[19] J. E. Jackson, *The Wiltshire Archaeological and Natural History Magazine*, 8 (1864), 252–3.

[20] A. V. Judges (ed.), *The Elizabethan Underworld* (1930), 83; Sir E. Coke, *The Reports* (1826), v. 219.

[21] *Sundrye strange and inhumaine Murthers, lately committed* (1591), A3ʳ–A4ᵛ.

[22] Ibid., B2ʳ–B4ᵛ.

[23] G. Dugdale, *A True Discourse of the practises of Elizabeth Caldwell* (1604), A4ᵛ–B1ʳ.

shillings and one cow, and, in an incident of 1580 showing just how little human life could be worth, an Essex baker, William Baker, accepted a good meal and the princely sum of five shillings to kill his hirer's opponent in a land dispute.[24]

Many of these cases are records of frustration on the hirer's part, with murder the last resort in quarrels they had failed to win by legal means. Killers were rarely hired merely on impulse, though there are exceptions, such as the case of a man named Harris, who was to receive a substantial legacy from one Keyt: when Keyt, in what appears to have been a fit of pique, threatened to change his will, Harris acted swiftly to forestall this, and hired a thresher to murder him.[25] The pattern is different when sexual antagonism is at the root: in the remarkably similar cases of Alice Ardern (burned for her husband's murder in 1551) and of Ulalia Padge, the adulteress's traditional weapon, poison, had been tried and had failed when the woman resorted to an assassin. The later case of Elizabeth Caldwell, incidentally, saw the sequence reversed: it was only Fernley's procrastination that led her to try poison. Cases such as these reflect the restricted social lot of women: poisoning is a first option because the preparation and serving of the husband's food fell within the wife's purview, but any more overt act of violence required the hiring of a man to perform it.

The native Englishness of these cases was reflected in the terminology that was used. As we shall see from the drama, the word most commonly denoting the paid killer was, simply, 'murderer'. 'Bloodhound' was also quite common in the early seventeenth century. Other terms were 'butcher', 'cut-throat', 'cutter', 'hackster', 'hacker', and 'ruffian', but, like 'murderer', these words do not refer specifically to the assassin: a man is hired to kill because he is a ruffian, not a ruffian because he has been hired to kill.[26]

Foreign terms began to enter the language only in the 1590s. The noun 'assassin' is first recorded in 1600, in its alternative form of 'assassinate', which indicates derivation from the French assassinat.[27] Usage was erratic, reflecting the original provenance: assassins, like the hashishiyyin of the Levant, could be political or paid killers, or both; as we shall see, the two were anyway not always clearly distinguished in the contemporary mind. The noun 'assassinate', though otherwise interchangeable with 'assassin', could also refer to a murderous attack.

[24] F. G. Emmison, *Elizabethan Life: Disorder* (Chelmsford, 1970), 160. This is the lowest fee I know of.

[25] J. Manningham, *Diary*, ed. R. P. Sorlien (Hanover, NH, 1976), 162–3. (Entry for 31 Dec. 1602; the incident is said to have taken place 'Not long since'.)

[26] *OED*; see also Stone, *Crisis of the Aristocracy*, 227.

[27] *OED* also quotes a 1531 reference to one of the corrupt texts of the *Summa Angelica*, which provides evidence against the word's being known in English at that time; indeed, the author quoted goes on to remark, 'there is no such terme of ascismus in the lawe of the realme': C. Saint German, *The Secunde Dyalogue in Englysshe wyth New Addycyons* (1531), O2ᵛ.

'Bravo' appeared at about the same time, being first recorded in 1597, again probably from French, which had had the word since the 1520s.[28] As with 'assassin', English usage was variable. The broadest sense of the word was simply 'ruffian'; judging by Thomas Coryate's description of the 'Braves' of Venice, this was also a sense of the Italian word.[29] The earliest specific sense in English was (as Thomas Dekker put it) a 'ruffianly he-bawd': a man who acts as a 'heavy' for a woman, who would usually though not always be a prostitute.[30] Such bravos appear as characters in Dekker's *If This Be Not a Good Play, The Devil Is In It* (1611), Thomas Killigrew's *Thomaso* (1654), and its derivate, Aphra Behn's *The Rover* (1677). Only by about 1620 does the word appear to have referred specifically to the hired killer.

Like the language, sixteenth-century law drew no distinction between the assassin and any other type of murderer: there were no special penalties prescribed as there were on the Continent. Indeed, the hired assassin raised difficulties of classification that were peculiar to English law. The basis of most continental legal systems was Roman law, in which to command a murder was the same as to commit it.[31] In England, however, the distinction between accessory and principal was drawn somewhat differently: 'if one commaunde an other to do a felonye and he doth it, if the commaunder be not present he is an accessory, but if he be present he is principal as wel as the other that did the dede'.[32] An assassin, then, would be the principal, the man who had hired him an accessory.

The jurist William Fulbecke had difficulty with this position:

By our Law the counsailor, commandor, or assistor are ... guiltie of homicide, & principall offendors: for al that be present, ayding, abetting or comforting him that doth murder, are principal offendors though they give no stroke, for the stroke of him that smiteth & woundeth is the wounding, and striking of all the others in law.[33]

This is true, but the initial generalization is misleading because Fulbecke has suppressed the question of the *absent* hirer or commander. The problem was that the legal terms appropriate in such a case implied a hierarchy of responsibility that ran counter to both ethics and the facts: less specialized terminology held the hirer-accessory to be the 'author' of the murder and the assassin-principal to be his 'instrument'.

Ethical commentators who mentioned the subject had no doubt that to hire a murderer was more blameworthy than to commit the crime personally.

[28] *OED* sb¹ 1; Imbs, *Trésor*, iv. 926.
[29] T. Coryate, *Coryat's Crudities* (Glasgow, 1905), i. 413.
[30] T. Dekker, *Selected Prose Writings*, ed. E. D. Pendry (1967), 137.
[31] S. P. Scott (ed.), *The Civil Law* (Cincinnati, 1932), xi. 63, 65–6.
[32] J. Rastell, *The Expositions of the Termes of the Lawes of Englande* (1572), A6ᵛ.
[33] W. Fulbecke, *A Parallele or Conference of the Civill Law, the Canon Law, and the Common Law of this Realme of England* (1601), M5ᵛ.

John Hooper metaphorically associates the practice with the contemporary taboo against projectile weapons which allowed a man to kill without personal risk: 'Some kill not themselves, nor will not be seen to break the peace; but shoot their bolts by other men, and wound and kill him that is an hundred mile from him.'[34] There was more than cowardice involved, however. In 1612, the Scottish nobleman Lord Sanquhar was tried by an English court for procuring the assassination of John Turner, a fencing-master who had accidentally put out one of his eyes several years earlier. Passing sentence, Sir Henry Yelverton told Sanquhar:

this your fault is far greater than if you had committed the fact yourself; for then it had been but your own single murder only; but now you have made them who were the executioners of your malice, murderers also with you: so you have made their bodies subject to the justice of man, and their souls subject to the justice of God, which, without his great mercy, they must endure.[35]

We may doubt whether a hirer's action would have any material effect on an assassin's chances of salvation, but for the theologian Heinrich Bullinger it was a real issue:

Another peradventure would not do the thing that he doeth, but because he seeth that thou hastenest him on; but because he knoweth he shall please thee thereby; and because he perceiveth that thy help upholdeth him. Although, therefore, that thou with thine own hand strike not the stroke, yet the murder, that another committeth by thy setting on, shall be imputed to thee as well as if thou thyself hadst killed the man.[36]

The point is underlined by Fulbecke in a striking misapplication of Roman law on the corruption of slaves:

if a man counsaile one to doe a murder, who if the counsaile had not bene would have done it, he that executeth the counsaile, and he that giveth the counsaile, are both in the eye of Lawe murderers. But when it is done by commaundement by persons executing the commandement, which otherwise would not have done it, then the commaunder onely is accompted guiltie of homicide.[37]

There was, then, a moral hierarchy of guilt which ran counter to the legal hierarchy of responsibility.

Of course, this moral hierarchy was recognized in the pursuit of justice. Yelverton clearly took it into account, as did King James earlier when, anxious that the guilty men should come to trial, he offered a reward of £500 for the apprehension of Sanquhar, but only £100 for Robert Carlisle, the assassin he hired.[38] Nonetheless, James was not averse to chicanery when

[34] J. Hooper, *Early Writings*, ed. S. Carr (Cambridge, 1843), 368.
[35] T. B. Howell (ed.), *State Trials* (1816–28), ii. 753.
[36] H. Bullinger, *The Decades*, tr. H. I., ed. T. Harding (Cambridge, 1849–52), i. 304.
[37] Fulbecke, *Parallele*, M5ʳ; cf. Scott, *Civil Law*, iv. 75–80.
[38] *A Booke of Proclamations*, 2nd edn. (1613), Y4ʳ–Y5ᵛ.

it suited him: after Lady Somerset's conviction in 1616 for procuring the poisoning of Sir Thomas Overbury, he pardoned her, claiming that, as the accessory and not the principal, she had been 'drawn to it by the instigation of base persons'; those base persons, her instruments, had already been hanged.[39]

The main problem arising from the incompatibility of the moral and legal discourses, however, was a procedural one. When Sanquhar gave himself up, denying his guilt, it was safe in the knowledge that Carlisle had fled overseas, and that as the accessory, he could not be convicted before the attainder of the principal. As Sir Edward Coke later explained, 'there cannot be an accessary, unless there be a principal, no more than there can be a shadow, unless there be a body.' Carlisle could, eventually, have been attainted by outlawry, but the King wanted his fellow-countryman executed with all due haste. To that end he used his double sovereignty to have the assassin rootled out of Scotland, where he had gone to ground, enabling Sanquhar to come to trial; he was hanged exactly seven weeks after the murder was committed.[40]

For a period of ten years under Edward VI and Mary I, there had been a more material difficulty in prosecuting the hirers of assassins. The problem lay in benefit of clergy, the system whereby criminals who could pass a literacy test were handed over to the church courts, which did not pass sentence of death. The early Tudor monarchs had curbed its availability, first by making it claimable only once for persons not in holy orders, then by withdrawing it altogether from various types of felony, including murder.[41] When this legislation was re-enacted on Edward VI's accession in 1547, an error in drafting produced a statute that omitted to mention accessories.[42] The effective result was that to employ an assassin became an attractive possibility for those with murder in mind: in the event of an arraignment, the hirer risked only branding on the thumb, whereas his instrument, if convicted, would go to the gallows.[43]

It was eight years before this loophole was brought to the attention of the authorities. The occasion was the murder of a Buckinghamshire man, Giles Rufford, by assassins in the pay of his neighbour, Benedict Smith. For more than two years, Smith had repeatedly failed to secure Rufford's conviction for the theft of certain items of property, and when Rufford sued him for attempting to procure a false indictment and was awarded damages in excess of £90, it appears that Smith lost his temper and paid two

[39] McElwee, 260.

[40] Coke, *Reports*, v. 215, 217–19.

[41] The statutes involved are: 4 Henry VII c. 13; 12 Henry VII c. 7; 4 Henry VIII c. 2, followed by re-enactments in 1531 and 1536.

[42] 1 Edward VI c. 12 s. 9.

[43] First offenders were branded to ensure that they could not claim the benefit a second time.

Londoners £40 for Rufford's death. His intention was clearly to exploit the loophole left open by the 1547 Act, for Rufford's widow took the singular course of petitioning Parliament 'that ... the said Benedicte shall not bee admitted to have or enjoye the pryveledge or Benefite of his Clergie, but shalbee put from the same; Any Lawe Statute or Custome in this your Realme to the contrarye notwithestandyng'. The Commons examined Smith and, with some difficulty, procured a confession; it was agreed that he was abusing a legal technicality, and Mrs Rufford's appeal entered the statute book as it stood.[44]

This Act was followed up, early in the business of the next Parliament, with a bill 'For the due punishement of suche as commaunde councell or hire any person or persons to committe perpetrate or doo anye Petie Treason wilfull Murder' or a number of other felonies; benefit of clergy was to be withdrawn from such people.[45] As such, the Act did not embody special penalties as were later ordained in France and the Netherlands, but merely restored the *status quo ante* 1547. Even so, the wording is very specifically directed against criminals such as Smith, and this may have a bearing on the case of Lord Stourton. Stourton, to recap, had hired murderers in 1557 and hoped to get away with it, not through benefit of clergy (he was ineligible, having been present at the killing and so a principal) but through Catholic favouritism in the Queen. For her part, even if she wanted to, Mary could hardly intervene to save a man who had committed the very crime that was to be the subject of legislation in the forthcoming Parliament that year, so Stourton was disappointed and, shortly, dead.

III

English practices and attitudes often differed significantly from those of the Continent, but England was not simply an island apart: there was a European dimension to the subject of the hired assassin. A disturbing trend of the late sixteenth century was the rise of poniard diplomacy: increasingly assassination became an instrument of international policy, used particularly, though not exclusively, by the forces of the Counter-Reformation against the heretic princes. Major Protestant leaders such as Admiral de Coligny and William the Silent were targets for the assassin's bullet, and two successive kings of France, Henry III and Henry IV, died at the hands of Catholic fanatics. In England there were countless plots against Queen Elizabeth, emanating from the Escorial as well as the Vatican after the defeat of the Armada. With the

---

[44] 2 & 3 Philip & Mary c. 17; G. Lipscomb, *The History and Antiquities of the County of Buckingham* (1847), iii. 351 n. 1.

[45] 4 & 5 Philip & Mary c. 4.

death of the monarch, all authority lapsed, and in the chaos that would follow an assassination there would be ample opportunity for a Catholic uprising and a foreign invasion.

These fears were at their height during roughly the last two decades of Elizabeth's reign, a result not only of the increased incidence of conspiracies, but also of what appears to have been a change in government policy in 1584.[46] Before that date, the authorities had played the subject down: after the arrest of John Somerville, a Warwickshire Catholic who set out for London in October 1583, announcing his intention to shoot the Queen, the government indulged in neither advertisement nor cover-up. The events of the following year produced a change of approach: William Allen published his *Defence of English Catholics*, William the Silent was assassinated, and weeks later papers were seized casting new light on the Catholic 'Enterprise' against England. The Privy Council responded by drafting the Bond of Association for distribution across the country: its signatories pledged to debar from the succession anyone 'by whom or for whom' the assassination of the Queen might be undertaken, and 'to prosecute such person or persons to the death'; it was, in effect, a commitment to lynch law.[47] By thus inflaming loyalist outrage, they made the threat to Elizabeth a public issue: soon afterwards Anthony Munday published his brief history of treason, *A Watchword to England*, the title implying a sudden need for increased vigilance. There was a new tone of hysteria in politics: 'It makes my heart leap for joy to think we have such a jewel. It makes all my joints to tremble for fear when I consider the loss of such a jewel,' one member told Parliament as it debated the Queen's safety in 1585.[48]

The ensuing Act passed in March of that year superseded the Bond, but the government continued its new policy of involving the common man, using the medium of the church.[49] When William Parry's plot was exposed, again early in 1585, special thanksgiving services were ordered throughout the kingdom and special forms of prayers ordained for the Queen's safety: with a tone strikingly more personal than that of the prayers following the crushing of the rebellious Northern Earls in 1570, congregations were told that God had 'hitherto wonderfully preserved [the Queen] from manifold perils and sundry dangers, and of late revealed and frustrated the traitorous practices and conspiracies of divers against her'.[50] Such prayers were in use until the end of the reign, regularly updated to include the names of the latest would-be regicides.

[46] Unfortunately this is hard to confirm, for the Privy Council records for the period between June 1582 and February 1586 are lost.
[47] J. E. Neale, *Elizabeth I and her Parliaments* (1965), ii. 17.
[48] Ibid. ii. 50.
[49] 27 Elizabeth I c. 1.
[50] W. K. Clay (ed.), *Liturgical Services* (Cambridge, 1847), 580.

Some of these men had purely mercenary motives. In 1569, Catherine de Medici offered to all comers a reward of 50,000 crowns for the assassination of Coligny.[51] Spain offered only half as much for the death of William the Silent, another open offer which the assassin Balthasar Gérard admitted had first inspired him.[52] A decade later, however, the Escorial was more generous to Dr Roderigo Lopez, Queen Elizabeth's physician: allegedly his fee for poisoning his mistress was to have been 50,000 crowns.[53] Others received less liquid but no less material rewards: although killing Coligny's lieutenant de Mouy in his place did not win Charles de Louvier, Sieur de Maurevert, the crowns on offer, he received an ecclesiastical benefice, the order of Saint-Michel, the appellation *le tueur du Roi* (the King's killer), and, three years later, a commission to gun down the Admiral.[54] These cases reflect the Italian and Spanish acceptance of the *bravo*, transferred to the highest level of power-politics.

The papacy, however, was more likely to offer treasure in heaven. Its chosen assassins were usually runagates, voluntary Catholic exiles convinced by their spiritual masters in the Continental seminaries that the English Jezebel deserved to die. We see the same religious mania in France and the Netherlands: Gérard endured four days of torture without any sign of penitence—rather he 'triumphed as if [the murder] had assuredly purchased him the eternal joys of Paradise'.[55] This resistance to torture reveals a fanaticism inculcated by the authoritarian structure of the Roman church: a Catholic could be instructed as to what works would secure his salvation, whereas a Protestant would have to search his own conscience. The English authorities, of course, denied such religious motives: runagates had fled the country 'partly for lack of living, partly for crimes committed', and those who returned as missionaries were really subversives, 'seedmen in their tillage of sedition'.[56] Those who attempted Elizabeth's assassination died not for 'poperie' but for 'most horrible and dangerous treasons against her Majestie': the distinction between the two was absolute, for the government was keen to deny that it practised religious persecution.[57]

In the official version, then, runagates were common criminals, traitors who had entered the service of a foreign potentate, the Pope. Not surprisingly, one

[51] J. E. Neale, *The Age of Catherine de Medici* (1963), 62.
[52] G. P., *The Trve Report of the Lamentable Death, of VVilliam of Nassawe Prince of Orange* (Middleborough, 1584), [14].
[53] *A Trve Report of Svndry Horrible Conspiracies of late time detected* (1594), B2ʳ.
[54] H. M. Baird, *History of the Rise of the Huguenots* (1880), ii. 337–8; H. D. Sedgwick, *The House of Guise* (1938), 211–12, 218.
[55] Neale, *Elizabeth I and her Parliaments*, ii. 45.
[56] P. L. Hughes and J. F. Larkin (eds.), *Tudor Royal Proclamations* (1964–9), iii. 88; Lord Burghley, *The Execution of Iustice in England* (1583), A3ᵛ.
[57] *A Trve and plaine declaration of the horrible Treasons, practised by William Parry the Traitor, against the Queenes Maiestie* (1585), E3ᵛ.

view of those who returned with murderous intent simply equated them
with the hirelings of secular powers. The first case to receive extensive
coverage was that of William Parry, who was brought to trial in 1585: Parry
himself claimed that his motive was 'the reliefe of the afflicted Catholiques',
but another view was that the Pope had hired him, just as he had 'suborned
many heertofore to kill her majestie'.[58] Foreign cases attracted similar views.
In 1589, for instance, the fanatical friar Jacques Clément stabbed Henry III
to death, and the Pope claimed that he was motivated by the Holy Spirit.
An English writer memorably retorted, 'it was no celestiall inspiration, it
was not the abundance of the spirit, but the spirit of abundance which
mooved him, the onely argument which perswaded *Judas*, we will give thee
thirtie peeces of silver, and he delivered them the man'.[59] As late as 1624,
Clément was remembered as the man who received five thousand ducats 'as
a gratuity for the killing of an heretical prince with a poisoned knife'.[60] There
is, of course, no known record of any such payments being made by the
papacy, to Clément or anyone else.

IV

Rightly or wrongly, then, the hired assassin had a high public profile in the
later sixteenth century. In the prose fiction of the time, however, such
characters, when they appear, receive somewhat exiguous treatment. In part,
this is simply a result of the stylistic briskness of some of the *novelle*: as
Gunnar Boklund says of Bandello's account of the Duchess of Amalfi, 'Many
names are mentioned ... but few characters emerge.'[61] This is certainly true
in Bandello's story of the adulterous Lady of Chabry, in which the assassin,
Giovan Tros, is no more than 'a man of very ill life' on hand whenever there
is another unwanted spouse or suspicious servant to be disposed of: of the
rest of his 'ill life' between his brief appearances we hear nothing.[62] In most
English stories, the assassin is not even named: indeed, both Geoffrey
Fenton and Barnaby Rich, independently retelling Bandello's novella from
Belleforest's French translation, choose to cut out the name of Tros and refer
to the man as, respectively, a 'knave' and a 'varlet'.[63]

There were also moral reasons for minimizing the assassin's role. The
principal figure of these stories is usually the hirer, and the burden of the

[58] Ibid. C4ʳ; P. Stubbes, *The Intended Treason, of Doctor Parrie* (1585), A2ᵛ.
[59] R. W., *Martine Mar-Sixtvs* (1591), D1ʳ.
[60] T. Middleton, *A Game at Chess*, ed. J. W. Harper (1966), IV. ii. 113–14.
[61] G. Boklund, *The Duchess of Malfi: Sources, Themes, Characters* (Cambridge, Mass., 1962), 7.
[62] Bandello, *Novels*, iv. 95.
[63] G. Fenton, *Certain Tragical Discourses of Bandello* (1898), ii. 104; B. Rich, *A Right Exelent and pleasaunt Dialogue, betwene Mercvry and an English Souldier* (1574), K1ʳ.

plot is generally his or her wickedness, of which the murder is one manifestation. To create too individual an assassin, then, would be to distract
attention from his employer and to reduce the impression of extreme
wickedness by implying relative degrees of evil, in that the killer does not
initiate his own crime, nor does he participate in the hirer's other activities.
A writer's aim, then, was to stress the hirer's responsibility for the murder
even if he does not personally commit it.

In many cases, language provided a useful device to this end. In *The Palace
of Pleasure* (1566–7), William Painter tells of how the Turkish prince Mustapha
was strangled by seven dumb men on the orders of his father, the Sultan
Solyman; yet he begins the novella with the extraordinary statement, 'This
Hellysh Champyon hys owne Sonne . ., in his owne presence moste Mys-
erably did kill.'[64] The sentence is over-earnest in its simplifying action: the
author and the victim of the murder are brought together and the killers
squeezed out, with only the odd-looking stress on Solyman's presence at
the event to imply their existence. Few cases are so clumsy, however: Sir
Thomas Hoby, translating Castiglione, reflects the usual practice when he
says that Synoris, desiring another man's wife, Camma, 'caused [the husband]
to be slaine'.[65] An assassin is there by implication, but he is an inexplicit
ancillary, and does not clutter up the story's sexual triangle.

There are tales in which the killer is more important, however. Painter
includes a story, derived from the *Heptameron* of Marguerite of Navarre,
which tells how the French King Francis I 'declared his gentle nature to
Counte Guillaume, that would have killed him'.[66] Guillaume is a gentleman
of the privy chamber who cannot live on the gifts and annuities he has
received from the King, and who has therefore accepted money to compass
his patron's assassination; the novella tells how Francis, warned of the Count's
intentions, exposes his faint-heartedness by giving him the opportunity to
commit the murder and making it clear what risks this would entail. The
King is the central figure of the story and the object of its praise (he was
the brother of the original author), but without a concrete opponent for his
'gentle nature' to vanquish, the point would be lost.

Similarly in Robert Greene's *Pandosto* (1588), the cup-bearer Franion,
whom the jealous title-character selects to administer poison to his supposed
rival, shows considerable independence in trying to persuade his master not
to order the murder, deciding not to commit it, and absconding with the
intended victim. This gives Greene the opportunity for a lengthy euphuistic
performance as Franion weighs up the pros and cons of murderous obedience.
There is also a distinct narrative advantage. Pandosto's jealousy derives from

---

[64] W. Painter, *The Palace of Pleasure*, ed. J. Jacobs (1890), iii. 395.
[65] B. Castiglione, *The Book of the Courtier*, tr. Sir T. Hoby (1974), 208.
[66] Painter, *Palace*, ii. 81.

'a certaine melancholy passion', and his murder plot is later said to please 'his humour'. It is all the result of a physiological imbalance in him, and Franion's function is to demonstrate this. He is not a paragon of virtue: Greene leaves the point moot as to whether his initial refusal is a product of 'a good conscience' or simply 'for fashion sake', and he is certainly tempted when offered the choice of preferment for compliance or death for disobedience. It is important that his behaviour is presented in terms of choice: first we see him offer arguments against his master's 'determinate mischief', and he becomes indeterminate later when set to 'meditate with himselfe'. As a rational man, he can see options that the obsessed Pandosto cannot, and thus he provides a point of contrast with the abnormal psychology of his king.[67]

In these two works the central figure is respectively the victim and the hirer; in Bandello's story of the Muhammadan slave, translated into English by Robert Smythe in 1577, it is the assassin. The plot concerns the Sultan of Orme, a tyrant who has murdered his way to the throne, but has overlooked one of his brothers, now in sanctuary, and two slaves, Mahomet and Cayme, who are devoted to the old order. The slaves he plans to eliminate by 'practisyng the one to be the murtherer of his companyon, and afterwardes to punish the murtherer according to the law, & his deserts'.[68] However, he reckons without the honesty of Mahomet, whom he first approaches, and who sees through his hasty assurance that this was done only to test him. Thus forewarned, Mahomet is able to persuade the more pliable Cayme to spare him and lie to the Sultan that his murderous mission has been accomplished. The Sultan stabs him for his pains and is caught red-handed by Mahomet and some soldiers.

The story could easily be focused on that common sixteenth-century bogeyman, the tyrant, but the Sultan lacks the consistency of character for such emphasis. His intrigue to destroy the two slaves is intelligent in conception, but not in execution: first he sticks doggedly to the original idea after Mahomet's refusal to co-operate, then inexplicably changes his plans and murders Cayme himself instead of allowing the law to take its course. His brother the Prince is another loose end that he seems to have no plans for (although at one point Mahomet thinks him the intended victim). These flaws are less central if we read the story as a demonstration of Mahomet's virtue, however: he is said to be the leading character, so it is not the Sultan's intrigue but his counter-intrigue that is the object of our attention. As for the Prince, who never appears, his function becomes clear in the closing moments, when the Sultan is killed and Mahomet is offered the crown: he has a prior claim which Mahomet upholds, refusing to do as the Sultan did

---

[67] Bullough, viii. 158, 159, 160.
[68] R. Smythe, *Stravnge, Lamentable, and Tragicall Hystories* (1577), H2^v.

and ascend the throne over his predecessor's dead body. The act sets the final seal on an exhibition of positive virtue.

Beyond the artistic considerations already stressed, the fact that in each of these three cases the assassin has scruples means that he must have some degree of personal independence. Even one who does fulfil his contract can be a character in his own right, though. Esdras the banditto in Thomas Nashe's *The Unfortunate Traveller* (1594) is a peripheral example. He is presumably one of the banditti who, 'hired for some few crownes ... will steale to *Rome* and do a murther', and in the past he has worked as an assassin for the Pope, who has 'authorised' his criminal activities in return; thus he is styled 'the Emperour of homicides', a secular arm of the papacy.[69] However, Nashe uses the character solely as a burglar, rapist, and murderer on his own account: the fact of having been an assassin and the nexus with the Whore of Babylon are included simply to add to his wickedness.

George Pettie's retelling of the Sinorix and Camma story in his *Petite Palace of Pettie's Pleasure* (1576) is more important. In the sixteenth century there were two traditions of this story, which derives from Plutarch's *Moralia*.[70] In the version told by Antonio de Guevara in *The Dial of Princes* (1529), faithful to the classical original, Sinorix kills Sinatus, the husband, personally.[71] In Castiglione's version, there is an assassin interposing. Pettie's treatment is in the latter tradition, with the difference that the killer is a speaking part rather than (as in *The Courtier*) an unrealized potentiality in the language. Here Sinorix selects 'one of his swearing swash buckler servauntes', who advises against murder, not on moral grounds ('For mine owne part it maketh no matter', he says) but simply because Sinorix will not get away with it: his reasons for wanting Sinatus dead are too well known, so suspicion will inevitably arise. The advice is rejected—is there not precedent for the murder in King David's treatment of Uriah?—and the servant told, 'if thou wilt not take it upon thee, I will either do it my selfe, or get some other that shall'. The servant is true to his pragmatism: 'seeyng how his Maister was bent bothe to satisfie his minde, and to gaine so good a summe of money [he] promised to perfourme his charge which with oportunity of time and place hee did'.[72]

Any discussion of Pettie's treatment of the episode must be tentative, for we do not know his immediate source—it may not have been Castiglione.[73]

---

[69] Nashe, ii. 282, 287, 320.

[70] Plutarch, *Moralia*, ed. F. C. Babbitt and others (1927–69), iii. 551–5.

[71] A. de Guevara, *The Diall of Princes*, tr. T. North (1557), r6ᵛ–s2ʳ.

[72] G. Pettie, *A Petite Pallace of Pettie his Pleasure*, ed. H. Hartman (Oxford, 1938), 31–3.

[73] There was at least one other sixteenth-century version, a (lost) ballad of '*SINOREX CANIA et SINATUS*' entered in the Stationers' Register in 1570: E. Arber (ed.), *A Transcript of the Registers of the Company of Stationers of London* (1875–94), i. 414.

If we suppose the innovation to be Pettie's, though, the reason for it is clear. C. S. Lewis comments, 'His art is at the opposite pole from that of the Italian *novella*. The story interests him solely as a trellis over which to train the flowers of rhetorical soliloquy and tirade.'[74] In particular, Pettie likes to introduce not dialogue, but set-piece speeches of debate in euphuistic style: in his hands plots spin out as reasoning precedes each decision. This is what has happened with the murder. The killing itself is rapidly accomplished: it is the exchange of speeches between servant and master that occupies Pettie's attention. It was presumably to create the opportunity for such speeches that he brought the assassin out of the prison-house of elliptical language.

There is a very positive portrayal of the hired murderer in Bandello's novella of Turchi and Deodati, which was translated into French by Belleforest in 1583 but did not proceed thence into English.[75] The plot concerns Turchi's revenge for a wound in the face which he believes his enemy Deodati has given him, and is based on an incident which occurred in Antwerp in 1551. To compass his design, Turchi hires a serving-man, Giulio of Romagna, who is to murder not only Deodati but also the Piedmontese servant he has to enlist to help him dispose of the body. Giulio is a major character, and much of the interest of the story derives from his relationship with Turchi. Nonetheless Turchi remains the novella's locus of wickedness: Bandello calls him 'a villain in grain', and though Giulio 'must ... have had a hand in an hundred murders', it is Turchi who initiates the two in the story—Giulio merely carries them out.

There is a place for the assassin in the novella because, besides evil, Turchi's principal characteristic is ineptitude. Bandello makes this clear from the start by stressing that he has jumped to the wrong conclusion about his assailant's identity, and by describing his intentions in somewhat contradictory terms—'to avenge himself on such wise that he might not be molested of justice and it should nevertheless abide in all men's minds that he had been the doer'. Even so, he rejects poison as a method, 'unknowing how he might avail to have thereof, without its being known'; nor is steel an option, since he is a weakling, 'gouty and feeble of arm and hand'. Turchi, then, has the *mens rea* for the murder, but it takes Giulio's skill and pragmatism to achieve the *actus reus*: Turchi cannot even succeed in killing Deodati when he is trapped in a trick-chair, and the job has to be finished off by Giulio.

It is Giulio too who is practical about arrangements afterwards. He and his employer have great difficulty in lugging the corpse down to the cellar, but when a house-to-house search makes its removal expedient, Turchi has

---

[74] C. S. Lewis, *English Literature in the Sixteenth Century Excluding Drama* (Oxford, 1954), 311.

[75] It may, however, have been known in England: it includes a trick-chair that is often cited in relation to *The Broken Heart*.

to be reminded that it is too heavy for one man to move—hence the employment of the Piedmontese to help Giulio. When the man rather inconsiderately runs off without waiting to be killed, leaving the corpse immovable in the middle of the street and exposure imminent, it is Giulio once more who knows how to cope with the situation: he flees to another state, leaving nothing to incriminate Turchi. All this casts him in an advisory role, and it is in such a capacity that he finally overreaches himself, by writing an incriminating letter telling Turchi how to behave if arrested; this falls into the hands of the authorities, and it is enough to condemn them both.[76]

This unusual relationship between assassin and employer is best seen as a variation on the hiring situation rather than a conscious exploration of character. Such variations provide the narrative interest in other stories too. Another of Bandello's *novelle*, retold in Painter's *Palace of Pleasure*, has its emphasis on the money involved. The plot concerns Didaco and Violenta, who are married in secret and do not cohabit, a situation which adversely affects Violenta's honour when gossip spreads about Didaco's regular visits. He has given her the sum of twelve hundred ducats to spend 'upon small trifles, such as be apt and convenient for householde'; but when she discovers that she is the victim of a bigamist, she decides that the money has been 'predestinated by the heavens for none other purpose but to paie them their hire, which shall do the vengeaunce upon his disloyall persone'.[77] In effect, Didaco has paid for his own assassination. It is only a momentary irony, for when the murder is committed our attention is with Violenta rather than Janique, the maidservant whose assistance she buys; and at the end of the novella (in the version told in French by Pierre Boaistuau and in English by Painter, though not in Bandello's Italian original), Janique escapes to Africa with the money, never to be heard of again, leaving her mistress to monopolize the trial and execution that are the conclusion.

As a final example, Greene's stress in the first story ('Venus' Tragedy') of his *Planetomachia* (1585) is on what happens when things do not go according to plan. It is often stipulated by hirers that the assassin should flee to another country after committing the murder: in some cases, indeed, the fee is said to be for travelling expenses or maintenance abroad. Such flight constituted a virtual admission of guilt, of course—remember the interpretation put on the disappearance of Malcolm and Donalbain in *Macbeth*—but international boundaries made for safe sanctuary. As for the hirer, the departure of his instrument left a void between him and the crime into which the trail would vanish. It is unsurprising, then, that Duke Valdracko in Greene's story should make this agreement with the 'desperate ruffian' he hires to murder the head

---

[76] Bandello, *Novels*, vi. 184, 182, 179.
[77] Painter, *Palace*, i. 224, 228.

of a family with whom he is feuding.[78] In this case, however, the killer does not have the chance to leave the country, for he is apprehended in the hue and cry following the murder, and brought before the Duke and Senate for trial. The two guilty parties play the situation differently: the assassin seems complacently assured of the Duke's co-operation, but the Duke is more apprehensive and orders the man's tongue to be cut out. Only then does the assassin realize the extent of his employer's deviousness, but the officers are too quick for him and he never submits his incriminating evidence. Greene's rather brief treatment does not fully exploit the scene's potential for tension as each party waits for the other to show his hand: Valdracko cracks too soon, and we see too little of the assassin's point of view. The interest of the episode as it stands is instead in the Duke's quick-thinking response to the changed circumstances, the mark of a successful intriguer.

It is important to realize that these works constitute a very small percentage of Elizabethan prose fiction, and even of the sub-category of crime fiction, in stark contrast with the ubiquity of the assassin in the drama after 1587, and indeed in John Reynolds's later collection of *novelle*, *The Triumphs of God's Revenge* (1621–35). Nonetheless, one of the writers, Greene, was also a dramatist, and some of the stories were to be the sources of plays: *Pandosto* was staged as *The Winter's Tale* (1610), of course, and the treatment of the assassin Lazarotto at his trial in *The First Part of Hieronimo* (?1600) may be based on the equivalent incident in 'Venus' Tragedy'.[79] Moreover, in some cases, as we shall see, the treatment of the hired murderer anticipates interests which received their fullest expression in dramatic form. What concerns us first, however, is the emergence of the assassin as a stock figure in the dramatic repertoire.

[78] R. Greene, *Complete Works*, ed. A. B. Grosart (1881–6), v. 90.

[79] Lazarotto is arrested immediately after the murder, brought before the King, and is about to expose his employer Lorenzo when his mouth is stopped and he is carried off.

2

THE ORIGINS OF THE STAGE ASSASSIN I:
1558–1587

I

THE early history of the Elizabethan dramatic assassin begins with Thomas Preston's tyrant-play *Cambises* (*c.*1561), which includes two episodes in which the protagonist employs a pair of killers, identified allegorically as Murder and Cruelty. The problem of lost plays makes it hard to trace the character's development thereafter: his next known appearance on the public stage was in Anthony Munday's *Fedele and Fortunio* (1583–4), and then in Thomas Kyd's *The Spanish Tragedy* (1587). There are also hired murderers in two academic plays dating from the intervening quarter-century: the Inner Temple's *Gismond of Salerne* (1568) and the third play in Dr Thomas Legge's Latin trilogy *Richardus Tertius*, performed at St John's College, Cambridge in March, 1580. What is clear is that playwrights used the assassin with great frequency in the years immediately following Kyd's seminal play: in English history plays like *Edward II*, *Woodstock* (1592), and *Richard III* (1592–3); in romances like *King Leir and his Three Daughters* (1589), *James IV* (1590), and *Mucedorus* (1590); in plays as miscellaneous as *David and Bethsabe* (*c.*1587), *Selimus* (1592), and *Arden of Faversham* (1590). By 1592, he had become an established figure in the repertory, if he was not one already.

Preston found no assassins in his principal narrative source, Richard Taverner's *The Garden of Wisdom* (1539). What he found was the same sort of elliptical expression we have already encountered in prose fiction. The first incident is described in one simple sentence: 'He murdered also hys owne brother smerdis, whom he prively caused to be put to deth, lest he might at any tyme be king.' Taverner's account of the second, in which Cambyses has his Queen killed for reminding him of Smerdis, includes more detail about the circumstances, but narrates the murder itself just as baldly: 'The kyng ... commaunded she shuld forthwith be taken out of hys syght and put to deathe.'[1] Neither of these passages imposes any specific enactment on the dramatist, and Preston had two options other than the one he chose in staging the incidents.

In both cases the killing could occur off stage, obviating any need to introduce functionaries to perform it. However, the theatrical merits of such

[1] R. Taverner, *The second booke of the Garden of wysedome* (1539), C4^r, C5^r.

a course are dubious, and Preston's aesthetic was, it has been argued, more theatrical than literary.[2] Alternatively, Preston could have chosen to follow the moral rather than the literal import of Taverner's words (explicit in 'he murdered ... smerdis'), and make Cambises kill his victims with his own hands. The use of intermediaries, it has been suggested, makes the episodes 'less illustrative of Cambises's cruelty'.[3] Preston, that is, achieves the theatrical immediacy of sensational violence, but passes up the opportunity to supplement it with moral immediacy; the violence exists more for itself than as a comment on Cambises, and our moral response to the play is diffused—so the argument might run. Such a view derives from a long-standing misconception of the characters of Murder and Cruelty.

'Most of the personifications in Cambises ... are not true allegorizations at all but generalized types set in historical context,' writes David Bevington. 'They might have been named specifically had the author so wished. ... Cruelty and Murder are in effect that pair so familiar in Shakespeare's chronicles and tragedies, signaled by the stage direction "Enter two murderers." '[4] Broadly speaking, Bevington's position is a valid one. Unlike individuals, personified abstractions are ineffective as dramatic characters unless their identity is communicated to the audience on their first appearance, whether verbally or visually: it is immaterial that (for example) until the closing moments of King Lear (1605–6) we are unaware that Lear has known the disguised Kent as Caius; but if Everyman were not identified at the earliest stage, he would become any man, more individual than type, and the whole effect of the play would be changed. Whether from ineptitude or unconcern, Preston is frequently clumsy over such matters. Two of the abstractions are never identified in the dialogue, and it is hard to imagine a visual device that would convey to an audience the concepts of 'Commons' Cry' and 'Preparation'; anyway, the naming of these characters relates more to their function in the action than to such concepts. Three other such characters (Small Hability, Attendance, and Diligence) are identified late in their appearances, after the audience has had the opportunity to draw its own conclusions. Execution is explicitly presented as an individual rather than a personification, the 'execution-man' (411, 434, 473); and Counsel could also be interpreted as such.[5] Three other characters (Proof, Trial, and Commons' Complaint) are named on introduction, though the abstractions serve primarily for shorthand purposes: Commons' Complaint allows one actor to represent many people, and Proof and Trial enable Preston to bypass enquiry into allegations which the audience already knows to be true. As

---

[2] B. J. Fishman, SEL 16 (1976), 201–11.   [3] D. C. Allen, MLN 49 (1934), 386.

[4] D. M. Bevington, From 'Mankind' to Marlowe (Cambridge, Mass., 1962), 186–7.

[5] He is consistently referred to as Cambises' Counsel; in the second quarto, the opening stage direction (though no other) calls him 'Councellor'.

Bevington says, these are not genuinely allegorical figures.[6]

Cruelty and Murder differ in that Preston makes the abstractions indices of character as well as of function. This is apparent from their first exchange of dialogue:

CRUELTY
My coequall partner, Murder, come away;
From me long thou maist not stay.
MURDER
Yes, from thee I may stay, but not thou from me;
Therefore I have a prerogative above thee.   (710–13)

One cannot murder without cruelty, that is, but one can exercise cruelty without committing murder; in personifying the abstractions, Preston has turned the principle into a question of status. It is a tautological parallelism when Murder subsequently tells Smirdis that they have orders from Cambises,

Upon thee to bestow our behaviour,
With cruelty to murder you and make you away.   (721–2)

Being Murder and Cruelty, no other 'behaviour' is to be expected from them. Finally, it is Cruelty who is given the most obviously sadistic lines:

Even now I strike, his body to wound.
Beholde, now his blood springs out on the ground!   (728–9)

There is no similar emphasis on the underlying abstractions at the murder of the Queen, but the action of a play, even an episodic one such as this, is cumulative, so we assume this groundwork when the characters reappear. Admittedly that groundwork is not perfectly executed: the fact that Cruelty is not named until after his first exit would blur the details somewhat in performance (although we can assume that he is a murderer and an abstraction like his companion). The point is, however, that Preston clearly intended these characters to be more than First and Second Murderer.

Being personifications, they never achieve substantive individuality. We see not only human beings but walking allusions, and, as in the morality tradition, these have a double application. There is more than one character in *Cambises* who is characterized by cruelty. Shame, black-trumpeting Cambises' misdeeds, makes three specific accusations:

Lechery and drunkennes he doth it much frequent;
The tigers kinde to imitate he hath given full consent.   (345–6)

The third of these, though the least explicit, is of most importance in the play. 'His cruelty we wil delate,' announces the Prologue (34), and it is as a series of four killings that Ambidexter sums up the action:

---

[6] I have omitted Shame from this survey in so far as her function is choric, not dramatic.

> Cambises put a judge to death,—that was a good deed,—
> But to kill the yong childe was worse to proceed,
> To murder his brother and then his owne wife,—
> So help me God and holidom, it is pitie of his life!   (1151–4)

Drunkenness could lead to murder in practice, as did lechery in contemporary theory, and each is narratively anterior to the crime in one of the main-plot episodes (the shooting of Praxaspes' son and the wooing of the Queen respectively). However, it is cruelty which the play stresses as Cambises' fundamental vice:

> He was akin to Bishop Bonner, I think verily!
> For both their delights was to shed blood,
> But never intended to doo any good.   (1148–50)

Accordingly, Ambidexter gives two variant accounts of the murder of Smirdis: first, 'Lord Smirdis by Cruelty and Murder is slaine' (734), but then, 'The king through his cruelty hath made him away.' (745) The character of Cruelty, then, is a vestige of the externalized psychology of the morality plays; except that, in a work far closer to Marlowe than to Prudentius, he is under the direction of the central character, not an influence upon him— Cambises' 'delight' (1100) at his arrival to take charge of the Queen is a sign of the inherent tendency that made him send for the character in the first place, not of the impressionable behaviour we find in a morality protagonist. Because of the nature of the intermediary he introduces, then, Preston has been able to retain the moral short circuit he found in Taverner's prose.

This account has been a partial one in several respects: it shows Preston's ingenuity in avoiding a corollary of the use of hired murderers without indicating why such characters need have been introduced at all; and it ignores Murder, who personifies an abstraction that is not an element of psychology. There is a public as well as a personal dimension to *Cambises*, much as the king had two bodies: Cruelty reflects a feature of Cambises' person, Murder of his tyrannical regime. Tyrants were archetypal employers of assassins: one of the commonest subjects in the medieval mystery cycles, for example, was the Massacre of the Innocents by soldiers acting under the orders of King Herod.[7] More recently, Castiglione had remarked that tyrants 'maintaine ... murtherers and cutthroates to put men in feare and make them to become faint harted'.[8] The appearance of such characters here allows Preston a further conventional index of the nature of Cambises' rule, but

---

[7] There are examples in all four surviving cycles, as well as one-off versions from Digby and Coventry, and a fragment of a seventh play, reprinted by R. H. Robbins, *Anglia*, 72 (1954–5), 31–4. These plays may have influenced Shakespeare in *Richard III* and *Macbeth*: see Jones, *Origins*, 80–3, and S. Colley, *Shakespeare Quarterly*, 37 (1986), 451–8. However, I see no evidence of indebtedness elsewhere.

[8] B. Castiglione, *The Book of the Courtier*, tr. Sir T. Hoby (1974), 278.

also the opportunity to explore the inverted values that flourish under that rule. The point is laboured by Smirdis, who tells them, pleading for his life,

> Consider, the king is a tirant tirannious,
> And all his dooings be damnable and parnitious.   (724–5)

They ignore him and proceed to effect the particular 'damnable and parnitious' doing that he was trying to prevent. The moral element is more effective on their second appearance, where the audience is allowed to infer it: there is something decidedly sinister about their declared intent to murder a defenceless woman 'With couragious harts' (1110) and 'with a good will' (1103). Moreover, it is at this point that their nexus with tyranny is made most explicit. Not only does Cambises license their criminal behaviour— 'Spare for no feare; I doo you full permit' (1108)—he also makes reference to their 'offices' (1105), underlining the fact that they have replaced Execution, who performed the legitimate killing of Sisamnes, and who also had an 'office' (459).[9] The base shall to the legitimate: such is the tyrant's regime.

Moral immediacy is also served by the use of personifications rather than individuals. Cambises employs Murder, not a murderer; he uses Cruelty to kill people, rather than killing them cruelly. Although they have a concrete relation to a particular individual and to a particular set of political circumstances, they also represent abstract concepts—this is the 'double application' mentioned above. The moral point becomes fundamental, fused with the actuality. It is a technique which should, in theory, be the more effective in a play such as this which mixes personifications with historical figures: in a more purely allegorical play, the audience is never forced to integrate morality with mimesis. In practice, there are the flaws noted above, and the characters are probably given too little stage time and attention to establish them clearly enough for success in this respect; but unfortunately we are unlikely today to find an audience sufficiently versed in the conventions of personification to test this aspect of the play in performance.

In creating a pair of hired assassins, then, Preston achieves (or at least intends) an illustration of his protagonist's wickedness with more facets than his alternatives, outlined above, would have allowed. The need to choose between these alternatives, the impetus behind the creation of Murder and Cruelty, lies in the nature of the dramatic medium itself. The writer of a prose narrative has considerable freedom in selecting those details he wishes to portray: everything is communicated to the reader through his words, so the impression made by brief or oblique references is minimal. Drama is more sharply focused, and the playwright's options are accordingly more

---

[9] This supplanting is especially clear from Bevington's analysis of the play's structure in relation to the characters involved ('*Mankind*' to *Marlowe*, 184–5).

limited: he cannot gloss over functionaries like the assassin, for everything on stage has its own substantive existence; and, once introduced, the hired murderer will naturally command audience attention, involved as he is in a violent act of narrative importance. Taverner's prose leaves us with little sense of the assassins; but we do not easily forget Murder and Cruelty.

II

We find other problems of adapting prose sources in the two academic plays, *Gismond of Salerne* and *Richardus Tertius*. The former is derived from the first novella of the fourth day of Boccaccio's *Decameron*, a story of paternal possessiveness, with a dark, incestuous sub-text, that achieved great popularity in Renaissance Europe. It was retold in English verse by Gilbert Banester in the fifteenth century, by William Walter in 1532, and later as one of Dryden's *Fables* (1700). There were numerous dramatic adaptations in many languages, beginning with Antonio Cammelli's Italian tragedy *Filostrato e Panfila* (1499); in England, the story was probably available to paying playgoers at the original Blackfriars theatre as well as to the Inner Temple's élite audience, though only a song has survived from the Blackfriars play.[10]

At the climax of the story, Tancredi, Prince of Salerno, captures Guiscardo, his daughter Ghismonda's lover, and has him strangled one night by his two guards. Boccaccio's narrative takes as its focus here Tancredi's orders, which are made very specific: the men are 'to strangle him noiselessly that same night, after which they were to take out his heart and bring it to him'. The act of murder is conflated into the act of commanding it, and Boccaccio only needs to add that the guards 'carried out his orders to the letter'.[11]

The murder is presented in similarly oblique fashion in the Inner Temple play, taking place off stage; but the angle of approach is different. When Guishard is taken to prison at the end of Act IV, it is clear that his death is to follow, and he speaks of it in anticipation; in Robert Wilmot's revision of the play, the fifth Act is preceded by a dumb show in which his guards drag him away with a garrotte around his neck.[12] However, the murder is most fully realized at the start of Act V, Wilmot's contribution to the original version, when it is described by Renuchio, a gentleman of Tancred's privy chamber who was among the party of servants sent to perform the killing, and who is now on the way to deliver the victim's disembodied heart to

[10] G. E. P. Arkwright, *N&Q* 10th ser., 5 (1906), 341–2.
[11] G. Boccaccio, *The Decameron*, tr. G. H. McWilliam (Harmondsworth, 1972), 339.
[12] R. Wilmot, *Tancred and Gismund*, ed. W. W. Greg (Oxford, 1915), H4ᵛ. This does not appear in the manuscripts of the earlier version, and there is no evidence that it was included in the original performance.

Gismond. In accordance with the classical form of the tragedy, he is the Senecan *nuntius* for whom 'the cruel fact is ever in myne eyes' (v. i. 32), and who is accordingly able to give a precise account of the horror he has observed.[13] However, he cannot simply be explained, as he has been by John Cunliffe, as a stock character, imported like Megaera and the Chorus from Seneca.[14] Seneca's messengers are witnesses: Wilmot has given the role to one of the murderers.

Up to a point, it is logical to use the assassin as a *nuntius*: with any other witness we would ask why they did not intervene in what was, after all, hardly the sort of unstoppable natural disaster that Seneca's messengers report. Even with the murderer, though, there is a similar problem when his part includes the conventional lamentation of the *nuntius*: if that is how he feels, why did he commit the murder in the first place? This is not simply a difficulty thrown up by the decision to conflate the Senecan messenger, a piece of dramatic machinery, with one of the actants in the narrative, a realistic character. That decision is itself a corollary of the need to dramatize interpersonal violence in a classical form which is better suited to mayhem on a grand scale.

An instructive comparison may be made with Cammelli's *Filostrato e Panfila*, which uses a similar technique in dramatizing the murder: it is described to King Demetrio by the servant, Tynolo, who has performed it. However, Cammelli evades the resultant problems by creating a chain of command not unlike that in *Richard III*: between Demetrio and Tynolo stands Pandhero, Demetrio's secretary, whose task it has been to procure the murderer. This allows a successful compromise between convention and character: Pandhero laments the killing at length, while Tynolo speaks up tersely for the virtues of obeying royal commands, then goes to make his report to the King; we see the servant's own self-recrimination gradually develop in the course of four scenes of fetching and carrying. The elements of the messenger's role survive, but the role itself does not; the lamenter need not have been present at the murder he bewails, for the reporter can always be another character.

Wilmot is more slavishly Senecan in his treatment, and so more clumsy. Nonetheless we need not take the contradictions inherent in Renuchio's dual role of messenger and murderer as a sign of the dramatist's ineptitude. The same tender-heartedness appears in all the murderers at the very moment of the killing:

---

[13] In the earlier of the two manuscripts of the play, indeed, he is designated as 'Renuccio the messenger': British Library MS Hargrave 205, fo. 18ʳ.

[14] J. W. Cunliffe, *PMLA* 21 (1906), 454, 458.

> They stretch the bandes, and even when the breath
> began to faile his brest, they slacked againe
> (so did their handes repine against his death)
> and oft times loosed, alas, unto his paine.   (v. i. 141–4)

In part, this behaviour makes for physical horror: however suitable for the sort of silent nocturnal execution that Boccaccio's Tancredi has in mind, strangling is too quiet a death for a Senecan play; so Wilmot makes the killing horrible, by having the murderers first unintentionally extend Guishard's death agonies and then fall to mutilation of the corpse, which even 'savage beastes do spare' (177). If horror were the dramatist's sole concern here, though, the killers' behaviour need not have been so contradictory: their reason for slackening the strangling-cords could have been different, or not specified at all; yet Wilmot chose not only to make them 'repine', but also allowed this detail to stand in his 1591 revision.[15] Clearly, then, there is a point to it.

The only person who does not find the murder of Guishard a 'dolefull destinie' (1) is Tancred himself: Renuchio reports him 'rejoysing to behold' (194) the heart brought in on a sword's point. The contrast in attitude is important. Renuchio and his fellow-murderers are instruments of their king's 'cruel hest' (69), and, here as in *Filostrato e Panfila*, there is some stress on the subject's obligation to obey. By emphasizing the killers' reluctance and revulsion, Wilmot assigns sole responsibility for the crime to Tancred, much as Greene later used Franion in *Pandosto*. The problem has been the same as that of *Cambises*, of avoiding the moral fragmentation of the play; but Wilmot has a different form of drama with different conventions to manipulate, and the result is a different presentation of the assassin.

III

Unlike Preston and Wilmot, Dr Legge did not have to create the murderers in Part Three of *Richardus Tertius*: he found them all, Brakenbury, Tyrrel, Dighton, and Forrest, in his sources, the accounts by Thomas More and Edward Hall of the tragical doings of Richard III; he also found a detailed narrative of the murder itself. One reason for this copiousness, in contrast with the reticence of most prose fiction, is the different concerns of the chroniclers: whereas fiction traces the career of an individual whose acts constitute the thread of the story, Tudor history traces a sequence of acts which are assigned to individuals. Accordingly, the chronicles scrupulously name names whenever possible, pinning their actants down as distinct and

---

[15] The revised version of the line, 'So did their hands repine against their hearts' (1513), adds to the impression of internal struggle.

historically identifiable personages. We may divine the reason for this from the speech made by Sir Piers Exton in Fabyan's *Chronicle* after he has assassinated King Richard II: 'alas, what have we doen, we have now put to death hym, that hath been our soveraigne and drad lorde, by the space of .xxii. yeres, by reason wherof I shall be reproched of all honor, where soever I after this daie become, and all men shall redound this deede to my dishonor & shame'.[16] Men were still doing so two centuries later. The more infamous the deed, the more important it was to catalogue its perpetrators for posterity: and few deeds were more heinous than killing a king.

Even so, More's *History of King Richard III* (c.1513), the basis for most subsequent accounts of that monarch, is suspicious in the degree of its specificity. The killing of the young King Edward V is described in every detail, and everyone involved is named, even the low-born assassins, Tyrrel's horse-keeper John Dighton, and the criminal Miles Forrest, 'a felowe fleshed in murther before time'.[17] We may allow imaginative licence in the description, but how could More have known these names? Such men do not usually draw attention to themselves, and in no other murder case was a chronicler able to identify the assassins when they were servants or other such persons of little account: yet Dighton and Forrest did exist and were connected in some way with Richard's court.[18] Unless we are prepared (as few historians now are) to accept More's claim that his source was Tyrrel's confession, and so to accept the truth of the murder as told, his account is problematic. Possibly the answer lies in the work's status as propaganda dressed as history: More's informants may have had reasons for casting specific individuals as murderers. Whatever the truth, the key point for our purposes is that the narrative is looser and less intensely focused than any to be found in the explicitly fictional sources available to dramatists.

Writing as he is in the Senecan form, Legge's initial problem is, again, to adapt that form to present a murder. Like Cammelli, he divides the role of *nuntius* among his participants: the murder scene is structured around four long speeches, beginning with Brakenbury attacking Richard's decision to have his nephews murdered, followed by reports from Tirell about his commission from the King, and from Dighton, closely following More, of the murder itself, to conclude with Brakenbury again lamenting the horrid deed. The scene is not so much drama as narrative for speakers, then. There are still touches of stagecraft, however. Legge's concern is to pitch the murder for maximum emotional effect, and the first three scenes of the play are constructed around the watershed of Dighton's account and the display of the corpses. Up to that point, midway through Act i, Scene ii, suspense is maintained as Brakenbury and Tirell talk of their commission and their

[16] R. Fabyan, *Chronicle* (1559), 214[r–v].

[17] T. More, *The History of King Richard III*, ed. R. S. Sylvester (1963), 85.   [18] Ibid. 265.

unease about executing it. Afterwards all is ululation, beginning with Brakenbury's reaction to the sight of the bodies:

> Videone corpora regulorum livida?
> funestus heu jam caede puerili thorus.
> quis lachrymas durus malis vultus negat?[19]   (I. ii. 97–9)

The sole purpose of the following scene is to show the mother's tears. In contrast, Dighton, on whom the sequence is centred, is the only person to view the murder dispassionately. He is a technician whose speech concentrates on the method he and Forrest have used:

> mox suffocantur adempto uterque spiritu
> quia pervium spirantibus non est iter.[20]   (94–5)

The effect would have been the more chilling in performance because of the man's physical size: in More, he is 'a big brode square strong knave', and Legge retains this, designating him in the *dramatis personae* as 'Dighton carnifex. a big sloven', whereas we may assume that Tirell and Brakenbury are of normal size.[21] When the bodies of two dead children are displayed, the stage contains a horrifying sequence from the enormous murderer to his tiny victims: without seeing any act of violence, we register a shocking brutality that justifies the somewhat prolix wail that follows.

The murder of the princes is an important turning-point in the Richard III story as told by More: Richard is tortured by guilt as a result, and his closest henchman, Buckingham, turns against him. Legge places the incident strongly at the start of Part Three of his trilogy, which is concerned with Richard's downfall. Although structurally logical, however, this positioning brings out a familiar problem which Legge, unlike Preston and Wilmot, has been unable to solve. Although the Argument to Part Three, clearly designed to be spoken before the performance as a prologue, describes Richard's villainies, as the play itself begins we see only his instruments: they refer to him, of course, and raise questions of loyalty and obedience, but Richard himself is not a physical presence on stage until Act III. More's *History* is not the easiest of sources to dramatize: it has a central villain in Richard, but because of its historical diffuseness as a narrative, there is much to include besides Richard. In Legge's play, the character's absence stretches his nexus with the murderers almost to breaking-point. Significantly, though, the difficulty did not recur in the later plays for the popular stage that were based on More; we shall see why in Chapter 3.

[19] 'Do I see the livid bodies of the Princes? Alas, their bed is now defiled with their youthful slaughter. What harsh countenance will refuse tears for these evils?'

[20] 'Soon both, their breath having been taken away, were suffocated, because there was no way accessible for their breathing.'

[21] More, *History*, 85; T. Legge, *Richardus Tertius*, ed. R. J. Lordi (1979), 156. *Carnifex*: butcher.

IV

Playwrights could also have found the assassin fully formed in *cinquecento* Italian drama, in which the *bravo* often featured as a variant form of the braggart, sometimes in the specific role of hired assassin (though often working for sexual favours rather than gold), and sometimes as a general underworld figure.[22] Two English plays require brief notice in this connection, Abraham Fraunce's Latin comedy *Victoria*, written at Cambridge in the early 1580s, and Anthony Munday's *Fedele and Fortunio*. Both are based on Luigi Pasqualigo's *Fedele* (1576), a play about the amorous intrigues sparked off when two men pursue the same woman, Victoria. When she feels that one of them has insulted her, she prosecutes her revenge by inducing a third suitor, Frangipietra, to murder him. Frangipietra is not only a *bravo* but a '*bravaccio*', and cowardly with it, and the upshot of the incident is that he is caught by the watch and publicly displayed in a net.[23]

Fraunce and Munday treat Frangipietra very differently. In *Victoria*, the role is cut down, excluding the business with the net: instead, Victoria simply communicates to the off-stage assassin that she has changed her mind, and we never see him again. In contrast, Munday adapts Pasqualigo's play by slimming down the number of servants, giving some of their action to Frangipietra, Anglicized as Captain Crackstone. The result is that Crackstone becomes the principal comic character, given to malapropism, confusion, and slapstick. His assassin's role in the second half becomes one of several humorous escapades, with a feigned fight under Victoria's window, and then the net incident.

The influence of *Fedele and Fortunio* on subsequent drama has yet to be studied in detail. Muriel Bradbrook has suggested that the play was 'outmoded' almost at once by advances in the Italianate manner made by Lyly.[24] However, its plot strikingly anticipates some of the motifs of Shakespeare's comedies, especially *The Two Gentlemen of Verona* (?1592), *A Midsummer Night's Dream* (1595), and *Much Ado About Nothing* (1598).[25] Crackstone seems to have been popular: the title given at the head of the printed text is 'The Pleasant and Fine Conceited Comedy of Two Italian Gentlemen, with the Merry Devices of Captain Crackstone'; and Nashe remembered the character in 1596.[26] His influence on the nascent assassin type seems to have

[22] See D. C. Boughner, *The Braggart in Renaissance Comedy* (Minneapolis, 1954), 60, 76–7, 80–2, 100, 102–3, 107.

[23] L. Pasqualigo, *Il Fedele Comedia* (Venice, 1576), D8ᵛ. *Bravaccio*: braggart.

[24] M. C. Bradbrook, *The Growth and Structure of Elizabethan Comedy*, new edn. (Cambridge, 1973), 41.

[25] On *Much Ado*, see Richard Hosley's edition (1981), 95–6. Hosley underrates the similarities with the other two plays, which lie in the central plot of mismatched pairs of lovers, and in the use of magical means to compel love.   [26] Nashe, iii. 102.

been negligible, however. This is because Munday, like Fraunce, is true to the original Italian play in that he assimilates the character to an already established type, the Plautine swaggerer or *miles gloriosus*: he is the captain of the guard on the city gates, not a professional *bravo*; in *Victoria* he is even referred to as 'Frangipetra glorioso milite' (1688) at one point. Nashe's later allusion coupled Crackstone with another dramatic braggart, Basilisco in *Soliman and Perseda* (1590), not with any of the stage assassins that were by then common.

The hired murderers who began to appear from the late 1580s owed little to the Italian *bravo*, either directly or via *Fedele and Fortunio*. Equally uninfluential were the three academic plays discussed in this chapter, none of which were available in print anyway. For the seminal influence on the later assassin, we must turn back to *Cambises*.

There are a number of very general similarities between Preston's work and that of his successors. Assassins often work in pairs in plays written later in the century; the dramatist of *Arden of Faversham* even adapts his source material to make a twosome, Black Will and Shakebag. Moreover, playwrights were still concerned primarily with a single central villain, so that the assassin is not so much a character in his own right as a means of casting aspersions on his employer: there are no plays of the 1580s and 1590s about hired murderers, only plays with hired murderers in them. The character is a subordinate one, something especially evident in the construction of Scene ii of *The Massacre at Paris* (c.1591), in which the Duke of Guise holds the stage and our attention, while his hirelings pass across it to receive their commissions.

However, there is no need to invoke the influence of a generation-old play in explanation of these similarities. The dramatists shared Preston's artistic and moral concerns, so naturally the assassin would continue to attract less attention than his employer; and if troupe numbers permitted, to have two murderers simply made for more effective drama, in that it gave each of them someone to talk to besides the victim.

Even if there is a debt to be considered, moreover, the quarter-century between *Cambises* and *The Spanish Tragedy* is a period for which more plays are lost than are extant, and in such circumstances Occam's razor becomes a blunt instrument: we cannot be sure that it was *Cambises* and not some other, lost play on which the later playwrights were drawing, and, even if it was, whether the characters were filtered through intermediary works before reaching them. Even a blunt instrument is better than none, however, if used with these caveats in mind. The direct influence of *Cambises* is not impossible: the play was printed and went through two editions (c.1570, c.1585); these were presumably intended for use by actors as well as readers (they included a doubling pattern), so the play may well have been on the stage as late as the 1580s. The gap of thirty years narrows, and we need only recall Falstaff's performance in 'King Cambyses' vein' (II. v. 390) in *Henry IV, Part 1* (1596–7) to show that *Cambises* was at least remembered into the 1590s.[27] Indeed, several scholars have suggested, largely on the basis of verbal parallels, that Shakespeare knew the play at first hand.[28] This being the case, a more particular influence of *Cambises* on certain plays may now be suggested.

The career of Cambises as it is dramatized by Preston consists of five episodes: an act of justice, three acts of murder, and a deserved death. It is the three murder episodes which concern us here: first Cambises shoots the son of his councillor Praxaspes, then he sends Murder and Cruelty to kill first his brother Smirdis and then his wife. There is a similar structure to the criminal careers of two of Shakespeare's characters. Richard of Gloucester first kills Henry VI with his own hands, in *Henry VI, Part 3* (1591), and then, in *Richard III*, suborns two sets of murderers to dispose of Clarence and the Princes; as in *Cambises*, the second murder has a brother for its victim and the third takes place off stage. Macbeth, too, follows the murder of Duncan, committed personally, by hiring assassins who kill Banquo and Lady Macduff and her son; she too (though not the boy) is killed off stage. The parallels between the two sets of incidents have been discussed by Emrys Jones; to his account must be added that in both cases Shakespeare adjusts his sources to create a structure like that of the murders in *Cambises*.[29]

In neither of the accounts of Macbeth that Shakespeare read (those of Raphael Holinshed and George Buchanan) is Lady Macduff killed by assassins in the manner of the play: in these versions, Macbeth has entered the castle at the head of an army and has her and her children slain, presumably by the soldiers and in his presence.[30] Shakespeare's alteration brings the action of the play into line with the murder and two hirings of the career of Richard III, but that sequence was itself his own creation. No prior account of the murder of Clarence corresponds with the version we see in *Richard III*. In the three works which allege Richard's responsibility (Hall's Chronicle, Shakespeare's main source for the play, does not), professional assassins do not appear. *The True Tragedy of Richard III* (1591) has Clarence for a ghostly Prologue, and it is said that he was 'cruelly murthered, by Richard *Glosters* Duke' (42), and 'By *Glosters* Duke drowned in a but of wine' (49). In *The Mirror for Magistrates* (1559), Richard commits the murder himself, in the

---

[27] There are further allusions to King Cambyses by Thomas Dekker in *Satiromastix* (v. ii. 249) and *The Gull's Hornbook* (*Selected Prose Writings*, ed. E. D. Pendry [1967], 98), while the play's Vice, Ambidexter, was remembered in *Alphonsus, Emperor of Germany* (II. ii. 48–50) and possibly in G. Chapman, *Bussy D'Ambois* (I. i. 204).

[28] M. P. Tilley, *MLN* 24 (1909), 244–7; K. Muir, *The Sources of Shakespeare's Plays* (1977), 76.

[29] E. Jones, *Scenic Form in Shakespeare* (Oxford, 1971), 200–1.

[30] Bullough, vii. 501, 515.

presence of accomplices.[31] Only in *Richardus Tertius* is there even a hint of his handing over the job to hired contractors, a hint not only as elliptical as in Taverner, but also dependent on one interpretation of an ambiguous piece of Latin: 'fratri suo mortem intulit Glocestrius'[32] (Part 1, I. i. 95). Shakespeare invented the murder of Clarence in the form that he presents it, just as he later invented that of Lady Macduff.

He could have derived this sequence from one, or perhaps two other plays besides *Cambises*. The crimes of Lorenzo in *The Spanish Tragedy* comprise three murders: first he participates in the killing of Horatio, then hires Pedringano to eliminate his accomplice Serberine, and finally engineers Pedringano's execution. Kyd emphasizes the murderous nature of the last of these by including a curious scene in which the hangman worries about his own culpability in the matter.

The other play, about which we can only conjecture, is the *Ur-Hamlet* (1589), also attributed to Kyd. The German play on the subject, *Der bestrafte brudermord* (? c.1603), includes a scene during Hamlet's voyage to England in which two '*banditen*', the equivalents of Rosencrantz and Guildenstern, land with Hamlet on an island near Dover and make an attempt on his life, for which they have been hired by the King. By trickery, Hamlet causes them to shoot each other and makes his own way back to Denmark. The play is linked in some way with the memorial reconstruction of Shakespeare's *Hamlet* that was printed as the first quarto (Polonius is called Corambis in this, Corambus in the German play), and George Duthie has suggested that this relation is via a common source in the *Ur-Hamlet*, which the first quarto's reporter has conflated with Shakespeare's version at some points. One of his suggestions is that the quarto text's reference to Hamlet's being set ashore, which is compatible with the German version of the story but no other analogue, may indicate that the earlier play included the episode with the two assassins instead of the diplomatic dealings of Belleforest and Shakespeare.[33]

Not all scholars have been convinced by this theory, and it would be unwise to lay too great a weight on so slender a foundation. All that can be said is that, if Duthie is correct, the *Ur-Hamlet* too would have had the three-murder sequence we have been discussing: Claudius (or Fengon, or whatever he was called in this version) kills Hamlet's father personally, hires assassins to dispose of the son, and, this failing, seduces Laertes (or Leonhardus) to perform the murder. (As in *The Spanish Tragedy*, the third 'hiring' is unorthodox.) Kyd (let us assume he wrote both plays) may also have derived the sequence from *Cambises*. Certainly the introduction of

---

[31] W. Baldwin and others, *The Mirror for Magistrates*, ed. L. B. Campbell (Cambridge, 1938), 18. 360–71.

[32] 'Gloucester instigated his brother's death'; *intulit* could also mean 'perpetrated'.

[33] G. I. Duthie, *The 'Bad' Quarto of 'Hamlet'* (Cambridge, 1941), 186–93.

assassins into the Hamlet story deviates from Belleforest, its source; but no narrative source is known for *The Spanish Tragedy*, so ultimately the extant material is too sparse to allow us to gauge questions of Kyd's indebtedness. Whatever the case, however, there is none of the corroborative evidence for these plays which, in the case of Shakespeare, suggests that he went back to Preston and not to his more recent predecessors.

It has been suggested that Shakespeare created the scene of Clarence's murder by transferring material from the Chronicle accounts of the murder of the Princes.[34] In fact, the only point of comparison is the appearance of Brackenbury to deliver up the keys to the murderers and place Clarence in their custody. In Hall the Princes are sleeping killed, and bloodlessly, by smothering; Clarence, in contrast, is awake and trying to talk his murderers out of their intention when he dies, and a post-mortem examination would reveal multiple stab wounds ('Take that, and that!', I. iv. 264) as well as lungs filled with Malmsey wine.

The basic form of the scene seems to have been developed from two principal sources. The first is Thomas Lodge's Roman history play *The Wounds of Civil War* (1588), which may have suggested some other features of *Richard III* to Shakespeare: Richard's comic villainy could owe something to the murderous sense of humour exhibited by Lodge's villain Scilla, and the two plays share the same *schema* of divine justice which may be directed by curses or prayers; Richmond's line 'Now civil wounds are stopped' (V. viii. 40), moreover, seems to echo Lodge's title. In Lodge's murder scene, the banished factionary Marius is in prison at Minturnum: his gaoler informs him of a forthcoming attempt on his life, and they talk about the differing attitudes to death and personal ruination taken by those of high and low estate; he resolves to accept his death and goes to sleep, at which point the murderer arrives. Shakespeare has omitted the forewarning and so made the conversation with the gaoler more subtly and diffusely ominous, but the two half-scenes are parallel in their underlying shape. However, the rest of Lodge's scene bears no resemblance to the rest of Shakespeare's: the murderer negotiates with his employers and decides on the basis of a hallucination not to take the commission, leaving Marius to wake up very surprised to be still alive.

For the enactment of the murder itself, Shakespeare turned to a second source, which seems to have been, again, *Cambises*—specifically, the murder of Smirdis. The scene begins with Smirdis alone, anxious for some respite from the 'unquiet' (707) court; the murderers enter and talk first among themselves and then to the victim, who tries to dissuade them; they 'Strike him in divers places' (728 s.d.), exchange words, and *exeunt* with the body. However compendious the execution, the structure is essentially the same

[34] R. A. Law, *PMLA* 60 (1945), 694–5.

as that of Shakespeare's half-scene: two blocks of dialogue, the murder, and closing conversation. If he did not simply invent it anew himself, Shakespeare could have found this structure in no other extant play.

Perhaps it was *The Mirror for Magistrates* that made Shakespeare think of *Cambises* in treating Richard. There, Buckingham laments his consenting to the murder of the Princes and compares himself and Richard to a number of classical murderers, among them Cyrus and Cambyses:

> Behold Cambises and his fatal daye,
> Where Murders mischief myrrour like is left:
> While he his brother Mergus cast to slaye,
> A dreadful thing, his wittes were him bereft.
> A sword he caught wherewith he perced eft
> His body gored, which he of liefe benooms:
> So just is God in al his dreadfull doomes.[35]

Nonetheless, Shakespeare makes no direct allusion of this nature, and the old play seems to have given him nothing more than scenic form and structure. Even that he developed for his own purposes. In *Cambises*, as Madeleine Doran has said, the sequence of the scenes seems arbitrary—'any other order would do as well'.[36] Not so in Shakespeare. Richard kills, hires assassins, and then hires an assassin who himself hires assassins—a distinct sequence of murders, all taking place in the Tower. The villain recedes from the crimes he has instigated, producing a kind of moral ripple effect as each murder involves more and more accomplices, and so more and more quanta of blood guilt.[37]

In *Macbeth*, a play of greater moral sensitivity, Shakespeare rejects this somewhat mechanical device in favour of a manipulation of point of view. We see murder first through the eyes of the murderer, then through hirer and assassin—for Banquo barely speaks in the scene, and Fleance not at all. Finally, the apparatus of hiring is removed and the killers' roles minimized (in the text as we have it, at least), so that our third experience of the crime is presented to us through the victims. Consideration of the effects of this change of viewpoint belongs to a study of *Macbeth* rather than of the hired murderers therein, but briefly: by distancing Macbeth the man from what we know remains his crime, Shakespeare objectifies our sense of that crime; the process continues in the following scenes, this being Macbeth's longest absence from the stage in the play; this complicates our response to him on his return with, if anything, an intensified existential command on our attention.

---

[35] Baldwin, *Mirror*, 22. 99–105.

[36] M. Doran, *Endeavors of Art* (1954), 298.

[37] In contrast, Kyd's tripartite murder sequence in *The Spanish Tragedy* suggests a trap closing around the victims as the villain 'erases' people to perfect his version of reality—in which he is innocent of murder, hence the hirings.

By now we have travelled a long way from *Cambises*, but in doing so we have established a probable link with its later Elizabethan successors: the particular relationship with *Richard III* strengthens the general similarities with other plays noted above. The intuition of David Bevington has been vindicated, even if his formulation of it has proved inaccurate: Preston's Cruelty and Murder may not be the equivalent of Shakespeare's 'two murderers', but they are at least their ancestors.

3

THE ORIGINS OF THE STAGE ASSASSIN II:
1587–1592

IN the last chapter, we saw the beginnings of the stage assassin, and the influence of one play on later examples; but we still have some way to go before the character becomes an established stage type. From the first two-thirds of Elizabeth's reign, *Cambises* and *Fedele and Fortunio* are the only surviving plays for the popular stage that include such figures. In the years after *The Spanish Tragedy*, however, the type mushroomed: we have no fewer than seventeen plays with assassins from the period 1587–92. In explaining this phenomenon, we must begin once again with the sources of the plays in question.

In some cases there are problems. I have already mentioned that no narrative source is known for *The Spanish Tragedy*, and the same is true of *Mucedorus*. For a third play, *The Massacre at Paris*, the source material we have is probably incomplete. Marlowe drew the events from recent French history, and he need not have relied solely on printed pamphlets for information on the subject: it is very plausible that there is also a lot of unrecoverable hearsay behind the play. Consequently, although we know that the numerous hired killers employed by and against the Duke of Guise were historical figures, we cannot be sure in what forms Marlowe found them nor what transformations he made in staging them.

In the cases where we can observe it, however, the transformation is the same sort of expansion that we have already seen in *Cambises* and *Gismond of Salerne*. However, the extent of the sources' brevity varies: few are quite as laconic as Taverner. In some cases the playwright found a little information about the assassin himself, which gave him something to build on in creating the character in detail for the stage. For instance, the original of the poisoner Abraham in *Selimus* is a nameless 'Jewe phisition' in Paulo Giovio's history of the Turks.[1] Thomas Lodge, drawing *The Wounds of Civil War* from an English translation of Appian, found that the assassin set on to kill Marius was a 'Frenchman' (as the Greek *Galaten* was rendered); accordingly, the

---

[1] P. Giovio, *A shorte treatise vpon the Turkes Chronicles*, tr. P. Ashton (1546), H4^r.

murderer in the play is a comic character speaking a kind of sixteenth-century 'franglais'.[2] The writers of plays on Richard III, of course, found names in Hall's Chronicle, but this too left much room for elaboration: a name may identify a specific individual, but it bestows neither personality nor character. A play requires more detail from moment to moment than the sources were able to supply.

This is true even in two cases where the assassin is a relatively substantial character. Both the account of the murder of Thomas Ardern in Holinshed's *Chronicles* and Cinthio's novella about King Astatio, staged as *Arden of Faversham* and *James IV* respectively, include series of failed murder attempts, and assassins who doggedly persist until they fulfil their contracts. The increased role means increased demands on audience attention, which the dramatists meet by introducing a strong vein of comedy: in *James IV*, for instance, Robert Greene turns Cinthio's home-grown killer into a farcical Frenchman, suggested no doubt by *The Wounds of Civil War*, but also by the traditional and, to English eyes, baleful links between France and Scotland.

Another feature of some sources is that they give a detailed description of the scene of the murder itself. This meant that a dramatist had a detailed block of narrative to work with, whereas (for instance) Hall gave Shakespeare only the knowledge that Duke Humphrey 'was found dedde in his bed' for *Henry VI, Part 2* (1591).[3] The assassin tends to be backgrounded, however: Appian gave Lodge a murder scene, but one in which interest is focused on the supernatural portents that save Marius, rather than the 'Frenchman' whom they scare off; it is Lodge who redirects attention by making these portents a hallucination of the murderer's. Similarly, in Hall's account of the murder of the Princes in the Tower, pathos is so important a part of the effect that the passive victims, the 'sely children', occupy us more than the men who smother them.[4] On stage, however, in *The True Tragedy of Richard III*, it is the violent action and therefore its perpetrators who command our attention; the dramatist struggles to restore the balance in favour of pathos by bringing on the boys as speaking parts, and then giving one of the murderers an attack of conscience. This predominance of the assassins may be why Shakespeare chose to keep this particular killing off stage when he covered the subject in *Richard III*: though we hear from Tyrrel of the two murderers Dighton and Forrest, our abiding impression is of 'the gentle babes | ... girdling one another | Within their alabaster innocent arms' (IV. iii. 9–11). Until a dramatist has to write a scene around him,

[2] Appian, *An Avncient Historie and exquisite Chronicle of the Romanes warres, both Ciuile and Foren* (1578), F3[r–v].
[3] Bullough, iii. 107.
[4] Ibid. iii. 279.

the assassin is a mere functionary, too minor a figure to warrant much notice.

What all this would seem to imply is that the emergence of the stage assassin in these years is really a consequence of the dramatists' choice of sources: hired murderers are there, and are naturally developed in the process of being staged. The question would then be what led playwrights to such sources, and might be answered in terms of the development of the drama as a whole during the 1580s: the growing obsolescence of the moral interlude and the corresponding tendency to realistic scenarios would naturally cause plot and story to be of greater importance, and so produce a greater demand for narrative sources, some of them with hired assassins ready to be exploited.

No doubt there is a grain of truth in this explanation, but it is not the whole truth. However prominent the murderers in their sources, these dramatists had options just as Preston had thirty years before, and not all of them made the same choices. For instance, among the incidents available to Robert Greene in *The History of Friar Bacon* (?c.1587), his source for *Friar Bacon and Friar Bungay* (1589), was Vandermast's attempt to avenge his disgrace at Bacon's hands by hiring a Walloon soldier to kill him; Greene did not include it. Obviously he could not use all the material in his source, a very disparate collection of jests; but in another case the assassin was cut from a more coherent narrative. William Percy's *A Forest Tragedy in Vacunium* (1602) is based on *Tancred and Gismund*, Wilmot's revision of *Gismond of Salerne*, but it omits Renuchio and has the Tancred-character perform the murder personally. It was not a common choice, but it was a possible one.

A third option is characteristic of one dramatist, George Peele. One of the incidents in his *David and Bethsabe* is the murder of Amnon at Absalon's sheep-feast. At the moment of the murder, Absalon addresses the drunken victim:

> Die with thy draught perish and die accurst,
> Dishonour to the honour of us all,
> Die for the villany to Thamar done,
> Unworthy thou to be King Davids sonne.   (756–9)

Here we must clear away a confusion sown into the text by its editor, Alexander Dyce, in 1861, and reproduced in many subsequent editions. Dyce adds a stage direction, without authority from the 1599 quarto, making Absalon say these lines as he stabs Amnon.[5] Taking her cue from this, Eleanor Prosser argues that Peele 'intensifies Absolon's guilt' by removing

---

[5] R. Greene and G. Peele, *Dramatic and Poetical Works*, ed. A. Dyce (1861), 472.

the proxies who commit the murder in the biblical source, the Second Book of Samuel.[6] In fact, the assassins *are* included, though they have no dialogue: the scene begins with Absalon giving them their instructions. It is reasonable to assume, then, that Peele was staging the action as he found it in the Bible, and that his stagecraft is subtler than Prosser gives him credit for. Absalon's lines are a passionate outburst if he speaks them in the act of stabbing, but altogether more sinister if he is merely watching while others do the killing; detached from the violent action, his words are a clearer and more shocking expression of hatred.

Peele achieves a similar effect in *The Battle of Alcazar* (1589). Two killings are enacted in the second dumb show: 'Enter the Moore and two murdrers bringing in his unkle Abdelmunen, then they draw the curtains and smoother the yong princes in the bed. Which done, in sight of the unkle they strangle him in his chaire, and then goe forth.' (36–9) The presenter then tells us:

> His fathers brother of too light beleefe,
> This Negro puts to death by proud command.   (42–3)

The published text of the play is very corrupt, but scholars have been aided in their attempts to reconstruct what Peele originally wrote by the survival of the theatrical 'plot'—a scene-by-scene outline listing the characters involved—of a revival in the late 1590s.[7] The evidence of this document suggests that the murderers in the dumb show do not act in concert with the Moor: it is they who bring on Abdelmunen and bind him to a chair.[8] Presumably what then happens is that they act under the Moor's direction, indicated by gestures of command. Because of the dumb-show medium, the effect is less sharply focused than in *David and Bethsabe*: we see the hirer's and then his assassins' actions in sequence without the simultaneity achieved by the earlier play's use of dialogue; but the image of the hirer watching the killing is the same.

Nonetheless, *The Battle of Alcazar* is the better guide to Peele's intentions in presenting assassins. Whereas *David and Bethsabe* faithfully re-creates the incident in the Bible, the murder of Amnon by servants in the presence of Absalon, *Alcazar* departs from the narrative of its source, John Polemon's *Book of Battles* (1587), in which Muly Mahamet's 'three cut throte villains' follow Abdelmunen to Tremissen and there shoot him while he is at prayer in the temple.[9] The manner of the killing in the play and, more importantly,

[6] E. Prosser, *Hamlet and Revenge*, 2nd edn. (Stanford, 1971), 55–6.

[7] The plot is transcribed in W. W. Greg (ed.), *Two Elizabethan Stage Abridgements* (Oxford, 1923); see 49–51 for a reconstruction of this dumb show.

[8] G. Peele, *Life and Works*, gen. ed. C. T. Prouty (New Haven, Conn., 1952–70), ii. 349.

[9] J. Polemon, *The Second part of the booke of Battailes* (1587), S2ᵛ.

the Moor's presence at the event are both Peele's invention. The staging he achieves by this invention is one in which audience attention is deflected from the assassins on to their employer, a stage approximation to the similar strategy that we have seen in prose works. In these plays, Peele has solved the problem of indicating the hirer's responsibility in terms of the newly realistic drama; but the solution is personally unique. Other representations of the hired murderer were far less minimalist.

Playwrights were not bound to dramatize their sources faithfully, then, and where Peele reduces the assassin's role, others introduce it. I have already said that, if the *Ur-Hamlet* included professional killers, this was a departure from any previous version of the story known to us. There are several other cases. The author of *The Troublesome Reign of King John* (1588) found in Holinshed that 'certeine persons' were appointed to blind Prince Arthur, and extended the crime to murder as well as mutilation, at the same time transferring the commission to the boy's keeper, Hubert.[10] The transition is not smooth: the blinding is pointlessly retained as part of the task—why bother if the child is to die anyway? Even so, Shakespeare saw fit to let this stand when he revised the play as *King John* (1596).[11] *King Leir* makes an even more striking contrast with its sources. The only hint of murder in the Lear story comes in William Warner's version in *Albion's England* (1586): '*Gonorill* ... did attempt | Her fathers death'.[12] In the play, however, this plot is the mainspring of the second half of the action, the crowning demonstration of the unnaturalness of Gonorill and Ragan. The assassin, the basis for Shakespeare's Oswald, is also a major figure and appears in four scenes. We may, in addition, count *The Spanish Tragedy* with these plays if we accept the current thinking that Kyd invented the plot himself.[13]

What these contrasting sets of cases demonstrate is that it is not sufficient to present the hired assassin appearing because he was already a part of the story, a part which the dramatic medium brought out better than prose. Playwrights could reduce his role or cut it out altogether, just as they could create it when it was not already there. Peele and Percy notwithstanding, then, there was something about the character that interested dramatists and audiences alike. The nature of this interest is a complex subject which will be treated in detail in the next three chapters. Here I wish to consider only certain topical and dramaturgical elements of it which

[10] Bullough, iv. 32.

[11] For the purposes of this discussion, I accept current opinion on the problem of the relation between Shakespeare's play and *The Troublesome Reign*.

[12] Bullough, vii. 335.

[13] A. Freeman, *Thomas Kyd: Facts and Problems* (Oxford, 1967), 50. The plot of *Mucedorus*, with its obvious overtones of Sidney's *Arcadia*, may also have been devised by the playwright.

might account for the character's sudden rise to prominence in the late 1580s.

II

We found in Chapter 1 that the 1580s saw a change in public awareness of the danger to Queen Elizabeth posed by Catholic Europe and its mercenaries (supposed or otherwise). As far as the drama is concerned, this development was important primarily because it produced a public consciousness in which political assassination and murder by proxy loomed large. This atmosphere alone helps to explain playwrights' growing use of the hired killer; but there is also the possibility of specific topical allusion, for a number of plays of the period address the international situation in patriotic tones. Fiction could be laminated with contemporary reality, as it is in *James IV* when Queen Dorothea confronts the French assassin Jaques. The allusion is signalled by her emotive statement,

> Shall never Frenchman say an English maid
> Of threats of foreign force will be afraid.   (IV. iv. 48–9)

There is surely another 'English maid' in this image of defiant royalty in danger; and, like the Virgin Queen, Dorothea makes a miraculous escape from death. Dating from about 1590, the play is probably too early for Jaques to be named after Captain Giacomo Francischi, the lieutenant of Sir William Stanley's regiment in the Spanish Netherlands and sponsor of Elizabeth's murder, also known to English writers as Jaques: his first appearance in the state papers is in the summer of 1591.[14] The allusion is broader, to the period's 'threats of foreign force' in general. However, there is one case in which a Catholic hireling may be identifiable behind a stage assassin.

The state papers for late 1591 and early 1592 include a fragmentary correspondence between the government spy-master Thomas Phelippes and one of his informers, William Sterrell, alias Henry Saintman.[15] These letters contain a number of references to a shadowy figure known as 'the Italian', an assassin who was to come over and kill the Queen in preparation for an invasion of England by Stanley's forces. In one letter, Phelippes refers to the man, significantly, as an 'executioner': this implies that he was no Catholic fanatic but a specialist killer, a *bravo* if not actually a hangman. The man was an employee of the Pope who had been placed in the camp of the French king, Henry IV, but was recalled before

---

[14] *Calendar of State Papers, Domestic Series 1591–1594*, ed. M. A. E. Green (1867), 99.
[15] Ibid. 110–11, 169, 182–4, 302.

he could assassinate him, in order that he should 'attempt the like' on Elizabeth.

It must be said that Sterrell was not a trusted informant: on one occasion he writes aggrieved that Phelippes has disbelieved him. We may, then, legitimately doubt whether the Italian ever really existed, and was not just the invention of a spy hard up for genuine intelligence. Nonetheless, the story did gain credence, for Phelippes passed it on. Apparently Sterrell was involved in an operation shortly before 7 January 1592, to foil an attempt to smuggle the assassin into England, although the man 'escaped by others' negligence', as he told Phelippes. The danger had not yet passed, though, for the invasion was still planned for June, and the following month Phelippes sent Sterrell to the Low Countries to trace the Italian and spread disinformation about the failure of the plot and about 'the letters procured from Sir Walter Raleigh to the executioner'. That, frustratingly, is the last we hear of the matter.

1592 is also the date usually assigned to Marlowe's *Edward II*, in which another specialist Italianate assassin, Lightborn, is employed to dispatch a monarch. In fact, Lightborn's nationality is not a clear-cut issue. The main evidence linking him with Italy is his catalogue of the lethal skills he learned in Naples, the most murderous of Italian cities. It is tempting to suppose that he is simply an Italianate English traveller, for this would make sense of his other associations. His name is certainly English: many commentators have pointed out that it Anglicizes 'Lucifer'. Moreover, the death he metes out to Edward, with its unpleasant implications of talion punishment, has been associated with the torments of the damned.[16] We should not be surprised, then, that the dungeon in which Edward is imprisoned is referred to as 'the lake' (v. v. 25)—a word that implied the pit of hell.[17] Perhaps, then, in Lightborn Marlowe was dramatizing the well-known Italian saying, '*Englese Italianato, e un diabolo incarnato*'—an Englishman Italianate is a devil incarnate.[18]

This speculation aside, the distinction between Italian and Italianate is not material: the point is that Lightborn is a trained *bravo*, and is associated with Italy. The play underlines the character's cultural specificity by structural means. Like Richard II in *Woodstock*, Edward is presented early on as a king corrupting England's national integrity by introducing foreign influences. These influences are centred on Gaveston, a man who wears Italian clothes and presents Edward with 'Italian masques' (I. i. 54) and other epicurean southern entertainments; nor should we forget that sodomy

[16] C. Marlowe, *Edward the Second*, ed. W. M. Merchant (1967), introduction, pp. xxi–xxii. All quotations are from this edition.

[17] W. D. Briggs, *MLN* 39 (1924), 437–8. Briggs does not himself adduce the connection with hell, but it is evident in most of his examples.

[18] R. Ascham, *English Works*, ed. W. A. Wright (Cambridge, 1904), 229.

was thought to be a particularly Italian practice.[19] The action works out a horrible tit for tat: Edward is punished in kind. Lightborn stands parallel with Gaveston at the other end of the play: the voluptuous particularity of the parasite's speech on his sensuous diversions recurs, sado-masochistically, in the assassin's description of his murderous techniques—the play's two best-known passages. He is an appropriate executioner for Edward, just as a hot spit is a horrifically 'apt' death for a homosexual: he represents another aspect of Italy of which the Italianizing King falls foul.

Lightborn is a scholar of Nashe's 'Academie of man-slaughter', as he termed Italy in his tirade in Pierce Penniless (also 1592).[20] Both these references are out of the ordinary. We saw in Chapter 1 how little Continental influence there was on the English view of the hired murderer, and this was reflected in the drama. The genre in which the assassin appeared most often in the period under discussion was the English history play. The earliest relevant play with an Italian setting (bar Gismond of Salerne) is Robert Yarington's Two Lamentable Tragedies (1594–5); even then it is not a particularly Italianate Italy. James IV has an Italian source, though it was probably mediated through a French translation; but the story's setting is Irish, and was transferred by Greene to Scotland. The assassin himself is French, though his broken English includes a few Italian words among the French; but it would take a very linguistically acute audience to pick up from this slender evidence that he is 'an Italianate Frenchman' as J. A. Lavin would have it.[21] His employer Ateukin is presented as a follower of Machiavel, but the allusion is more to the philosophy than the nationality of Machiavelli: as G. K. Hunter has pointed out, the Elizabethan Machiavel frolicked with his friends in many countries. Hunter's thesis is that Italy became a setting for villainy in plays only with John Marston's début as a dramatist in 1599; before that date the stage Italian was generally a comic foreigner.[22] If this is correct, then Marlowe could have made Lightborn explicitly an Italian national only by turning him into the sort of farcical assassin we find in The Wounds of Civil War and James IV; as he is, he constitutes something of an anomaly.

This is not the only problem with Lightborn. The character is Marlowe's invention: his sources, principal among them Holinshed's Chronicles, name Maltrevers and Gourney as the murderers, whereas these characters merely assist the assassin in the play. Lightborn is someone who should simply not be there, in the narrative of Edward II as in dramatic and cultural history.

[19] Nashe, iii. 177; see also A. Bray, Homosexuality in Renaissance England (1982), 75.
[20] Nashe, i. 186.
[21] In his New Mermaid edition (1967), note to III. ii. 112.
[22] G. K. Hunter, Dramatic Identities and Cultural Traditions (Liverpool, 1978), 110–12.

Could Marlowe then have taken his cue from a recent plot against the Queen, as uncovered by Sterrell? We have three pieces of evidence, all appearing at roughly the same time: Sterrell, Marlowe, and Nashe. If Sterrell's reports to Phelippes were fictitious, it is possible that both the writers and the spy were influenced by a hypothetical wave of anti-Italian feeling at about this time. The alternative is that, whatever the truth of Sterrell's claims, they were themselves the source of that feeling. I do not wish to press the suggestion strongly: obviously we are dealing in an area where absolute proof is impossible. However, it is not implausible that Marlowe could have had access to the information, even if it was not deliberately promulgated by the authorities: he certainly knew Ralegh, and if Ralegh's involvement was, as seems likely, just part of the trail of false information being laid by Phelippes, his circle of acquaintances also included government agents who had worked for Sir Francis Walsingham, and so for Phelippes, the co-ordinator of Walsingham's intelligence network. Nashe, in turn, could have composed his allegations after seeing Lightborn in the theatre.

Edward II itself has one contemporary sub-text which has already been recognized: Edward's sexual and political habits could be associated with those of the recently assassinated Henry III of France, a leading character in another Marlowe play of similar date.[23] This only makes another allusion the more plausible. Moreover, any portrayal of the killing of a king, particularly a king of England, would have some political overtones given the climate of the time; and Lightborn himself, with his Neapolitan connection, hails from Spanish Italy, and so has an immediate national association with one of the powers threatening Elizabeth. The audience, of course, may not have known about the particular case of Sterrell's 'Italian'; but if Marlowe did, is it not possible that in Lightborn we have the man, translated into dramatic terms and acting with greater and more shocking success?

III

A development of more fundamental importance to the drama in the 1580s was *The Spanish Tragedy* itself. Many critics have discussed the seminal originality of Kyd's play: particularly important in relation to the history of the stage assassin is Alfred Harbage's view that Kyd introduces to tragic drama a new and hitherto comic form of action, intrigue. 'The appeal of intrigue', he argues, 'is intellectual. Moral judgement stands partly in abeyance as we check the villain's calculations. Whereas we watch Macbeth

[23] W. Sanders, *The Dramatist and the Received Idea* (Cambridge, 1968), 123.

commit a murder, we watch Iago play a game.'[24] It is the appeal of plot (in both senses of the word) which is exploited in Kyd's presentation of the villain Lorenzo's machinations, and in many subsequent plays; and plot had, of course, gained in importance with the change to realistic scenarios mentioned above, a change which the success of *The Spanish Tragedy* must have greatly hastened.

Lorenzo's devotion to plots has meant that he is often cited as the first 'Machiavellian' villain in English drama, albeit as a *post hoc* judgement by modern scholars, for Machiavelli is never directly alluded to in the text. However, a number of similar characters in slightly later plays are explicitly associated with his name. Ateukin in *James IV*, the employer of Jaques, has made 'annotations upon Machiavel' (III. ii. 53), we are told, and the first scene of *Alphonsus, Emperor of Germany* (?1594) shows the Emperor's secretary, also Lorenzo, giving his master advice, derived ultimately from *The Prince*, on topics that include a prince's dealings with assassins. While these villains are students, the Duke of Guise, hirer of murderers in *The Massacre at Paris*, is said elsewhere by Marlowe to have been possessed by the spirit of 'Machevill' himself; and Shakespeare's Richard III even boasts that he can 'set the murderous Machiavel to school'.[25]

Not all critics, it is true, have been convinced of Lorenzo's position as the first of this group, because he lacks overtly political motivation, whereas the work of Machiavelli was in the science of statecraft. But this is to confuse Machiavellians with Machiavels: to confuse, that is, characters who follow the precepts of the historical Machiavelli, such as (arguably) Shakespeare's Henry V, with villains like Lorenzo who follow the 'mythical' version of Machiavelli exemplified in the work of Gentillet among others. I do not suggest that these characters were conceived in ignorance of Machiavelli's own writings, which were in circulation in England in the form of manuscripts and surreptitious printed editions.[26] On the contrary, we shall see in subsequent chapters that the hirer's behaviour in several plays appears to show the direct influence of Machiavelli's thought.[27] The Machiavel, that is, embodies not a second-hand misunderstanding of that thought, but a biased reaction against it.

One of the principal traits of this type of character is the delight he takes in intrigue and stratagem. Elaborate, deceitful plots are cited again and again as the work of Machiavel: 'sleights', 'scrues, . . . engins', 'rare tricks'; in a word, policy.[28] We must bear in mind, though, that the pejorative connotations of

[24] A. Harbage, in R. Hosley (ed.), *Essays on Shakespeare and Elizabethan Drama in Honour of Hardin Craig* (1963), 38.
[25] C. Marlowe, *The Jew of Malta*, Prol. 1–3; W. Shakespeare, *3 Henry VI*, III. ii. 193.
[26] F. Raab, *The English Face of Machiavelli* (1965), 52–3.
[27] See also M. Scott, *RenD* NS 15 (1984), 147–74.
[28] H. E. Rollins (ed.), *Old English Ballads* (Cambridge, 1920), 117, 187; J. Webster, *The White Devil*, V. iii. 193.

the word 'policy' antedate the impact of Machiavelli in England; as Bernard Spivack has argued, Tudor England was aware of Machiavellianism before it was aware of Machiavelli.[29] To understand the origins of the Machiavel myth, then, we must ask not why a concept of 'Machiavellian' evil emerged, but why the name of Machiavelli became attached to a prior conception of evil.

At this point, we may turn to the other major charge against Machiavel: atheism. This was a more immediately understandable reaction to the writings of Machiavelli: because his political ideology was ultimately pragmatic, it represented a challenge to the dominance of the church over all areas of human conduct, and so conjured up 'the spectre of the Secular State'.[30] Clearly the problem was academic so long as the politician remained within the bounds of church-sanctioned morality: the Machiavellian ideology was most dangerous and subversive in so far as it was amoral, and therefore permitted acts which the prevailing, moral ideology did not. This was the locus at which the mythical Machiavel was generated—a sanctioner and practitioner of evil. That evil was defined, of course, in the terms of the conservative opinion that produced the bugbear: the established wickedness of policy, and the most heinous crime of murder. When the character came to the stage, therefore, it was as a villain who murders by devious stratagems such as poisoning and, most importantly for our purposes, suborned third parties.

This account, of necessity, simplifies a complex process that requires a study of its own. My points here are that the Machiavel-hirer (as distinct from the tyrant) is a new type of villain in the late sixteenth century, first used on stage, albeit not by name, in *The Spanish Tragedy*; and that he combined tradition and topicality to produce characteristics which made him employ assassins out of a sheer intellectual relish for devious villainy.

Kyd did not create the taste for tragic intriguers, for other non-dramatic texts which probably antedate his play, such as *Planetomachia*, show the same interest. His contribution was in developing dramaturgical techniques for staging this kind of action. Emrys Jones's account of the play's recurrent use of eavesdropping takes us some way towards understanding these techniques: 'When Lorenzo ... lays his villainous plots and goes on to double-cross his hapless accomplices, he appears to be in a position of unqualified superiority; his power seems invulnerable. And this invulnerability is an effect of his apparent command of the stage: he seems to be the most powerful person on it.' Subsequently, however, Jones seems

[29] N. W. Bawcutt, *English Literary Renaissance*, 1 (1971), 195–209; B. Spivack, *Shakespeare and the Allegory of Evil* (1958), 375–8.
[30] Raab, *English Face*, 61.

dissatisfied with Lorenzo in comparison with Marlowe's Barabas or Shake-speare's Richard III: he is 'a flatly conceived character, without flamboyance or histrionic gusto'.[31] Nonetheless, Jones is not contradicting himself: to infer this is to misunderstand the nature of the power involved. Lorenzo is a manipulator of others, so his mastery does not depend on personal or stage-presence. As he explains himself after setting on his accomplice Balthazar to procure the trial of Pedringano,

> I lay the plot, he prosecutes the point,
> I set the trap, he breaks the worthless twigs
> And sees not that wherewith the bird was lim'd.
> Thus hopeful men, that mean to hold their own,
> Must look like fowlers to their dearest friends.
> He runs to kill whom I have holp to catch,
> And no man knows it was my reaching fatch.   (III. iv. 40–6)[32]

The keyword here is 'reaching', articulating his ability to control events seemingly at a distance from himself. The consummate demonstration of his power, the hanging of Pedringano, takes place with its architect nowhere in sight. His role is one that we perceive intellectually; any other emphasis from him would be fatal.

Kyd signals Lorenzo's intrigues in two distinct ways: where he is learning information, we see the fact in space, but when he initiates action, we follow it in time. The former is the technique used in the eavesdropping scenes that Jones discusses: Lorenzo is a sinister, understressed figure at the rear of the stage, seeing and hearing (as he thinks) all, with nothing going on behind his back.[33] However, after his participation in the murder of Horatio, it is usually through agents that he acts, and our sense of his absence is an important part of the effect. Kyd needed, then, to create the equivalent in time of the character's presence in the upstage area, never monopolizing our attention but always there.

Just as his spatial presence is a kind of framing device for the action under observation, so Lorenzo frames the episodes of his intrigues. He appears before the murder of Serberine, giving Pedringano his commission, and after it, to receive the report of the killing's successful execution: there are lines of force leading back to him from the murder scene. But we must not only see the command; we must understand the stratagem, the nature of the control that is being exercised. We see him as a confidence trickster at work, persuading the worried but dubious Pedringano that Serberine is a threat. He is effecting a transference of the responsibilities of guilt: Pedringano too

[31] Jones, *Origins*, 198, 215.
[32] References to the play are to the Revels edition of Philip Edwards (1959).
[33] Jones, *Origins*, 197–9.

is implicated in Horatio's murder, and so has no choice but to act; but Lorenzo has cunningly introduced a division of labour, giving the butchery to the assassin while reserving the planning to himself. Then, once Pedringano has gone, he consolidates the casting by explaining to us the full scope of his design, the death of both his accomplices. As this grows more complex, Kyd inserts the short scene in which the page opens the box he is delivering, that supposedly contains the assassin's pardon, to find it empty. We have been meticulously prepared for the events that are to unfold; our pleasure is in watching that happen.

Then the frame is broken. At the moment when we expect to see Lorenzo hearing the news of his success, we are presented instead with the executioner, who has found an incriminating letter on Pedringano's body. The villain's mastery has been an illusion: Kyd has shown us the absence of one document, but concealed the presence of another. Just as Revenge and Don Andrea form a layer of eavesdropping behind Lorenzo, so his reshaping of reality is left imperfect here. In another manifestation of the egoism which Jones sees in the concentric spatial staging, Lorenzo has forgotten that Pedringano can act as well as be acted upon.[34] From this mistake his downfall proceeds: wily beguiled.

Kyd's innovations were of the first importance in the history of the stage assassin: he not only set a theatrical vogue for a kind of villainy that operates naturally through such characters, but also created a new dramatic and narrative structure for the episode in which they appear. Preston had cramped his murderers into single scenes: he was less concerned with them as characters than as instruments of tyranny, less with plot than with theatrical spectacle. In contrast, setting up a murder takes time in *The Spanish Tragedy*, and in that time we see more of the assassin and, in particular, more of his relationship with his employer: the stress on this nexus solves the problem of indicating the hirer's responsibility. Indeed, Lorenzo's position as main villain is largely dependent on his role as a manipulator of tools. Other dramatists followed suit: Richard III's stage presence in *The True Tragedy of Richard III* is as minimal as in *Richardus Tertius*, but the later dramatist preceded the murder of the Princes with a scene in which Richard plans it. By the time Peele attempted to deal with it in *The Battle of Alcazar*, the problem was obsolete. At last the hired murderer was a viable stage character.

[34] Jones, *Origins*, 199.

IV

What this argument assumes is that an important influence on playwrights as they transformed their sources was the treatment of similar incidents in other plays. We have already seen how Shakespeare drew on *The Wounds of Civil War* and *Cambises* in creating the scene of Clarence's murder in *Richard III*. We cannot proceed with confidence far into stemmatics, however. For one thing, the difficulty of dating plays exactly means we can rarely be certain which is the debtor. For another, not all the evidence is extant. We know of several lost plays that probably contained hired assassins. From one we have preserved a single line—'oh slave art hyr'd to murder me, to murder me, to murder me?'—whose rhetorical style suggests a date of around 1590.[35] The play seems to have been a well-known one: who knows how it could have influenced an original-seeming minor dramatist? There is a crop of suggestive titles in the impresario Philip Henslowe's records of payments to authors: to Robert Wilson, Thomas Dekker, Michael Drayton, and Henry Chettle for their collaborative play *Pierce of Exton* (1598), presumably about the murderer of Richard II; to Dekker and Ben Jonson for *Page of Plymouth* (1599), based on the case of Ulalia Padge; and to Jonson for *Richard Crookback* (1602), obviously yet another variation on the Richard III theme.[36] As for the academic stage, Gismond of Salerne was presumably the subject of Henry Wotton's tragedy *Tancredo*, acted at Queen's College, Oxford in 1586; and over Christmas 1597–8, St John's College, Oxford presented *Astiages*, about a classical tyrant whose main claim to fame was attempting to have the young Cyrus murdered.[37]

If we cannot document playwrights' borrowings in detail, though, we can at least observe them in general. To borrow can be to learn, and some things recur again and again in plays, a cumulative approach producing, by a kind of snowball effect, a conventional narrative sequence for assassin episodes. The similarities with *The Spanish Tragedy* are unlikely to be coincidental. The sequence begins with a scene between hirer and assassin, in which the contract is made and instructions given. The murder scene itself follows, omitted only in *Richard III* and one of the two versions of *Henry VI, Part 2*. Finally, and less commonly, the assassins themselves end up dead, by various means, but most frequently double-crossed by their employer. A few plays shuffle the order of these elements: in *Henry VI, Part 2* and one sequence of *The Massacre at Paris*, we see a meeting between the murderers and their

---

[35] T. Dekker, *Satiromastix*, IV. iii. 130–1. The line is quoted by the posturing, Pistol-like Horace when his enemy Tucca pretends to stab him.

[36] P. Henslowe, *Diary*, ed. R. A. Foakes and R. T. Rickert (Cambridge, 1961), 88, 123, 203.

[37] E. K. Chambers, *The Elizabethan Stage* (Oxford, 1923), iii. 517; R. E. Alton, *Malone Society Collections*, 5 (1960), 78–9.

master only after the killing has taken place. Nor do all playwrights give the episode the time and attention that Kyd does. *Mucedorus* is a gallimaufry paced as fast as *Cambises*, and the murder is rushed through in minutes: the dramatist's interest is in the narrative complications which the incident enables the villain to spin around Mucedorus, who kills the assassin in self-defence. Even so, the basic structure is still visible: evidently old habits died harder than new ones were acquired.

The typical scenic form and content of the assassin episode will be analysed in detail in the next chapter; it is important here in that it indicates the gradual establishment of that episode as a conventional situation. By 1592, it seems that this process was largely complete. We can determine this point in the character's history by the assumptions which playwrights make about audience sophistication: the devices and techniques described above became conventional not simply by repetition but through the audience recognition that ensued. It is probable that such familiarity existed by the time *Edward II* was written, for some of the play's effects depend on it.

The play has several references to the hiring of assassins before the appearance of Lightborn in Act v. It is the younger Mortimer who introduces the idea to the political scene, proposing that if Gaveston were brought back from exile,

> How easily might some base slave be suborned,
> To greet his lordship with a poniard,
> And none so much as blame the murtherer,
> But rather praise him for that brave attempt,
> And in the chronicle, enroll his name
> For purging of the realm of such a plague.   (I. iv. 265–70)

When asked why no one has attempted this before, he replies, 'Because ... it was not thought upon' (273); but nothing comes of it now that it is. Nor, when Gaveston returns the compliment and proposes to have Mortimer 'privily made away' (II. ii. 235), does the King take up the suggestion. Later, when he has given up the crown, he jumps to the conclusion that he is to be a victim—'I know the next news that they bring | Will be my death' (v. i. 125–6)—and, on the arrival of Sir Thomas Berkeley immediately afterwards, he bares his breast to receive that news. It is a comically pathetic example of Edward's self-dramatizing: the news is in fact of a change of gaoler. These references, none of them drawn from Holinshed, implant an idea of murder by assassins long before the murder itself is planned.

However, the text supplies very little substance to this idea: the audience necessarily draws on its own preconceived notions of the business of hiring an assassin and, in particular, the way it is portrayed in drama. Thus Marlowe induces expectations which the murder sequence itself plays upon. At first, everything seems straightforward: Mortimer appears and lets us know that we are about to witness the usual scene between hirer and assassin, and that the latter will himself be murdered in the end. It is when Lightborn enters that things begin to go awry. The content of Mortimer's discourse is not unusual: he is checking the man's resolution, as stage hirers often do.[38] Lightborn, however, refuses to go through the appropriate motions:

MORTIMER
Art thou as resolute as thou wast?
LIGHTBORN
What else, my lord? and far more resolute.
MORTIMER
And hast thou cast how to accomplish it?
LIGHTBORN
Ay, ay, and none shall know which way he died.
MORTIMER
But at his looks, Lightborn, thou wilt relent.
LIGHTBORN
Relent, ha, ha! I use much to relent!
MORTIMER
Well, do it bravely and be secret.   (v. iv. 22–8)

There is an impatience in the murderer's tone here, especially in his second line: he is a seasoned professional, so Mortimer's questions should not need asking; after an irritable 'ay, ay', he goes on to demonstrate his grasp of what is required. The warning not to relent is especially common: it is given to several assassins in plays, and though all brush it aside, only Lightborn finds the idea ridiculous.

Now the assassin takes the lead, eschewing detailed instructions and listing some of his Italianate methods. This kind of brutal catalogue was quite common: it had obvious sensational appeal, but was also used as a source of comedy. The earliest example is in *The Troublesome Reign of King John*, where the Abbot of Swinstead partially overhears his deputy's disquisition on various ways of killing the King, an act for which he anticipates promotion; this makes for a moment of anti-clerical farce as the Abbot, misunderstanding, fears for his own life. The list was incorporated into some scenes between assassin and hirer, with the laugh on the assassin. In *The True Tragedy of Richard III*, it is the comedy of professional incompetence as the three killers are told that there must be no bloodshed, but

---

[38] The word 'resolute' and its cognates are recurrent in such scenes.

then propose the absurdly inappropriate methods of shooting the children, beating their brains out against the wall, and cutting their throats. As in *The Troublesome Reign*, the first three ideas are rejected and the sequence closes with the method to be adopted. There is another such scene in *Woodstock*, though there the first murderer is over-enthusiastic rather than stupid, and his employer Lapoole has to douse his proposals with the instruction not to leave any visible sign of violence. As we might expect, Lightborn does not need telling: in his mouth, the list becomes a mark of professional expertise, and none of the techniques he describes would leave any trace. Neither here nor anywhere else in his part is there any scope for comedy.

Lightborn is out of the ordinary, then, in ways that go beyond his Italian connection; and an audience would realize this from its prior experience of assassins on the stage. The result is a feeling of unease with the character, which contributes to the ongoing change in our attitude to the victim, Edward, at this point in the play. 'Edward's follies alienate us, and ... his trials win us back', argues Harry Levin.[39] We have just seen the ex-King washed and shaved in puddle-water, and we are about to hear of his physical endurance when kept in conditions that revolt even the keepers, Matrevis and Gurney. Lightborn is cast as the arch-tormentor, and Marlowe is careful to give him nothing that an audience might find likeable—one reason for the avoidance of comic elements. The unease he generates therefore translates into further sympathy for Edward. This is especially so when the two come into confrontation before the murder. Edward vacillates in his estimation of the assassin's purpose: when Lightborn protests innocence, he is taken in sufficiently for the deception to be cruel, but not for so long that we count him a credulous fool—a delicate equilibrium sustained by Marlowe. Finally, there is the sheer physical horror of the hot spit.

The careful cultivation of our sympathy for the victim is one thing which gives this moment its power to shock; another is that we are not over-prepared for it. When Lightborn first appears, a sophisticated audience of the day, such as Marlowe seems to require, would have its own ideas about what the character should be like: he may not fit those expectations exactly, but at least the conventions are there in some form. With the murder, however, we are given nothing to expect. Lightborn's list of techniques makes a distracting series of images which he, unlike previous exponents, refuses to end with a description of the 'braver way' (37) he intends to use. Later, when he orders the instruments of death he requires from Matrevis and Gurney, he is somewhat reticent about what he intends to do with them; Gurney, indeed, seems surprised that to kill a man he needs no more than a

---

[39] H. Levin, *Christopher Marlowe: The Overreacher* (1961), 121.

hot spit, a table, and a mattress (v. v. 32, 34). The murder is a blank which is suddenly, horribly filled in.

The point is that Marlowe has tried to differentiate the murder of Edward from his audience's prior experience at the playhouse: he distinguishes it from earlier dramatic fictions to create a terrible reality of physical suffering. This suggests that so many murders and assassins had been available to the audience, in very similar form, that there was a danger of its becoming blasé. Five years after *The Spanish Tragedy*, the hired murderer had become a frequent and distinctive character on the English stage.

4

THE ASSASSIN AND HIS EMPLOYER

I

It follows from the circumstances of the assassin's birth into English drama, delivered out of the indirect language of prose sources, that, early on, his role was a secondary one. He has the function of an instrument in the schemes of a more important figure, who is usually either protagonist or antagonist in the play; his appearances tend to be confined to one or more episodes, and he does not initiate action himself. The role is, in short, a bit-part.

One way of demonstrating this is to consider the typical length of an assassin's role. During the period 1587–92, a leading male part could run to anything between 550 and 800 lines; a leading female role, played by a boy apprentice in an adult company, would usually be shorter, between 200 and 350 lines.[1] Most assassins' parts, in contrast, are tiny: Tremelio in *Mucedorus* speaks 11 lines, the two murderers in *Henry VI, Part 2* have 7 between them, and Abraham in *Selimus* has 22. Even memorable, distinctive, and influential characters do not have extensive dialogue: in *The Spanish Tragedy*, Pedringano has 95 lines, his employer Lorenzo, 330; and *Edward II*'s Lightborn has just under 50, whereas Mortimer speaks three and Edward more than four times as much in Act v alone.

There are in fact three plays of this period which give assassins moderately large parts: *King Leir*, *Arden of Faversham*, and *King John*. The Messenger in *Leir* is one of a group of six secondary leads, all of them with between 200 and 300 lines.[2] Shakespeare's Hubert is a major subsidiary of the latter half of the play with 135 lines, about the same as the Dauphin.[3] *Arden of Faversham* is the most remarkable of the three. At 270 lines, Black Will's part is one of the longest in the play, behind only the fatal triangle of Arden, Alice, and her lover Mosby; the other principal assassins, Michael and Shakebag, also have substantial roles, at 230 and 130 lines respectively. Black Will, indeed, was cited with Arden as a main character in the title

---

[1] e.g. Hieronimo (*The Spanish Tragedy*)—770 lines; Edward II—725; King Leir—580; Queen Margaret (*2 Henry VI*)—315; Tamora (*Titus Andronicus*)—255; Katherina (*The Taming of the Shrew*)—215. All lengths of parts quoted in this chapter are approximate.

[2] He has 225; the others are the three sisters, Perillus, and the Gallian King.

[3] I work from the assumption that Hubert is not the same character as the Citizen of Angiers; see Jones, *Origins*, appendix D.

registered by the play's publisher in 1592: '*The tragedie of ARDEN of Feversham and BLACKWALL*'.[4]

The size of these parts can be understood as expansion to fill a vacuum. The King John Shakespeare found in his source, *The Troublesome Reign*, was a leading role of 695 lines; Shakespeare cut him down to 430, emphasizing at the same time the unimpressive aspects of the character.[5] The transformation also entailed building up some of the secondary roles, including Hubert by 40 lines. Where this seems to have been a result of an artistic choice by Shakespeare, simple necessity operated in the case of *King Leir*: the story requires two female villains, each of them limited by the typical length of a leading boy's part. With the usual concentration of evil in one character impossible, the dramatist takes the opportunity to maximize the threat to Leir by increasing the assassin's role. Finally, in *Arden of Faversham*, the basic thread of the narrative is a series of murder attempts, so it is only to be expected that there should be a proliferation of murderers. Alice Arden is the leading character with almost as many lines as Arden and Mosby combined, but she barely meets Black Will and Shakebag until the murder is finally committed; and Arden himself goes through the play ignorant of danger. With no other character to dominate his scenes, Black Will is free to take the lead.

In each case, then, we can see that the development of the murderer is contingent upon a diminution of the role of the hirer. In other words, the assassin is usually a minor character because of his position as a tool: mediating between protagonist and antagonist, he is neither the instigator nor the victim of the murder. One French writer, discussing Henry IV's murderer, expressed the point paradigmatically by observing that, just as the knife was 'but the instrument of *Ravailac*', so Ravaillac was just the instrument of his Jesuit masters.[6] Because narrative interest usually centres on the people who do and who are done to, an intermediary like the assassin is relatively unimportant. Writing for performance, dramatists had to bear in mind the limited personnel of a theatre company; clearly most decided their leading players could be better employed elsewhere.

It may be objected that mere length is not a sufficient criterion of a character's importance: my analysis so far has ignored the content of the lines, and the non-verbal elements of a performance. For instance, some assassins are characterized by their silence. Shakebag is on the stage for as long as Black Will, and is the more sinister for his taciturnity; and in John Marston's *Sophonisba* (1605), it is remarked of the poisoner Gisco,

---

[4] E. Arber (ed.), *A Transcript of the Registers of the Company of Stationers of London* (1875–94), ii. 607.

[5] Cf. Jones, *Origins*, 239–40. The diminution is the more striking in that *King John* is shorter than *The Troublesome Reign* by just under 370 lines.

[6] W. Crashaw (tr.), *A Discovrse to the Lords of the Parliament* (1611), A2ᵛ.

> Be't well or ill, his thrift is to be mute;
> Such slaves must act commands, and not dispute.   (II. i. 44–5)

Such a part is intrinsically minor, however: silence may generate a response to the character, unease, but it communicates little about him. The more a character has to say, the more opportunity a dramatist has to develop characterization.

In practice, however, the assassin's principal interest during this early period was not as a character in his own right. It came, instead, from his relationship with his employer. The conventional structure of the murder episode emphasized that nexus: hiring scene, murder scene, aftermath. In particular, it stressed the drawbacks of the relationship.

II

'Ah whome shall a man trust?' asks More's Richard III as he tries to find someone willing to make away his nephews.[7] The problem was a perennial one for would-be employers of assassins. In such enterprises, Machiavelli had argued, 'the necessity of consulting others means danger to yourself', so the 'one-man conspiracy' was the least dangerous kind: 'if you, perforce, have to divulge it, it should be told to but one other person, and this a man of whom you have had very considerable experience, or else one who is actuated by the same motives as you are'.[8] A hired murderer hardly qualifies. In *The First Part of Hieronimo*, the later 'prequel' to *The Spanish Tragedy*, Lorenzo has taken the maxim to heart:

> The fewer in a plot of jealousy
> Build a foundation surest, when multitudes
> Makes it confused ere it come to head.   (vii. 22–4)

Nonetheless, there were also strong arguments against committing one's murders personally. Elsewhere, Machiavelli suggests that the prince should delegate unpopular measures in order to retain the love of the people: in his world, it is more important to seem than to be virtuous.[9] Moreover, some hirers are squeamish about undertaking the job themselves. King Astyages in William Alexander's *Croesus* (1604) illustrates both concerns when he employs Harpagus to kill the infant Cyrus:

> Though pitty none, some horrour did remaine,
> Whil'st damn'd in substance, to seeme cleere in show,
> Your bloud his heart, but not his hand should staine.   (2226–8)

[7] T. More, *The History of King Richard III*, ed. R. S. Sylvester (1963), 83.

[8] N. Machiavelli, *The Discourses*, tr. L. J. Walker, corr. edn. (Harmondsworth, 1974), 422, 401, 409.

[9] N. Machiavelli, *The Prince*, tr. G. Bull, rev. edn. (Harmondsworth, 1981), 106.

Social prejudice, too, could play its part:

> It is not for a prince to execute,
> Physicians and apothecaries must know.[10]

It was, in short, the sort of task that was better delegated to underlings. Moreover, one type of hirer was unable to engage in violence personally: 'woman's poor revenge | . . . dwells but in the tongue' unless she hires a man to take it further.[11] In several cases she wishes she were male and so able to act for herself:

> O God, that I had bin but made a man;
> Or that my strength were equall with my will!   (2371–2)

wishes Ragan in *King Leir* when she finds that her assassin has let her down; the Beatrices in *Much Ado About Nothing* and *The Changeling* (1622) express similar desires when contemplating murder, before getting men to do it for them.[12] As late as 1700, when attitudes to the assassin had changed radically, he continued to be presented as a woman's weapon: 'I'll have him murder'd! I'll have him poison'd! . . . I'll marry a Drawer to have him poison'd in his Wine' (III. i. 108–11), threatens Congreve's Lady Wishfort in *The Way of the World*.

Obviously it was essential to choose one's instruments carefully. An Essex case of 1590 shows the consequences of a mistake: John Chaundler hired Rowland Gryffyth to kill the husband of his mistress, but Gryffyth chose instead to expose his employer by turning Queen's evidence.[13] A good bet, in line with Machiavelli's recommendations, was a man with a grudge against the intended victim. In fact, the assassin and the revenger were understood as two distinct types, each killing for a different reason: a 'hired revenger' was a contradiction in terms. It is a discrimination that lies behind the question asked of the assassin by his target in John Fletcher's *Valentinian* (1614): 'is it revenge provoked thee, | Or art thou hir'd to kill me?' (IV. iv. 133–4) Nonetheless, a revenger had obvious attractions as a potential assassin. In 1613, for example, when Lady Essex wanted Sir Thomas Overbury murdered, one of those she approached was Sir David Wood, who had already tried to fight a duel with the man.[14]

It was also a wise move to select a man who was already inured to violence: folk tales offered examples enough of hired killers who found

---

[10] *Alphonsus, Emperor of Germany*, I. i. 166–7.
[11] J. Webster, *The White Devil*, III. ii. 283–4.
[12] W. Shakespeare, *Much Ado About Nothing*, IV. i. 304–8; T. Middleton and W. Rowley, *The Changeling*, II. ii. 107–8.
[13] F. G. Emmison, *Elizabethan Life: Disorder* (Chelmsford, 1970), 199.
[14] McElwee, 68.

themselves unable to go through with the murder when the time came.[15] Many stage assassins are soldiers by profession. Two soldiers are given murderous instructions by the Duke of Guise in *The Massacre at Paris*, and there are hints in *The Wounds of Civil War* and *James IV* that their murderers are also military men.[16] In peacetime, soldiers were a social problem in England: discharged from their profession, some turned to crime.[17] In John Awdeley's taxonomy of criminal types, such men figure as rufflers: 'A ruffler goeth with a weapon to seek service, saying he hath been a servitor in the wars, and beggeth for his relief. But his chiefest trade is to rob poor wayfaring men and market women.'[18] On stage, they turn assassin: in *Mucedorus*, for example, Tremelio has fought valiantly as a captain in the wars, but with peace declared he readily accepts Segasto's charge to kill Mucedorus; Black Will in *Arden of Faversham*, too, was a corporal in the garrison at Boulogne before turning to crime upon his discharge.

Prior experience in criminal activities was another advantage: 'Yt is easye to corrupt him which is evil of himselfe', remarked Geoffrey Fenton.[19] For example, Dighton and Forrest in Shakespeare's *Richard III* are 'fleshed villains' (IV. iii. 6), while their counterparts in *The True Tragedy of Richard III*, Black Will and Denten, are said to be 'such pittilesse villaines, that all London cannot match them for their villanie' (1213–14). *Arden of Faversham*'s Black Will, a different character, and his partner, Shakebag, are also known criminals; both appellations seem to have been typical criminal nicknames, like 'Fingers' today.[20]

One feature marking out several assassins as villains is their long, tangled hair, a sign of criminality in the sixteenth century. Many underworld figures in plays of the 1590s have it: Jack Fitten in *Arden of Faversham* has 'Long hair down his shoulders curled' (ii. 50); Pilia-Borza in *The Jew of Malta* (1589) is 'shaggy' (IV. iii. 6); and Faulkner in *Sir Thomas More* (1595) has a 'shag fleece hung dangling on [his] head' (III. i. 99), a result of three years' absence from the barber. As late as 1638, long hair is part of Benatzi's outlaw disguise in *The Lady's Trial*: 'a' has chang'd | haire with a shagge dogge' (1201–2), it

---

[15] S. Thompson, *Motif-Index of Folk Literature*, rev. edn. (Copenhagen, 1955–8), K. 512. The tale turns up around the world with different participants: in ancient Persia with Harpagus and the young Cyrus, in medieval England with Hubert de Burgh and Prince Arthur, in Germany with a huntsman and Snow White.

[16] T. Lodge, *The Wounds of Civil War*, III. ii. 68–9; R. Greene, *James IV*, III. ii. 100.

[17] G. Salgādo, *The Elizabethan Underworld* (1977), 117.

[18] A. V. Judges (ed.), *The Elizabethan Underworld* (1930), 53.

[19] G. Fenton, *Certain Tragical Discourses of Bandello* (1898), ii. 117 n.

[20] Leaving aside the possibly derivative character in Samuel Rowley's *When You See Me, You Know Me* (1604), the appearance of two distinct Black Wills in two separate bodies of source material—the murders of the Princes in the Tower and of Thomas Ardern—suggests a type-name; see also Rochester, *Letters*, ed. J. Treglown (Oxford, 1980), 120. On Shakebag, see *Gesta Grayorum*, ed. W. W. Greg (Oxford, 1915), G4ᵛ, and *OED* on 'shack-rag', 'shag-rag', and 'shake-rag'.

is remarked. The adjective 'shag-haired' is applied to three assassins—the messenger in *King Leir* (2277), Blunt in *The Fair Maid of Bristol* (1604; E1ᵛ), and one of the murderers of Lady Macduff in *Macbeth* (IV. ii. 84). In *Arden of Faversham*, moreover, the assassins' hair is the subject of a textual crux: the quarto reads 'bolstred', which some editors have interpreted as 'bolstered', envisaging some kind of sixteenth-century punk style; but others have emended to 'boltered', and so placed Black Will and Shakebag among the ranks of the unkempt.[21]

To a dramatist, there was supplementary value in attributing prior criminality to the assassin, in that it cast discredit on his employer: in meddling with the crime of murder, he becomes a criminal and therefore associates with criminals. A mistranslation of Bandello is notable here. In the original version of the novella about the Lady of Chabry, the lawyer Tolonio hires the assassin Giovan Tros, who gets the assistance of 'a fellow of his own sort', but in Fenton's translation, it is Tolonio who hires 'a knave of hys owne disposicion': hirer and assassin are conflated into the single category of murderers.[22] Nonetheless the distinction between the 'respectable' hirer and the 'criminal' assassin retained a residual significance in most cases. Robert Yarington even derives a moment of wry comedy from it in *Two Lamentable Tragedies* when Fallerio,

> A man to whom the true unpartiall swarde,
> Of equall justice is delivered,   (C4ᵛ)

assures the ruffians he is about to suborn that he has not summoned them to inquire into their 'passed lives' (C4ᵛ). The irony cuts against his assertion of his judicial integrity: the nervous ruffians are behaving as one would expect in the presence of a judge, but the judge is not correspondingly acting his office.

Whoever a hirer chooses to employ, however, there is usually difficulty in the process of commissioning the murder. An influential example appears in *King Leir*, which contains one of the most thoughtful and sophisticated early treatments of the hired murderer. The commissioning process extends in this play over three different scenes and two different employers. It begins with Gonorill: she has fallen out with her father, and to save her credit needs to destroy his, or else see him dead. To this end she intercepts the messenger her husband has sent to check on Leir's safe arrival in Cambria and, by opening the letters he is carrying, puts the man in her power: he worries about the consequences when he delivers them with the seals broken, and she promises to defend him from hanging. In the ensuing dialogue, the

---

[21] *Arden of Faversham*, iv. 72. For discussion of the crux, see Wine's note to the line in his Revels edition (1973).

[22] M. Bandello, *The Novels*, tr. J. Payne (1890), iv. 95; Fenton, *Tragical Discourses*, ii. 104.

Messenger shows three things in quick succession. First, his absolute loyalty to her:

MESSENGER
    Kind Queene, had I a hundred lives, I would
    Spend ninety nyne of them for you, for that word.
GONORILL
    I, but thou wouldst keepe one life still,
    And that's as many as thou art like to have.
MESSENGER
    That one life is not too deare for my good Queene.   (1007–11)

Here she nudges his fulsome gratitude to see how far he will go, and, satisfied, proceeds to test a second quality in him: avarice. She flings him a purse 'In token of further imployment' (1017), and he responds appropriately. When she declares her satisfaction, he goes on to give her further evidence of his pecuniary concerns by relating how he has brought down the price of property in his parish, presumably as the first stage of a speculation, by making himself impossible to live with: 'My toung being well whetted with choller, is more sharpe then a Razer of Palerno.' (1027–8) What is more important for Gonorill is that this violence and choler, a murderous humour, makes him 'a fit man for my purpose' (1029); so she goes on to test the third, most important quality: corruptibility. She orders him to neglect his commission from the King, instead to deliver her fraudulent letters to Ragan, and to affirm on oath that the allegations they contain are true ones. It is his willingness to do all this that suits him to be a murderer for her: she asks the key question, will he murder Leir, and is answered in the affirmative—

        Few words are best in so small a matter:
        These are but trifles. By this booke I will.   (1056–7)

After the long build-up, it is a shockingly off-hand climax: Gonorill has probed and pushed the man so far that the final escalation, from perjury to murder, is for him the least significant.

    From this point, the Messenger is ready to commit the murder; but the play delays him. Gonorill is playing her sister on a long string: she sends her an 'inditement' (1344) of Leir, along with a suitable assassin, but leaves it to her to connect the two and conceive the crime. As a result, the hiring scene is re-enacted, with the difference that this time we have no doubt of what Ragan has in mind. For her part, she readily asks the murderer if he will 'act a stratagem, | And give a stabbe or two' (1210–11), but holds back from telling him the victim's name. The process stretches into another scene the following morning, the killer's impatience underlining the suspense: 'it might have bin dispatcht, | If you had told me of it yesternight.' (1307–8) When Ragan still continues coy, he declares his trustworthiness:

Were it to meet the Devill in his denne,
And try a bout with him for a scratcht face,
Ide undertake it, if you would but bid me.   (1313–15)

Knowing what his task is to be, of course, he can promise anything. It is not mistrust but shame that restrains Ragan's tongue, however, shame to admit her desire for parricide. The deadlock is only broken when the murderer himself states what he is to do, and receives monosyllabic affirmation. With this, the delay is ended and the narrative can proceed to the long-expected murder.

In this protracted sequence of hiring scenes, the play exposes the mechanics of engaging an assassin's services. We have seen that there are two basic reasons for using a third party in murder: either the hirer wishes to maintain a fiction of his innocence, or he is squeamish about undertaking the killing personally. Either way, he must pull back from naming the deed he wants done: to do so is to incriminate himself, in one case before his own conscience, in the other before someone who may have more scruples than the job requires. In play after play, hirers are shown negotiating their way around this difficult moment. In *The True Tragedy of Richard III*, Richard shies three times as he is about to tell his page he wants the Princes murdered, drawing from the boy assurances that he can be trusted. This still leaves him with a leap of faith to make, however. It is far more satisfactory for the hirer when, as in *Leir*, the assassin is the first to mention murder: once he has proved his criminal inclinations, the hirer can admit to his also. Thomas Heywood's version of Richard III, in *Edward IV, Part 2* (1599), hands Tirill his instructions in the form of a cryptic note, and waits for him to explicate it. Others are even more circumspect. In *The First Part of Hieronimo*, Lorenzo sees Lazarotto with every intention of using him to murder Andrea, but asks him in only the broadest terms about how to cross his sister's love, and listens patiently to the villain's proposals until a lethal one comes up.

The risks involved are usually only implicit; but they are spelt out in an episode of Shakespeare's *Richard III* in which the instrument refuses to take the hint. After his coronation, Richard tries to lead his henchman the Duke of Buckingham to propose the murder of the Princes, urging him, 'Think now what I would speak' (IV. ii. 11). The aim is to have Buckingham arrange the killing, to secure his 'consent' (24), as he later puts it.[23] But the Duke is 'dull' (18), and, when Richard loses his patience and explicitly wishes the bastards dead, non-committal; the job goes to Tyrrel soon afterwards.

This incident seems to be Shakespeare's invention: the sources do not mention it. One reason for its inclusion is to tighten the narrative. Buckingham turned against Richard soon after the murder, an act variously explained in different versions: in Hall's Chronicle, he is piqued at being

---

[23] i.e. 'consent' in the sense of being an accessory (cf. *OED* sb. 1*b*).

denied the lands of Hereford, in *Richardus Tertius* and *The Mirror for Magistrates*, repelled by the murder.[24] Shakespeare links the two causes: another of his inventions is that the lands were promised in return for Buckingham's connivance in the judicial murder of Hastings; his refusal to go further and have the Princes killed without process of law precipitates the King's retention of the lands, and so the Duke's grievance. Thus Richard gives his principal accomplice first refusal on the job rather than inexplicably turning to Tyrrel.

It is significant that Buckingham should balk at this point, immediately after Richard is secured on the throne. To put him there, he has dirtied his hands with many a crime, but now destruction sickens. 'I would be king', Richard tells him, and he replies, 'Why, so you are' (13–14); more killing is mere excess. The effect is to isolate Richard in his villainy: if Buckingham, with whom he has come so far, will not play the murderer for him, then whom indeed can he trust?

III

Once the murder was committed, the problem of secrecy and trust became acute. It was essential to leave no evidence that might connect the hirer with the crime. Written instructions, for example, could easily go astray, as they do in *King Leir* and *James IV*. In *Titus Andronicus* (1592), Tamora exploits this fact in order to incriminate Titus' sons of the murder of Bassianus, by forging a letter from them to a fictitious huntsman-assassin.[25] Moreover, killers sometimes kept such letters, either to protect themselves or for later use as blackmail material.[26]

One way of avoiding these dangers was to issue instructions that were ambiguous. A well-known, somewhat literary example, was the use of a form of words that could read differently according to punctuation: for example, '*Reginam interficere nolite timere bonum est et si omnes consenserint ego solus non contradico*' can be interpreted as a command to kill or a command to desist.[27] Marlowe's Mortimer, issuing similarly worded orders for the murder of Edward II, spells out his intent:

[24] Bullough, iii. 280; T. Legge, *3 Richardus Tertius*, II. i. 34–5; W. Baldwin, *The Mirror for Magistrates*, ed. L. B. Campbell, (Cambridge, 1938), 22. 337–43.

[25] W. Shakespeare, *Titus Andronicus*, II. iii. 268–79.

[26] M. C. Bradbrook, *John Webster: Citizen and Dramatist* (1980), 70; McElwee, 269.

[27] *Either* 'Fear not to kill the Queen. It is good, and if everyone agrees, I alone shall not oppose it' *or* 'Do not kill the Queen. It is good to fear, and if everyone agrees, I alone do not: I oppose it': G. C. Moore Smith, *Times Literary Supplement*, 9 Aug. 1928, 581.

> Unpointed as it is, thus shall it go,
> That being dead, if it chance to be found,
> Matrevis and the rest may bear the blame,
> And we be quit that caused it to be done.   (v. iv. 13–16)

In other words, to use such a device is not only to protect oneself, but also to double-cross one's instrument.

This was a necessary measure: the assassin could be as dangerous a witness as a letter was evidence. The success of the enterprise depended on his silence, therefore, and this could not be taken for granted. Obviously a killer who talked would implicate himself as well as his employer, but *in extremis*, the principles of self-interest changed: the death-bed is a place where God's justice looms larger than man's. It was in such circumstances that the Overbury murder finally came out: two years after administering the fatal enema, William Reeve fell seriously ill at Flushing, and confessed to the murder in the belief that he was dying.[28] Others, taken and facing execution, might try to drag their hirers down with them. In *The First Part of Hieronimo*, Lazarotto threatens to 'peach' (viii. 46) on Lorenzo unless he arranges a pardon, and, double-crossed, tries to make his accusations before he is gagged. In contrast, the assassin in John Jones's *Adrasta* (1635) confesses 'in hope of life' (K4ʳ): evidently he regards incriminating his employer as his best chance of a pardon. Others keep their silence only in the certainty that they will escape. Procured to murder Arden of Faversham in return for the hand of Susan Mosby, the servant Michael promises he will not talk if caught: even a murderer could make a last-minute escape from execution, it was believed, if a virgin claimed him for a husband, so in Michael's case, 'Susan, being a maid, | May beg me from the gallows' (i. 166–7).

It may be added that in the second decade of the seventeenth century there appears a quite different concept of the assassin's behaviour under interrogation. In 1612, Sir Francis Bacon stated the basic principle: 'they that are resolute in mischief, are commonly obstinate in concealing their procurers'. The occasion was Lord Sanquhar's trial: Sanquhar had hoped, he suggested, that the assassin Carlisle, 'a resolute man', would keep his name out of the case.[29] This was pure conjecture on Bacon's part, but not long afterwards a hired murderer was called upon to save his employer's neck in this manner. The case was, as so often, that of the Overbury murder: Richard Weston, the man entrusted with arranging the crime, was persuaded to stand mute by Sir Henry Yelverton, who had been judge in the Sanquhar trial but was now serving factional political interests. Without Weston's plea, the trial could not proceed, the crime could not be proven, and the accessories to the murder could escape; but the law reserved special penalties for those

---

[28] McElwee, 163–4.
[29] T. B. Howell (ed.), *State Trials* (1816–28), ii. 751.

who obstructed justice like this. Yelverton was assuming that, to protect his employer, the assassin would willingly swap a quick death at the rope's end for having his rib-cage slowly crushed in the ordeal of the *peine forte et dure*, the torture used to force a defendant to plead, or kill him in the attempt. Weston played along with Yelverton's scheme for several days, but finally made his plea and gave the law the means to proceed against his accomplices and procurers.[30]

What is remarkable here is not simply the notion that a doomed man would protect his employer, but that he could be relied on to do so under ordinary circumstances ('commonly', as Bacon puts it). It is an idea that is apparently unique to the 1610s, and probably stems from the contemporary interpretation of the behaviour of François Ravaillac, who assassinated the French king Henry IV at the start of the decade. The authorities believed that the murder had been instigated by the Society of Jesus, and subjected the unfortunate killer to brutal and protracted torture to make him confess. The assumption was probably wrong, and certainly despite appalling torments, Ravaillac was consistent in his denial that he was procured by anyone. Concerned for his soul and bound for execution, it seems likely that he was unwilling to die affirming a lie; but the general belief was that he was holding the truth back from his interrogators.[31] His extreme physical courage was remembered as defiant obstinacy: 'Arraigne me, rend me peece-meale, ile confesse nothing', says Thomas Dekker's stage version.[32] This was credible because it was not entirely unprecedented: earlier political assassins such as Gérard had shown a remarkable resistance to torture. Nonetheless, Ravaillac's case supplied a new and widely publicized example of human behaviour in an exceptional situation.[33] Based on an erroneous assumption, it was an example contrary to received wisdom, and proved false when put to the test with Weston: assassins were indeed men who could not in the end be trusted.

Dependence on the uncertain loyalties of a hired murderer was not simply a danger to the hirer, moreover. I have already intimated that the assassin was almost always of lower social status than the villain who suborns him. There was a stigma attached to such work that went beyond a distaste for the criminality of the undertaking. Outside drama, men could take offence when offered money to kill an enemy: in Italy, a Milanese asked to assassinate Antonio Bologna refused the commission, saying that he 'had no mind to turn butcher at another's hire'; and in England Sir David Wood spurned Lady Essex's offer of £1,000 to kill Overbury, because he 'would play the

[30] McElwee, 185–90.

[31] E. Goldsmid (ed.), *The Trial of Francis Ravaillac* (Edinburgh, 1885), *passim*.

[32] T. Dekker, *If This Be Not a Good Play, The Devil Is In It*, v. iv. 140.

[33] There is no evidence that either Bacon or Yelverton were thinking of Ravaillac; but I know of no similar case that could account for Bacon's extraordinary statement.

hangman for nobody'.[34] Wood's remark indicates the nature of the stigma: the assassin was the criminal equivalent of the public executioner. The name of one such character, Verdugo in *Imperiale* (1639), means 'executioner' in Spanish. Another, in *The Duke of Milan* (1621), is said to play a 'hangmans part' (II. i. 415); and the bravo in *The Custom of the Country* (1620) even looks 'like the figure of a hang-man' (p. 352).[35] It was a parallel with social implications: to be a hangman was considered the lowest kind of honest work: Pompey in *Measure for Measure* (1603–4) starts at the bottom when he leaves his illicit trade of bawd. As for the assassin, then,

> To kill men scurvily, 'tis such a dog tricke,
> Such a ratcatchers occupation;

the job was one fit for 'some base slave', for 'peasants'.[36]

The class difference made the situation socially embarrassing as well as dangerous for the hirer. It could, indeed, be the murderer's class background that made for the danger:

> servile fear or counsel-breaking bribes
> Will from a peasant in an hour extort
> Enough to overthrow a monarchy.[37]

Fear of one's betters is presented as an inherently lower-class trait which can all too easily induce an assassin to talk. But this assumption bites back at the hierarchical consciousness that produced it: if 'peasants' are in every way inferior to aristocrats, then it is intolerable that the security of an aristocrat should hang on the good grace of a peasant.

Of course, the situation looked very different from the peasant's point of view. A link with the nobility was something that James Franklin, the apothecary who supplied the poison in the Overbury case, could not resist boasting of when he was pensioned by Lady Essex.[38] Moreover, the assassin could always enforce the connection by blackmailing a recalcitrant employer. This was the course taken by the thresher in the Harris–Keyt case reported by John Manningham: 'This poore knave having effected this villany began to growe resty, could not endure to worke any more, but would be maynteyned by Harris for this feate, otherwise most desperately he threatened to reveall the matter.'[39] There is a tone of understated outrage here that

---

[34] Bandello, *Novels*, ii. 54; McElwee, 68.

[35] The play is quoted from the Glover and Waller edition of Beaumont and Fletcher (Cambridge, 1905–12).

[36] J. Fletcher, *The Island Princess*, IV. ii. 21–2; C. Marlowe, *Edward II*, I. iv. 265, and *The Massacre at Paris*, xxi. 69.

[37] *Alphonsus, Emperor of Germany*, I. i. 168–70.

[38] McElwee, 142.

[39] J. Manningham, *Diary*, ed. R. P. Sorlien (Hanover, NH, 1976), 162.

emphasizes the class issue: a poor knave who cannot endure to work is clearly getting above himself.

It was necessary, then, for hirers to have some means of ensuring their instruments' silence, and various strategies were used. In the case of the Great Turk, the problem was easily dealt with: allegedly he kept seven mutes in his retinue, 'as partakers of his secretes, and redye wickedlye to accomplishe all kyndes of murther, and heynous actes'; in England, these men were famous as the killers of Mustapha.[40] However, such figures were specific to the Christian notion of Ottoman culture, on a par with eunuch slaves; dumb assassins were not represented elsewhere. Moreover, even without a tongue, a man can still write, as the audience of *The Spanish Tragedy* and *Titus Andronicus* would have known: it was safer to prevent the murderer being interrogated in the first place. In prose fiction, it was not infrequent for assassins to agree to flee the country after the murder; but this still presupposes a degree of trust between parties to the contract. On stage, the scenario was uncommon. Dramatists tended to favour a more spectacular and more final way of stopping the murderer's mouth.

IV

Murdering the murderer was one of the 'Italionate conveyances' of a Machiavel listed by Nashe in *Pierce Penniless*:

> to use men for my purpose and then cast them off, to seeke his destruction that knowes my secrets; and such as I have imployed in any murther or stratagem, to set them privilie together by the eares, to stab each other mutually, for feare of bewraying me; or, if that faile, to hire them to humor one another in such courses as may bring them both to the gallowes.[41]

The stratagem was known from historical examples such as that of Vortigern, who hanged the guards he employed to kill King Constantine.[42] It was also suspected in some contemporary cases: in 1582, when Juan Jauréguy was cut down after shooting William the Silent, the rumour ran abroad that he was killed by his own confederates; and after the Overbury murder, Weston worried that all Lady Essex's instruments were themselves to be poisoned.[43] It was, in short, a well-known conclusion to a hirer's dealings with his assassins.

This action was the most satisfactory for a hirer to take, for a number of

[40] B. Ðorðević, *The ofspring of the house of Ottomanno*, tr. H. Goughe (1570), L4[v].

[41] Nashe, i. 220.

[42] J. Higgins and T. Blenerhasset, *Parts Added to The Mirror for Magistrates*, ed. L. B. Campbell (Cambridge, 1946), 1578 edn.: 4. 71–7.

[43] C. Plantin (tr.), *A Trve Discovrse of the Assavlt Committed vpon the Person of the most noble Prince, William Prince of Orange* (1582), A4[v]; McElwee, 142–3.

reasons. First, it was a thoroughly effective means of silencing the key witness to his involvement: 'dead folkes doe neither harme, nor tell tales'.[44] Moreover, done openly, the act could positively establish the doer's innocence: it dissociates hirer from assassin, being so opposite to the way one normally treats one's servants and employees. And thirdly, it was also an aggressive reassertion of class proprieties: if peasants are useful in committing aristocrats' murders for them, they can be equally useful in giving up their own lives afterwards to protect their erstwhile employers—'Who Princes can upbrayd, tis good they die.'[45] To kill the assassin is to impose one's superiority upon his body, and by that act to reclaim control over one's destiny.

On stage, although several plays of the early 1590s kill off the assassin by other means (suicide in *Selimus*, and brawling amongst themselves in *Two Lamentable Tragedies* and *Alphonsus, Emperor of Germany*), it was murder by the hirer that was most frequent over the longest period. Again, the influence of *The Spanish Tragedy* is an element in this tendency. Lorenzo exemplifies all the suspicion and class attitudes of the hirer in his treatment of Pedringano and Serberine:

> better it's that base companions die,
> Than by their life to hazard our good haps.
> Nor shall they live, for me to fear their faith:
> I'll trust myself, myself shall be my friend,
> For die they shall, slaves are ordain'd to no other end.
>
> (III. ii. 115–19)

In engineering these deaths, he demonstrates the superior intellect and cunning of the Machiavellian intriguer. The point is signalled most succinctly when he promises Pedringano that he will 'mount' (93) for the murder, punning on mounting to preferment and mounting to the gallows; but only he can hear the *double-entendre*. Pedringano has a naïvety that makes him take things on trust—that it will be preferment to which he mounts, that the empty box contains his pardon. His discomfiture, involving (presumably) the opening of the box, his reaction and immediate hanging, makes a dense and memorable stage moment.

Contemporary allusions and imitations testify to the impact which this episode must have had. In his poem, *Leicester's Ghost* (c.1603), for example, Thomas Rogers added an immediately identifiable detail when he retold the story of the Earl of Leicester's dealings with his servant and tool Gates. The story came from the political libel *The Copy of a Letter* (1584)—now better known by its seventeenth-century title *Leicester's Commonwealth*—and

[44] J. Reynolds, *The Triumphs of Gods Revenge* (1635), L4ᵛ. The saying was proverbial: Tilley, M. 511.

[45] T. Dekker, *The Whore of Babylon*, III. i. 93.

related how Leicester promised Gates, sentenced to death for a robbery, a pardon that never came. Rogers makes Leicester remark,

> For his reprivall, like a crafty fox,
> I sent noe pardon, but an emptie box.[46]

The reference identifies Leicester, Machiavellian villain of Elizabethan politics according to *The Copy of a Letter*, with Lorenzo, Machiavellian villain of the Elizabethan stage.

Among plays, the fate of Pedringano most obviously influenced *James IV*, which includes a more laboured version of Lorenzo's punning: Ateukin's servant Andrew tells Jaques that he is bound for the gallows, and describes what is to happen there. Whereas Pedringano was simply obtuse, however, Jaques misses the point only because he lacks competency in the English language—in particular, he does not understand the word 'gallows'.[47] The distinction between the characters is significant, reflecting another feature of Greene's response to Kyd: where Pedringano was naïve, Jaques is sophisticated. An audience already familiar with the assassin scenario through *The Spanish Tragedy* would know what was in store for Jaques; but so does he. 'Me do your service, but me no be hanged *pour* my labour' (III. ii. 130), he tells Ateukin, who assures him that he will be covered by a warrant— an equivalent for the pardon which was so significant an absence in the earlier play.

Jaques, then, is canny enough to escape Pedringano's fate: 'me will homa to France and no be hanged in a strange country' (v. ii. 23–4) are his last words in the play. Many others were not so lucky. Several factors explain the recurrence of the situation. Just as, for the hirer, it signalled the conclusion of his business with the murderer, so for the dramatist it secured narrative closure in the murder episode itself: in plays like *Edward II* and *Woodstock*, it rounds off that episode with its own internal justice, whilst leaving the lead villain free to continue his career or meet his nemesis in subsequent scenes. However, this explanation is far from all-sufficient. Closure and justice are achieved by the death of the murderer, no matter how that may occur, which is no doubt why some early plays kill him by other means for variety's sake. Moreover, some plays, such as *Richard III*, have entirely self-contained murder episodes without such a conclusion, while others, such as *King Leir*, show hirers intending to kill the assassin but failing, in the event, to find the opportunity.

It is the content of the incident which makes it an attractive means of closing the episode, whether enacted or only projected. The murder of one party by the other makes a powerful emblem of the continuing mistrust

[46] T. Rogers, *Leicester's Ghost*, ed. F. B. Williams, jun. (Chicago, 1972), ll. 797–8.
[47] R. Greene, *James IV*, IV. iii. 5–20.

between them. This is especially clear in *Claudius Tiberius Nero* (?1605), when
Sejanus stabs his instrument Spado:

> I did him a great favour, had he lived
> Tiberius would have had him tortured,
> Hang'd by the Navell for confession.   (2549–51)

With bizarre logic, perfidy becomes a good turn; the irony only underlines
the truth of the matter. In this situation, the hirer does as he expects to be
done by, and betrays the assassin before the assassin can betray him.

Moreover, for the hirer to murder his instrument neatly reverses the
action with which the episode often begins, and with which the theme of
mistrust is first introduced. His reluctance to utter his crime is a reluctance
to *outer it*, to entrust the knowledge of it to another person. Instinctively he
tries to hold it back within himself, whilst knowing that he cannot, if he
wants it committed at all. With the death of the murderer, that instinct
triumphs: the crime is sealed back into the hirer's mind, with no need to
trust anyone but himself. The sequence ends as it began, with a skeleton in
the cupboard.

v

This archetypal form of the murder episode is rarely represented in full, but
it helps to define a recurrent requirement of the characterization of the
assassin himself. On the one hand, he is narratively subordinate to the hirer;
but on the other, it is because he is a separate individual that he is a threat
to the hirer. The dramatist must develop a limited characterization that gives
the illusion of potential development, and which makes the assassin engaging
enough in his own right to hold the stage in the hirer's absence during the
murder scene.

Let us consider, for example, Shakespeare's treatment of Banquo's killers
in *Macbeth*. In the first and last scenes of the sequence, the dramatic tension
comes from the interaction of the murderers with Macbeth: mutual suspicion
in the first scene, and in the last, mutual anxiety, for different reasons, over
Fleance's escape. In the murder scene, this tension is likely to dissipate—
hence the Third Murderer. He is a source of friction which serves to
differentiate the characters. The Second Murderer accepts him, but the First
is suspicious: he is the one who likes to give the orders (III. iii. 4, 15), and
this well-informed newcomer may represent a challenge to his authority in
the group. The Third Murderer's main contribution to the scene, accordingly,
is to needle the First. As the assassins listen to Banquo's horses arriving, the
First remarks that he can hear them 'go about' (11). The Third replies, at
length, that this is only common practice: 'So all men do' (13), and so, it is

78 THE ASSASSIN AND HIS EMPLOYER

implied, should his companion have known. Similarly, after the murder he asks who struck out the light, and the First Murderer, thrown, asks, 'Was't not the way?' (20) The Third seizes his advantage and points out that it was not the way, because it allowed Fleance to escape. In the source, Fleance gets away 'by the benefit of the darke night'; in the play, the First Murderer's enthusiasm creates that benefit, and so loses them 'best half of our affair' (22).[48] The jockeying for position between the two is understated, but it is what makes the scene something more than a quick act of violence while Macbeth is off stage.

Other assassins have their own independent appeal through comedy. This is not incongruous, for the underside of laughter is fear: humour and ridicule are a means of taming the things we are afraid of. Violence, then, can be comical as well as horrific. A case in point is the use of the murderers Hans and Jerick in *Alphonsus, Emperor of Germany*. The characters are German 'boors' set on to kill the hero, Richard, who sees that he cannot defend himself and plays dead; they then fight over the division of the spoils, and Jerick kills Hans before being killed himself by Richard. What is remarkable is that the dialogue of the scene is almost entirely in German, and that there is no presumption that the audience will understand this: Richard translates the two key points, the text of Alexander's letter proposing the murder to the boors, and the fact that Jerick is ignorant of its author; everything else is communicated visually by the action. In consequence, it is hard to play the scene straight. It is true that the dialogue is not gibberish, but it must have seemed so to an audience unacquainted with the language, especially when the two murderers become agitated over which of them is to have Richard's chain. As a result, the performances must be overstated as in mime, while the presence of dialogue dissociates it from that medium of representation: we see not a dumb show but chattering, grotesque caricatures. When they attack each other, the scene rises to slapstick, to end with exaggerated irony when Jerick is gathering up his loot and the 'corpse' of Richard gets up and kills him. The overall effect was probably similar to that of the twentieth-century animated cartoon.

It is notable how stylized a form of violence this is: we can laugh at it (as we can laugh at *Tom and Jerry*) because, no matter how graphic the representation of the pain inflicted, the participants are treated in a way that allows us to forget that they are people who can get hurt. The avoidance of empathy with the victim is crucial to the development of comic possibilities in murder—it is why we cannot laugh at the death of Edward II, for example. Fletcher exploits the limitation in *The False One* (1620): Pompey never appears in the play, so humour can be drawn from the aftermath of his murder. Act II opens with a sequence in which, anticipating a reward from

[48] Bullough, vii. 498.

Caesar, hirer pulls rank on assassin in taking the credit, and then gets the same treatment from his superior; but after this build-up, Caesar rejects the crime. Such an overturning of expectations can be sardonically comic—as when Antonio rejects Vindice at the end of *The Revenger's Tragedy* (1606)— but this is not what we laugh at here. The scene's grotesque humour comes instead from the use of Pompey's severed head as a correlative for the murder, passed from character to character as they scramble for the honour of presenting it to Caesar. The treatment of the head is shocking, but its juxtaposition with the murderers' banal values allows us to vent our horror in laughter. Caesar's rejection is not comic, therefore, because it asserts a more appropriate response to the violence the head betokens, and so kills the joke.

Often, then, the comedy of murder turns on black irony. The sexual connotations of violence (and particularly of the word 'stab') give the opportunity for bawdy wisecracks:

> Why, heres a wench that longs to have a stabbe.
> Wel, I could give it her, and ne're hurt her neither.[49]

In *Selimus*, the physician Abraham gives his patient 'a drinke ... | Which soone will calme your stormie passions' (1826–7)—of course, the prescription is poisoned. In *Rollo, Duke of Normandy* (1617), there is even a scene of deadly slapstick as the kitchen staff, suborned by the parasite Latorch, 'accidentally' drop poison into Otto's food:

> Here stands my broths: my finger slipps a litle,
> Downe drops a dose, I stirre him with my ladle,
> And there's a dish for a Duke: *Olla podrida*:
> Here stands a bak't meate, he wants a litle seasning
> A foolish mistake, my spice-boxe gentlemen.
> And put in some of this, the matters ended.   (II. ii. 144–9)

In each case, the murderer's joke transforms killing into something else— copulation, medical practice, an unfortunate mishap. We laugh in simul-taneous awareness of the reality and the deviation: without the former, laughter would be unnecessary, without the latter, undesirable.

The assassin is not always the joker, however: he can also be the butt. The joke then lies in the undercutting of his pretensions or expectations. Sometimes this simply reflects his equivocal position as both instrument and victim of the hirer. In *The Spanish Tragedy*, for example, Pedringano casts himself as joker at his trial: he abuses the court and hangman, confident that the laugh will be on them when they find that, his pardon signed, they cannot hang him; but the real joke is that he has been outsmarted by a wilier trickster. In other cases, however, the irony comes from character, not

---

[49] *King Leir*, ll. 1227–8; cf. Greene, *James IV*, III. ii. 128–9.

circumstances. For example, we saw in the last chapter how, in *The True Tragedy of Richard III* and *Woodstock*, the assassin's catalogue of murder methods shows him to be less clever than he would like to think. The victim of the most sustained example of this sort of humour is Black Will in *Arden of Faversham*.

The play is tragedy dressed as farce. The plot, drawn from Holinshed's *Chronicles*, is an episodic series of unsuccessful murder attempts, and by staging them in the space of a few hours of real time, the dramatist imposes a unity on them that is comic in effect. On the one hand, we are conscious of the victim going about his everyday business, blithely unaware of the intense effort going on about him to end his life and of his own repeated narrow escapes—a comic technique more recently associated with Buster Keaton. On the other, the characters attempting the murder must be farcically inept to let him get away so often. Whereas Holinshed's Black Will is 'a terrible cruell ruffian', a 'desperat villaine' who 'maketh no conscience of bloudshed and murther', therefore in the play he is a comic braggart, an ex-*miles gloriosus* who is forever boasting of his prowess in villainy but never seems able to pull off this particular crime.[50] For much of the play, he looks like a conventional murderer, covered in blood, but we can see through the pose, aware as we are that it is his own blood, shed accidentally when the window cracked his head in Scene iii: he has sworn not to wash it off until Arden is dead. Consequently he is rather touchy when Michael asks how his face was bloodied, and threatens the servant with violence for his 'sauciness' (iii. 132).

Again, the joke turns on the juxtaposition of the fearsome and the harmless: the 'terrible cruell ruffian' and the inept man trying to live up to the role. The difference is that, this time, the reality is harmless, and the danger lies only in the deviation. This is why Shakebag is expanded from a very minor figure in Holinshed, who assists in one of the many unsuccessful murder attempts, into a full-time foil for Black Will. Where Will effusively declares his intention to kill Arden, Shakebag is quietly pragmatic: 'I'll stab him as he stands pissing against a wall, but I'll kill him' (ii. 97–8), says Will, but it is Shakebag who asks where he actually is. Similarly, after breaking his head, Will childishly angles for sympathy from Greene and leaves it up to Shakebag to answer the question of how it happened. It is Shakebag, too, who is concerned that the pistols be checked and in good order:

> Come, Will, see thy tools be in a readiness.
> Is not thy powder dank, or will thy flint strike fire? (ix. 1–2)

Will replies by telling him, at length, to stop trying to teach his grandmother to suck eggs. By now, Shakebag has the measure of his partner:

[50] *Arden of Faversham*, appendix II, 150, 151.

> Zounds, I hate them as I hate a toad
> That carry a muscado in their tongue
> And scarce a hurting weapon in their hand. (19–21)

The barb goes home, for Will takes offence. Finally, it is Shakebag who actually stabs Arden; Will merely pulls him down. Throughout, Shakebag's efficiency shows up Black Will's bravado for the empty ostentation it is: he supplies the danger that activates the joke, the reality of the 'terrible cruell ruffian' that Black Will would like to be.

Ultimately, the use of comedy in these characterizations is functional: the dramatists need to keep the audience's attention on the assassin, and endow him with traits that will induce a reaction, laughter. However, the character could appeal on other levels too. Any criminal enterprise raised fundamental problems of trust and secrecy, and therefore produced a relationship between the parties such as we have seen. However, beyond this there were two distinct types of nexus, defined by the assassin's inducement to the crime. Consequently, they produced two different figures, with different characteristics: men who commit murder because they are told to, and those who do so because they are paid to. Each type raised a different set of issues, as we shall now consider.

5

MURDER BY DECREE

I

ONE of the concerns which the stage assassin focused, from *Cambises* onwards, was tyranny. A tyrant was classically defined as a ruler who used his power not for the common good but to suit his own inclinations.[1] In the sixteenth century, that power was growing: in France, Jean Bodin defended absolutism in theory, and the Tudors practised it in England. With it grew the fear that a corrupt ruler might abuse it. The contemporary genre of the *speculum principis* sought to avert such an eventuality by imbuing potential princes with a sense of responsibility. According to many humanist thinkers, the principal bulwarks against tyranny were a good education and good advice.[2] Conversely, the thing most likely to corrupt a prince was flattery, 'the Nurse of Tyrants'.[3] It was easier to blame the flatterer than the prince for the latter's tyrannical behaviour, for in English law the monarch could do no wrong; critics of Queen Elizabeth's regime pointed accusing fingers at her ministers, never at the Queen herself.[4]

These are factors which underlie Robert Greene's portrait of the making of a tyrant in *James IV*. The plot moves King James by degrees towards an act of tyranny, the murder of his wife Dorothea by an assassin, in order to dissolve their marriage and leave him free to pursue another woman; but he does not come to this unaided. One of the changes Greene makes in turning Cinthio's character Astatio into James, is to invent Ateukin, the court parasite: Cinthio's prince behaves tyrannically on his own account, but Greene's has a flatterer helping.

Ateukin makes an easy scapegoat: it is he who has brought the assassin, Jaques, to court and procured him for the task, and he whom Jaques regards as his patron, his '*bon gentilhomme*' (III. ii. 36–7). Greene arranges the action so that we never see Jaques meet the King before the murder: his usual companions are the other comic characters, Ateukin's servants. We see the flatterer pressing for James's signature on a warrant for the murderer, but

[1] Aristotle, *The Politics*, tr. T. A. Sinclair (Harmondsworth, 1962), 116.
[2] Q. Skinner, *The Foundations of Modern Political Thought* (Cambridge, 1978), i. 213–14, 216–21.
[3] *Pathomachia* (1630), G2ʳ.
[4] Sir W. Holdsworth, *A History of English Law*, 4th edn. (1927–72), iii. 465–6.

the signing itself is done off stage. The prime mover in the affair, we are told, is Ateukin, who

> With vile persuasions and alluring words,
> Makes him make way by murder to his will.   (Chorus II. 6–7)

We later see him bringing Jaques to meet the King, again off stage, and murderous intent is assigned to him alone as he picks up an unintended pun in his directions:

ATEUKIN
   Say, gentlemen, where may we find the king?
HUNTSMAN
   Even here at hand on hunting;
   And at this hour he taken hath a stand
   To kill a deer.
ATEUKIN   A pleasant work in hand!   (IV. i. 1–4)

James intends to shoot a wild animal, but for Ateukin the victim is to be the King's 'dear', Dorothea.

Even so, James's involvement in the murder is gradually receiving heavier emphasis. We may not see him meet Jaques at this point, but we know that a meeting has taken place, and subsequently it is to him, not Ateukin, that the murderer looks for security. Leaving Dorothea's wounded body, he flees the scene of the crime: 'me will run *pour* a wager, for fear me be *surpris* and *pendu* for my labour. *Bien, je m'en allerai au roi lui dire mes affaires.*' (IV. iv. 56–8) If caught, he will be hanged by the King's officers and in the King's name; but if he can reach the King himself, he will be safe, and knighted. Finally, the next scene decisively shows James for the accessory he is. He and his retinue process one way across the stage, and Jaques, his sword drawn and bloody, runs the other. The King stops him:

> Stay, Jaques, fear not; sheathe thy murdering blade:
> Lo, here thy king and friends are come abroad
> To save thee from the terrors of pursuit.   (IV. v. 1–3)

It is a great stage moment: the killer's flight is suddenly arrested, and the stage becomes the locus for the convergence of the highest and the lowest in the land. Unprompted by Ateukin, the King legitimates the crime, and in that action plumbs the depths of royal depravity.

James is identified as a tyrant, then, by his association with an assassin. The two figures were often connected in the sixteenth century. In a tyranny, the ruling principle of justice was supplanted by the monarch's will: 'tyrant lust doth stande for lawe', as George Turberville put it.[5] The archetypal tyrannous act, therefore, was criminal: a breach of the law which tyrant lust abrogates. Murder was the ultimate incursion on the rights of the subject:

[5] G. Turberville, *Tragicall Tales* (1587), E4ᵛ.

not only does the tyrant instigate crime in hiring an assassin, he also bypasses the correct legal procedures, which would entail enquiry into the justice of any death sentence. Thus, for example, *The Mirror for Magistrates* stigmatized the murder of Thomas of Woodstock by royal hirelings as 'execucion doen before judgement'.[6]

In several plays, the point is underlined by juxtaposing the tyrant's assassins with the legitimate instruments of royal power. We have already seen how, in *Cambises*, Murder and Cruelty supplant the executioner when the King's deeds become unjust. In *The Massacre at Paris*, too, the murder of the Duke of Guise has hints of the legal execution it is not: King Henry lays great stress on Guise's offence of treason, and one of the assassins revealingly anticipates the murder with the line 'O that his heart were leaping in my hand!' (xxi. 6)—the climax of an English execution for treason being the removal of the victim's heart still beating.

In *Edward II*, it is a different public official whose role is usurped. In his first scene as Protector, Mortimer sets about removing those who are a danger to his new regime. The scene begins with him commissioning Lightborn to murder the old King. It ends with his soldiers dragging away the Earl of Kent, Edward's supporter, to be beheaded by 'martial law' (v. iv. 88). Between the two episodes there is the challenge of the King's Champion, the legitimate defender of the new King's right:

> If any Christian, Heathen, Turk, or Jew,
> Dares but affirm that Edward's not true king
> And will avouch his saying with the sword,
> I am the Champion that will combat him.   (74–7)

There is an embarrassing silence: 'None comes,' (78) observes Mortimer. It seems a pointless little incident, but in context it is the pointlessness that matters: the legal, formal, chivalric assertion of power lies impotently sandwiched between two cases of the sordid reality of tyrannical policy.

II

The tradition of medieval thought on tyranny, stretching back to John of Salisbury in the twelfth century, concerned itself less with preventative measures in the manner of the *speculum principis* genre, than with the practical consideration of what subjects might do about a tyrant once they had him. According to scholastic thinkers, a subject's options were determined by the right by which the tyrant governed: a *tyrannus absque titulo* (tyrant without title) who had acquired his throne unlawfully might be deposed, but under

---

[6] W. Baldwin, *The Mirror for Magistrates*, ed. L. B. Campbell (Cambridge, 1938), 3. 189.

a legitimate monarch ruling tyrannically (*tyrannus exercitio*), a subject had no choice but to submit. This influential distinction effectively subdivided the issue: active resistance and passive obedience were the possibilities offered, and the ethics of one might be considered independently of the other. Each was relevant to a different type of assassin. Resistance theory was politically important in the later Elizabethan period in that it was used by Catholic activists such as William Allen to promote civil disobedience amongst the recusant community, and to provide the ethical basis for the assassination of the heretic princes. The question of whether a private individual might take up arms against his ruler, then, was raised by plays dealing with political murder, such as *Julius Caesar* (1599). The question of how far a subject might go in obedience to a prince's commands, however, was one which playwrights addressed by putting a subject in the invidious position of being ordered to commit murder.

This subject had already been treated in the first-century Latin tragedy *Octavia*, which the Elizabethans knew, and which was translated into English by Thomas Nuce in 1566. The play was believed (probably wrongly) to be the work of Seneca, a major influence on sixteenth-century thought on tyranny, who also appears as a character in the drama.[7] The plot deals with the murder of the title character on the orders of her husband, the Emperor Nero, an archetypal tyrant in sixteenth-century eyes. At the play's core is a debate between Nero and Seneca on the nature of monarchical power: Nero argues for descending authority, with his power absolute and bestowed upon him by the gods, while Seneca stresses his responsibility to his subjects. The key question is whether he can expect obedience to any command, or only those which a subject can carry out in good conscience:

NERO
Well hardly then our will let them obay.
SENECA
Will nothing then but that which wel you may.
NERO
We wil decree what we shall best suppose.
SENECA
What peoples voyce doth joyntly bynd or lose,
Let that confirmed stand.   (p. 167)

There is no doubt that Seneca's view is right, but Nero's carries the day. The play stresses three immoral commands, all to commit murder. The Chorus reports how he sent a soldier to kill his mother Agrippina, and soon afterwards we see him order his Prefect to have Plautus and Sulla beheaded, an action which sparks off the debate with Seneca. Finally, the Prefect is told

[7] See W. A. Armstrong, *RES* 24 (1948), 20–5, 34–5.

to kill Octavia herself. But despite these practical cases, the issue remains essentially theoretical. The Prefect's attitude seems to be typical:

> Declare whose death your moode doth most require,
> Let not my hande be stayde from your desire,   (p. 186)

he tells Nero. He demurs a little when told Octavia is to die, but goes to perform the charge nonetheless. The play's stress is on the ethics of giving the order, not the dilemma of the subject receiving it.

There was more emphasis on the latter question in the sixteenth century. Although the monarch could do no wrong, the issue of a subject acting under orders was still a grey area in English law. In a hierarchical, absolutist state, obedience was regarded as a virtue, and it is true that in most situations it was possible, though not necessarily easy, to square fidelity with the other dictates of conscience. In *The Tempest* (1611), for example, Gonzalo manages this precarious balancing act when he ensures the survival of Prospero after supervising his overthrow as ordered; he is thus, as Prospero says, 'My true preserver, and a loyal sir | To him thou follow'st' (v. i. 69–70). When the order is to commit murder, however, the subject is on the horns of a dilemma: one or other moral imperative must be disregarded. Of course, moralists argued against unquestioning obedience: 'You ought ... to obey your Lord in all thinges that tend to his profit and honour, not in such matters as tende to his losse and shame'; if commanded to kill a man, or to conspire to commit treason, 'ye are not onely not bound to doe it, but yee are bound not to doe it'.[8] But this was not, as we shall see, a principle which was accepted without anxiety until the early seventeenth century.

One reason for the difficulty of the situation was that a second question, of practical rather than ethical import, clouded the issue. John Tiptoft, one of the few self-righteous ghosts in *The Mirror for Magistrates*, articulates the problem when he tries to justify himself concerning the murder of the Earl of Desmond's sons:

> the kinges charge doth me clere discharge,
> By strayt commaundement and Injunctions:
> Theffect wherof so rigorously runnes,
> That eyther I must procure to se them dead,
> Or for contempt as a traytour lose my head.[9]

It is easy to write off Tiptoft as a wicked man who protests too much, but the problem is no less real for the virtuous subject. Perhaps the clearest summary of the problem is given by Thaliard, the assassin sent by the tyrant Antiochus against the hero of *Pericles* (1607): it is a choice, he says, between hanging abroad for murder or at home for disobedience, 'for if a king bid a

---

[8] B. Castiglione, *The Book of the Courtier*, tr. Sir T. Hoby (1974), 112–13.
[9] Baldwin, *Mirror*, 15. 59–63.

man be a villain, he's bound by the indenture of his oath to be one' (I. iii. 7–8).

Plays treating the issue are interested partly in the subject's options under a tyrant, but also in his behaviour. Some characters seek a solution in evasiveness. William Alexander's Harpagus in *Croesus* is a case in point. King Astyages' instructions to kill the infant Cyrus induce a kind of paralysis in him:

> Whil'st horrour did congeale my bloud, a space
> I stood perplex'd, not knowing what to doe,
> And (as to purge my part) even shedding teares,
> By troupes of passions griefe, my soule assail'd.   (2239–42)

All he can do is what Astyages, also afflicted with 'horrour' (2226), has already done: pass the job on. All he achieves by doing this is to start the process again: the herdsman to whom he assigns the task undergoes the same anxiety. Only divine intervention can break the cycle: the herdsman's wife, 'No doubt inspir'd by some celestiall pow'r' (2274), proposes that they substitute their own new-born son for Cyrus. Faced with the alternatives of committing murder or undergoing it, Harpagus tries to avoid making any decision at all; but when Cyrus turns up alive, he learns that even inaction is a decision of sorts, and his punishment from Astyages is a Thyestean banquet. Moreover, he has failed in morality as well as in murder: by passing the buck, along with threats of 'many a cruell death' (2251) for non-compliance, he is simply making himself a tyrant too. The historical Harpagus, it may be added, was remembered as 'more compassionate then *Astiages* (though too remorcelesse)'.[10]

Another character who tries to fudge in such a situation is Shakespeare's Brackenbury, commanded to hand over the keys of the Tower to the two murderers who have come for Clarence. It is instructive to compare the character's behaviour in the same situation (albeit with the two Princes as victims) in the other Richard III plays of the 1590s. In *The True Tragedy of Richard III*, he knows that Terrill has come to kill the Princes, for Richard has sent to him to do the same many times, and he has refused; but now, as Terrill points out, he is no longer a party to the matter; his only option is to relinquish the keys 'with teares' (1204). In Heywood's *Edward IV, Part 2* he has only suspicion; but he also knows his duty. These are both men with a share of guilt, but their grief for it atones. Shakespeare's character is more fastidious: reading his orders, he states,

> I will not reason what is meant hereby,
> Because I will be guiltless of the meaning.   (I. iv. 90–1)

---

[10] R. Brathwait, *Natvres Embassie* (1621), C3^v

The lines only emphasize his suspicions and so make his refusal to think about them the more reprehensible. Where Heywood's Brackenbury wishes he could ask the King his intentions, 'to rid me of my doubt' (p.151), Shakespeare's sees moral security in a cloud of uncertainty. He never learns better ethics, as Harpagus does: after giving up the keys he disappears from the play. But it is worth remembering that another Lieutenant of the Tower, Sir Jervis Elwes, found himself in a similar situation in 1613 when he was told that Overbury was to be poisoned. Like Brackenbury, he chose to look the other way: 'Let it be done so I know not of it.'[11] The words were enough to hang him.

A command to commit, or to aid and abet murder leaves its recipient in a position where he must fall on one side or the other, then. One way in which dramatists approach the question is to contrast the behaviour of two characters in similar situations. In *Gismond of Salerne*, for example, Tancred's men Julio and Renuchio are ordered to put into effect different stages of the murder of Guishard: Julio's charge is to arrest him, Renuchio's to take part in the killing and present the disembodied heart to Gismond. When he first approaches Julio, Tancred is, like most hirers, diffident about making the proposal, and he feels the need to underline his position: 'We must commaund, and yow may not refuse.' (IV. ii. 126) Julio responds by stating

> How by your graces bountie I am bound,
> beyond the common bond, wherin eche wight
> standes bound unto his prince.   (127–9)

The King deserves well of him, having advanced him at court, he says, so like the Prefect in *Octavia*, he shows willing by promising compliance before he knows the task, though it be suicide.

As we saw in Chapter 2, obedience is more difficult for Renuchio, whose involvement with the murder is more direct. The question is emergent during his report of the killing, but comes to a head with the delivery of Guishard's heart, hacked from his body:

> Now were it not that I am forced thearto
> by a Kinges will, here wold I stay my fete,
> ne one whit farther go in this entent.
> But I must yeld me to my princes hest,
> and tell, alas, the dolefull message sent.   (v. i. 215–19)

He performs his task to the letter, and not beyond. His lines as he hands over the grisly token are Tancred's, reported by Renuchio in the previous scene and now repeated virtually word for word:

[11] McElwee, 84.

> Thy father, o Quene, here in this cup hath sent
> that thing, to joy and comfort thee withall,
> which thow loved best, even as thow weart content
> to comfort him with his chefe joy of all.   (v. ii. 1–4)

There is a stiff, formal quality in this repetition of lines we have heard only moments before, noticeable even in the stiff, formal context of a Senecan tragedy. It suggests Renuchio's embarrassment and shame; he says nothing to Gismond in his own person, and slinks off during her lengthy lamentation, never to reappear. It is as though by keeping strictly within his charge, by doing nothing on his own initiative, he hopes to erase his own responsibility as an actant in Tancred's crimes.

Gismond of Salerne was performed before Queen Elizabeth, and its authors were anxious to avoid giving offence: the Epilogue specifically denies any application to England. This may explain why there is no suggestion that Renuchio has an option to disobey his prince. When Dr Legge dealt with the same issue in *Richardus Tertius*, the possibility is at least implicit in his use of the rhetorical form of the debate when Tirell and Brakenbury argue about their orders. However, the two characters are more similar than the form might suggest: both have moral doubts about the murder, and both suppress them. Tirell first enters asking himself,

> Ignava mens quid jussa regis exequi
> dubitas? inanes et metus fingis tibi?[12]   (i. i. 56–7)

He argues his way round his scruples—'rex imperat: erit innocens necessitas'[13] (60)—before taking a stand for obedience against Brakenbury. Loyalty is the burden of his argument—it is a 'Caedis fidele munus'[14] (i. ii. 20) that is to be done—but his loyalty is reinforced by the rewards the King can offer:

> ego quis moneret intuens, qualis simul
> ipse fuerim, lamenta nec regis ferens
> meam ultro regi tum lubens opem tuli.[15]   (74–6)

Brakenbury, he suggests, has even more obligation, for he has already received advancement: 'Hanc immemor regi reponis gratiam?'[16] (i. i. 90) The Lieutenant's position is less honest, for though his moral objections are loud and demonstrative, the halo slips when he is asked a direct question:

[12] 'Listless mind, why do you hesitate to execute the orders of the King? And why do you fashion foolish fears for yourself?'

[13] 'The King commands: it will be a guiltless necessity.'

[14] 'loyal office of murder'.

[15] 'Considering who advised this, besides what I myself should become, and not considering the lamentations of the King at all, I then voluntarily offered my aid to the King with pleasure.'

[16] 'Will you, forgetful of the King, pay him this return?'

TIRELL

Tua interest vivat puer vel occidat?

BRAKENBURY

Parum: nisi ut occisore me non occidat.[17]   (86–7)

Like one of Thomas Middleton's characters, all he really cares about is keeping his own hands clean. Tirell argues himself into his debating position, then argues Brakenbury out of his, so the moral option is never translated into moral action. Nonetheless, the possibility is still there: Brakenbury's choice commits him, but it does not invalidate the alternative; he ends the scene with the line, 'discede pietas, et locum quaerat fides'[18] (I. ii. 140).

So long as the subject is caught between murder and mutiny, neither 'pietas' nor 'fides' is an entirely satisfactory course, however. Some plays presented on the public stage, more overtly moralistic than the academic, sought a resolution by incorporating the clashing ethical principles in a hierarchy. In *The Troublesome Reign of King John*, for example, the matter is approached through another formal debate, between Hubert, commanded to put out Arthur's eyes, and Arthur himself. Hubert sums up the essence of the argument as he reaches his decision not to carry out his orders:

> My King commaunds, that warrant sets me free:
> But God forbids, and he commaundeth Kings.   (vii. 123–4)

The logic is inescapable: though kings offer 'blisse' (69) or 'torture' (6) for obedience or otherwise, so too does God—but in his case, eternally. Throughout the scene, the punishment receives more emphasis than the reward, but this reflects on Hubert's character. He seems essentially a kindly man, from the little we hear from him before he is burdened with immoral orders:

> Frolick yong Prince, though I your keeper bee,
> Yet shall your keeper live at your commaund.   (iv. 36–7)

When he has those orders, he tells his accomplices, 'I would the King had made choyce of some other executioner: onely this is my comfort, that a King commaunds, whose precepts neglected or omitted, threatneth torture for the default.' (vii. 3–7) He is a man forced to perform torture upon Arthur in order to avoid it himself: the threat is far stronger inducement than any reward. In arguing as he does that he is simply a subject executing a decision that is John's responsibility, he is trying to justify to himself his way of dealing with an impossible situation.

It is because Hubert is essentially compassionate that Arthur's arguments hit home: when he tries to silence them with

---

[17] 'Does it concern you whether the boy lives or dies?' 'Little, except that he is not killed by me as executioner.'

[18] 'Depart, piety, and let loyalty seek your place.'

> My Lord, my Lord, this long expostulation,
> Heapes up more griefe, than promise of redresse,   (97–8)

we know that the converse is probably true. (Otherwise why not just blind the boy and have done?) But he has been thinking in confused terms: with John's sanctions looming in his mind, he has confounded the moral with the practical element of the problem facing him. The scene is an opportunity for him to rethink the position, and so separate the two: he first establishes what action is morally right, then looks for a practical way of reconciling that action with his own survival. Compared with the evil of mutilation, lying to his King is a venial way of protecting himself.

A corollary of this approach is that it holds the subject personally responsible for his own actions, even if they are committed under orders. This is also the import of the murder episode that begins *The Maid's Metamorphosis* (1600). The play presents a situation not unlike that of *Gismond of Salerne*: Duke Telemachus considers Eurymine, the low-born maid of the title, to be an unsuitable match for his son, and the action opens with two gentlemen, Orestes and Phylander, escorting her in embarrassed silence to the place where they are to murder her. But here the situation is contrived to minimize its political resonance: though Telemachus is called a tyrant (I. i. 214), he has not used his prerogative of command to enforce his wishes; instead, Orestes and Phylander are bound 'by vertue of a solemne oath' (74). Our attention, moreover, is on them rather than the Duke, who has yet to appear. When they debate whether or not to kill Eurymine, therefore, the key issue is one of personal morality, not public duty: keeping their vow, not disobeying their prince. Only when they have agreed that 'A lawfull oath in an unlawfull cause' (167) cannot bind them, do they turn to the political question of remaining in favour, and decide not only to lie to Telemachus but to fake evidence to show their compliance. The problem resolves into the same hierarchy seen in *The Troublesome Reign*.

III

The plight of the virtuous under tyranny drew attention for the ethical difficulties it raised, but it was also held that a tyrant's regime attracted evil men: one writer remarked 'how prompt and prepared men of depraved or vicious disposition are, to put in execution the pleasure of great ones, how indirect or unlawfull soever their pleasures be'; another denied that 'wickit Princis ever wantit ministeris of thayr wyckit treachereis'.[19] In Shakespeare, such figures focus the issue of tyrannical commands from a different

---

[19] Brathwait, *Natvres Embassie*, L3ʳ; G. Buchanan, *Ane Detectiovn of the duinges of Marie Quene of Scottes* (?Edinburgh, ?1572), H2ᵛ.

perspective: shocking because of their readiness to obey, they are also creatures of moral emptiness, embodiments of the mediocrity of evil.

A case in point is Hubert in *King John*, a very different person from the Hubert of *The Troublesome Reign*, probably Shakespeare's source. He too is a punctiliously loyal subject, willing (he tells John) to obey orders even at the expense of his own life; but he is also a bad man. He accepts his task of murder with terrible alacrity, hesitating only to make sure of John's intentions:

JOHN
  Death.
HUBERT My lord.
JOHN   A grave.
HUBERT   He shall not live.
JOHN   Enough.   (III. ii. 66)

The words volley back and forth in the space of a single verse line. For Hubert, this service is perfect freedom, as he later makes clear to Arthur:

ARTHUR
  Must you with hot irons burn out both mine eyes?
HUBERT
  Young boy, I must.
ARTHUR   And will you?
HUBERT   And I will.   (IV. i. 39–40)

The exchange turns on the substitution of 'will' for 'must': 'Goes thy heart with this?', Arthur is asking; and Hubert tells him with brutal simplicity that it does.

Even so, he has taken his time to do the job: a scene, and possibly an interval, interposes between command and execution, and it is clear that time has passed in that interim.[20] But the effect does not work, as one might expect, in Hubert's favour. We learn in the murder scene that he and Arthur have struck up a friendship during the child's imprisonment; but the period is not one of hesitancy or scruples. When Hubert reappears at the start of the scene, he is as resolute in his intentions as before: we infer a continuity. The intervening period, we must conclude, is one of premeditation, during which he deceives the boy he is to murder with a show of kindness.

Hubert's depravity is also stressed using the device of contrast. Even the executioners who are to assist him prove more compassionate: they have 'Uncleanly scruples' (7), and are 'best pleased to be from such a deed' (85) when sent away. Arthur's mishandling of the situation here underlines the point: he trusts to appearances, to the evidence of the eyes he is (it seems)

----

[20] The murder scene begins what Emrys Jones regards as the play's second movement: Jones, *Origins*, 253.

about to lose, so he still believes in the benign façade Hubert has shown him for so long, while the 'fierce looks' (73) of the executioners also characterize them for him. The truth, he soon realizes, is more complex: the leading executioner 'hath a stern look, but a gentle heart' (87); and with Hubert, the reverse is the case. Arthur goes on to suggest a further contrast: the very irons and fire refuse to co-operate in the blinding—'Deny their office' (118), as he significantly puts it. Only Hubert seems willing to do his duty when that duty is murder.

Emrys Jones, seeing a 'strangely serpentine development' in the narrative of this part of the play, remarks that, with Hubert's change of heart, 'we are left with the perhaps slightly callous feeling that the scene was not really necessary, since the situation at the end remains much what it was at the beginning'.[21] The same might be said of the corresponding scene in *The Troublesome Reign*: in both, the very lack of development emphasizes Hubert's decision not to perform the key act. In Shakespeare, however, there is a sense of pointlessness even beyond this. *The Troublesome Reign*'s Hubert is a basically good man whose moral vision is fogged, and the scene has a development in so far as he gains a clearer view. Accordingly, it works through debate and argument: Arthur is simply a moralistic voice, bound to a chair and therefore static, able to out-think Hubert at every turn. Shakespeare eliminates the intellectual element and orients the scene instead towards pathos. Arthur is less self-possessed and more childlike, and therefore more vulnerable; since, it appears, he is never tied up, he also has more stage-presence than his earlier counterpart. This Hubert is moved not by any ethical considerations, but simply by the normal human feeling of pity—in Jones's terms, an unexpected intervention from his inner self disabling him in his public role of torturer and assassin. Though the outcome is good, the impression of Hubert the scene leaves us with is ultimately one of banal ineptitude.

He gains nothing in moral understanding from the experience, as we see in the next scene. Having second thoughts about the murder, John tries to evade responsibility by misrepresenting the situation. First he treats Hubert as a wicked opportunist, Exton to his Bolingbroke:

> It is the curse of kings to be attended
> By slaves that take their humours for a warrant
> To break within the bloody house of life.   (IV. ii. 209–11)

Hubert belies him by producing a written warrant, so he tries another argument:

21 Ibid. 233–4.

> How oft the sight of means to do ill deeds
> Make deeds ill done!   (220–1)

Hubert tempted him to the crime by standing by and looking murderous, he asserts. All this is palpable sophistry, the floundering of a guilty man looking for an alibi. Then Hubert damns himself by joining in: the boy is alive, he tells John, and he himself is morally unblemished—

> Within this bosom never entered yet
> The dreadful motion of a murderous thought.   (255–6)

It is a direct lie; and he continues to assert it in the following scene when confronted by the barons. It is a shell of honour which proves empty within: he muddles along in John's service to the end, taking no moral position at all. It is an index of the irrelevance of ethics in his failure to murder Arthur.

A similar character is Oswald, Goneril's steward in *King Lear*, who ends his career with an attempt on Gloucester's life; but the emphasis is different. He is loosely based on the hired assassin in the source play, *King Leir*; but whereas that character, like Hubert, is employed as a murderer from his first scene, the function comes to Oswald late in his part. We see him first as, essentially, a loyal if somewhat odious servant—his name, in fact, means 'steward'.[22] That loyalty is emphasized by a parallel drawn with Caius (the disguised Kent), Lear's faithful servant: both are sent to Regan with letters at the end of Act I, and they fight with each other on arrival. Critics since Samuel Johnson have stressed this aspect of Oswald. A. C. Bradley writes,

twice we are able to feel sympathy with him. Regan cannot tempt him to let her open Goneril's letter to Edmund; and his last thought as he dies is given to the fulfilment of his trust. It is to a monster that he is faithful, and he is faithful to her in a monstrous design. Still faithfulness is faithfulness, and he is not wholly worthless.[23]

Bradley not only misreads the action (as we shall see), he also simplifies the play's ethics. Loyalty is a virtue, to be sure, in certain circumstances; but here, as the situation worsens, the question arises, how far does loyalty go?

Besides actively good and actively evil characters, *King Lear* has several who are morally indeterminate. For all the abuse that is rained upon him, Oswald is one of these: one who stands by, who does as he is told, but who does not initiate action himself. One by one, these characters drop away from the evil ones over the blinding of Gloucester: Cornwall's servant is moved to kill him, and Albany sees the truth. Oswald is conspicuous in supporting Goneril even through this brutality: in this he is, as Edgar remembers him,

---

[22] S. Musgrove, *RES* NS 7 (1956), 294.
[23] A. C. Bradley, *Shakespearean Tragedy*, 2nd edn. (1905), 298.

> a serviceable villain,
> As duteous to the vices of thy mistress
> As badness would desire.   (F: iv. v. 250–2)[24]

Throughout the episode and its aftermath, he is quietly linked with the victim, emphasizing his complacency: he announces Gloucester's capture (F: iii. vii. 13–18), discusses his treachery (F: iv. ii. 6), and finally undertakes his murder. It has been like watching Malvolio turn into Lightborn.

In agreeing to be an assassin, he at last achieves moral determinacy; it is the point, too, at which his loyalty finally breaks. Regan spends a short scene attempting to subvert his allegiance: he will not allow her to open Goneril's letter, nor will he pass on information; but he silently agrees to carry her letter to Edmund, despite knowing that the two sisters are rivals for his favours. Finally, the murder is broached:

REGAN
    If you do chance to hear of that blind traitor,
    Preferment falls on him that cuts him off.
OSWALD
    Would I could meet him, madam. I should show
    What party I do follow.   (F: iv. iv. 37–40)

His meaning is clearer in the unrevised text of the last line: 'What lady I do follow' (Q: xix. 40). At this point he is non-committal: we do not know whether he will commit the murder, or deliver the letter. But when he meets Gloucester, he does indeed show what lady he follows: hoping (as he says) to raise his fortunes, he attempts to kill the old man, and, slain himself, tries to make provision for both letters to reach Edmund.

Edgar's lines on his duteousness in villainy which follow are inappropriate at this point, then: they are another case of the sort of crass, moralistic over-simplification that Edgar is prone to. Where Albany stands out for good, so does Oswald for evil: where Albany stands away from the blinding, Oswald switches his loyalties from Goneril, who proposed it, to Regan, who helped perform it. It is his first act of self-interest in the play; and it also proves to be his last.

IV

Regan never specifically commissions Oswald to murder Gloucester: instead of a command, there is an understanding; instead of obedience there is a show of loyalty. It was, indeed, often held to be preferable that the killer should act without orders. In 1570, when Mary Stuart heard that James

---

[24] In references to *King Lear*, I use the letters Q and F to distinguish between the quarto and Folio versions, printed in The Oxford Shakespeare as the 'History' and the 'Tragedy' respectively.

Hamilton of Bothwellhaugh had assassinated the Regent Moray, she expressed her approval in these terms: 'What Bothwellhaugh has done, he did without my orders, for which I am as much indebted to him, *and more*, than if he had consulted me. I shall not forget the pension of the said Bothwellhaugh.'[25] When we first see Macbeth with the murderers of Banquo, he is trying hard to make them do the deed on their own initiative. He persuades them that Banquo has brought them to their present beggary, and attempts to induce them to take their revenge:

> Do you find
> Your patience so predominant in your nature
> That you can let this go?   (III. i. 87–9)

After a laborious process of hinting, during which the murderers remain infuriatingly obtuse, Macbeth has to state openly that he wishes Banquo dead, 'And thence it is | That I to your assistance do make love' (124–5). Still the murderers stick out for a direct order: 'We shall, my lord, | Perform what you command us.' (127–8) These men move only in command, nothing in love.

The reason for this attitude is clearest from an incident in *Antony and Cleopatra* (1606). At the party on Pompey's galley for the triumvirs, Menas proposes to Pompey that he should cut the boat adrift and murder the guests, leaving a power vacuum for his master to fill. Pompey regretfully rejects the idea:

> Ah, this thou shouldst have done
> And not have spoke on't. In me 'tis villainy,
> In thee 't had been good service. Thou must know
> 'Tis not my profit that does lead mine honour;
> Mine honour, it. Repent that e'er thy tongue
> Hath so betrayed thine act. Being done unknown,
> I should have found it afterwards well done,
> But must condemn it now.   (II. vii. 72–9)

For all his protestations of honour, however, it is not an honourable position to take: as Geoffrey Bullough says, 'Pompey ... is willing for his henchman to do the basest treachery for him but not to do it himself'.[26] He wishes both to benefit from the crime and avoid being an accessory before the fact—wishes, in effect, to be pardoned and retain the offence.

There is an inconsistency in Pompey's stance which makes one wonder, Bradley-like, what he would have done if Menas had killed the triumvirs

[25] 'Ce que Bothwellhaugh a fait, a été sans mon commandement, de quoi je lui sais aussi bon gré *et meilleur*, que si j'eusse été du conseil. Je n'oublierai la pension du dit Bothwellhaugh.': J. Knox, *The History of the Reformation of Religion within the Realm of Scotland*, ed. C. J. Guthrie (1898), 69 n. (my italics).
[26] Bullough, v. 241.

without telling him first: for though he wants to dissociate himself from the crime for appearances' sake, appearances would hardly be served by pardoning and rewarding the criminal. The only reason for avoiding prior commitment would be to leave a way open to reject the murderer afterwards.

Such a disavowal was an appropriate response from a just ruler to a subject hoping to win favour by villainy: King David executed the killers of Ish-bosheth, the son of his enemy; and Caesar served the murderers of Pompey similarly in two plays on the subject, the anonymous *Caesar's Revenge* (1595) and Chapman's *Caesar and Pompey* (1605).[27] In *The Mirror for Magistrates*, King Canute rises to wit when Edricus presents him with Edmund Ironside's head:

> O heynous acte, O bloody crueltie.
> But sith that love did move thee doo that deede,
> Thou for thy paynes shalt be preferde with speede.[28]

Edricus' preferment consists of having his own severed head set on the highest part of London's city walls. Edward Daunce, discussing several examples of this situation, commented, 'These are ... presidents of rare justice, & most excellent to be followed of them that care to maintaine the high reputation of their calling.'[29]

Even following those examples could be suspicious, however—it was proverbial that kings loved the treason and hated the traitor.[30] This is the final ambiguity in Shakespeare's presentation of Henry Bolingbroke in *Richard II* (1595). Throughout the play, there is nothing intimate in the portrayal: he is a silent, enigmatic, upstage figure, whose lines tend to be formal rather than personal. Therefore we can never know what he is thinking: the first scene begins with Richard enquiring into his motives, but even his father, Gaunt, can offer only a qualified answer (I. i. 12–14). About his actions, the play is equivocal: it is uncertain whether he seizes power or whether Richard simply assumes that to be his aim and hands it over; and once on the throne, it is uncertain what part he has in Sir Piers Exton's murder of his predecessor.

Writers of the time were undecided about the question, and their interpretations of Henry's behaviour grew increasingly subtle. According to the chronicler Fabyan and *The Mirror for Magistrates*, Exton was sent by the King.[31] In Holinshed's *Chronicles*, however, the murderer is an opportunist who 'incontinentlie' acts on Henry's stated desire for Richard's death; but Samuel Daniel, in his epic poem *The Civil Wars* (1595), holds that statement

---

[27] 2 Samuel 4: 8–12.
[28] J. Higgins and T. Blenerhasset, *Parts Added to the Mirror for Magistrates*, ed. L. B. Campbell (Cambridge, 1946), 1578 edn., 11. 40–2.
[29] E. Daunce, *A Briefe Discovrse Dialogvevvise* (1590), C3ᵛ.
[30] Tilley, K. 64.
[31] R. Fabyan, *Chronicle* (1559), 214ʳ; Bullough, iii. 422.

to be a sly hint to a villain whom he knew 'soone could learne his lesson by his eie'.[32] John Hayward, writing after Shakespeare, concludes, 'whether hee did expressely commaund his death, or no, it is a question; out of question he shewed some liking and desire to the action, and gave allowance thereto when it was doone.'[33] In the play, even that certainty is gone: an incident added by Shakespeare is Bolingbroke's rejection of the murderer in the final moments.

In the little scene before the murder, we see Exton present his accomplices with an interpretation of a remark by the King: 'Have I no friend will rid me of this living fear?' (v. iv. 2) The emphasis is on the glossing: we never see Bolingbroke actually say these words. They are, moreover, words which are capable of many interpretations. Shakespeare has cultivated ambiguity in them, as comparison with the equivalent statement in Holinshed, his principal source, makes clear: 'Have I no faithfull freend which will deliver me of him, whose life will be my death, and whose death will be the preservation of my life?'[34] The line in the play, in contrast, explicitly desires no one's death. We still do not know what Bolingbroke is thinking; but Exton believes he does. It is quite possible that he has misinterpreted.

Bolingbroke's behaviour when he rejects Exton does not help us decide. Despite the disavowal, he is also candid enough to admit that he wanted Richard dead:

> They love not poison that do poison need;
> Nor do I thee. Though I did wish him dead,
> I hate the murderer, love him murdered.   (v. vi. 38–40)

Moreover, though he is legally and morally innocent of the crime in the situation as he presents it, he accepts a share of blood-guilt and plans a pilgrimage to the Holy Land to cleanse himself. It looks like the horrified over-reaction of a good man: because the murder fulfils his secret, sinful desires, he has an irrational feeling of responsibility which he seeks to expiate. But with this character, we cannot be sure that that is not precisely the effect intended.

Orders are, ultimately, a crude way for tyrants to impose their will. As George Buchanan pointed out, even the selection of agents is problematic: 'they dare not hire good men, nor can they trust bad men'.[35] It is far more efficient to exploit the bad men's villainy without trusting to their fidelity. This is what Daniel's Bolingbroke does; but in Shakespeare the situation is pushed further into an insoluble uncertainty. Either Exton is an assassin who has been double-crossed, or Bolingbroke is a virtuous king purging his court

---

[32] Bullough, iii. 413, 457.

[33] J. Hayward, *The First Part of the Life and raigne of King Henrie the IIII* (1599), S2^r–v.

[34] Bullough, iii. 413.

[35] G. Buchanan, *De jure regni apud Scotos*, tr. Philaletes (n. pl., 1680), D6^r.

of a villain; but we do not know which is true. With *Richard II*, an Elizabethan bugbear becomes a political reality; the assassin shades into the ordinary murderer; and tyranny reaches its vanishing point.

v

Shakespeare returned to the question of tyrants and murderers in his later plays, as part of a wider consideration of the theme of service.[36] The realities of the situation remain unchanged: 'To do't, or no, is certain | To me a break-neck' (I. ii. 363–4), comments Camillo in *The Winter's Tale* after Leontes has commanded him to poison Polixenes. What is new is the integration of political and moral responsibility into a single imperative, where earlier plays had only set priorities between the two. Camillo accepts his orders, telling Leontes, 'If from me he have wholesome beverage, | Account me not your servant.' (347–8) He then relays his King's intentions to Polixenes and helps him to flee to Bohemia; but despite this treason, the oracle names him 'a true subject' (III. ii. 133).

A contrasting figure is Antigonus, who has orders to take Hermione's baby and burn it. From here the narrative diverges a little from what one might expect: Perdita is abandoned in the wild, but it is not because, as in folk tales, the assassin finds he has not the heart to murder her; it is Leontes who mitigates his sentence to exposure.[37] Antigonus simply carries out his commission to the letter, and he is held morally responsible for doing so: the vision of Hermione tells him,

<blockquote>
For this ungentle business
Put on thee by my lord, thou ne'er shalt see
Thy wife Paulina more.   (III. iii. 33–5)
</blockquote>

Camillo, in turn, is 'rewarded' in the same terms, with marriage to Paulina at the end of the play. He has been a true subject and Antigonus a false in so far as he has recognized that Leontes is 'in rebellion with himself' (I. ii. 356): there is, so to speak, a schism between the King's two bodies, and to obey the rebel is to join him in his treason.

Obviously the full implications of this position would be politically sensitive, so it is in *Cymbeline* (1609), at the pettier level of private service, that the theme is most explicitly articulated. The character of Pisanio is represented as a man utterly loyal to his master, Posthumus: 'when to my good lord I prove untrue, | I'll choke myself' (I. v. 86–7), he says, and the remarks of several other characters confirm his fidelity. Throughout the play,

---

[36] See H. Weinstock, *Studia Neophilologica*, 43 (1971), 446–73.

[37] Contrast S. Thompson, *Motif-Index of Folk Literature*, rev. edn. (Copenhagen, 1955–8), K. 512.

he remains loyal to Posthumus, despite attempts by the wicked Queen and later by her son Cloten to subvert his loyalties with offers of preferment. His behaviour in these situations steers a middle course between principle and pragmatism. On the one hand, he goes along with his seducers: he agrees to the Queen's proposals with his tongue (if not his heart), and later obeys Cloten in deed as well as word, fetching a suit of Posthumus' clothes for him. These actions are necessary, especially when dealing with Cloten, to protect himself—Cloten has, after all, threatened his life. Nonetheless he does not transfer his allegiance, despite the persuasive contrast Cloten draws between 'the bare fortune of that beggar Posthumus' (III. v. 118–19) and the rewards which those in favour can bestow. Pisanio's co-operation with him shows not a devotion to the main chance but the ability to temporize. The most perceptive summing-up of his character comes from the Queen: 'A sly and constant knave' (I. v. 75).

Slyness and constancy are most evident in his response to his master's letter ordering him to murder Imogen, which presents him with a simple choice between fidelity and infidelity: 'thou, Pisanio, must act for me, if thy faith be not tainted with the breach of hers. Let thine own hands take away her life. ... if thou fear to strike ... thou art ... to me disloyal.' (III. iv. 25–31) His reaction is morally laudable: 'If it be so to do good service, never | Let me be counted serviceable.' (III. ii. 14–15) Yet his behaviour seems suspiciously at odds with this position: he follows his instructions in giving Imogen the letter that summons her to Milford Haven, and in escorting her there. When he explains the situation to her and assures her that he has no intention of committing murder, it is a pertinent question that she asks: 'Wherefore then | Didst undertake it?' (III. iv. 101–2) The doubt is invoked only to be banished: Pisanio has not simply been procrastinating, putting off the decision to obey or not; he has actively been working through a plan of his own, as is evident from his foresight in packing boy's clothes for Imogen. The point is that he emerges as an independent agent rather than an obedient puppet.

To be genuinely loyal in *Cymbeline* requires such independence of judgement. The penitent Posthumus later insists,

> Every good servant does not all commands,
> No bond but to do just ones.   (v. i. 6–7)

This has been the import of the quibbles on truth and falsehood in servants that recur throughout the play: 'Wherein I am false I am honest; not true, to be true.' (IV. iii. 42) The implications go further: Pisanio's loyal service has not consisted solely of obedience or disobedience, but in acting on his own initiative to the good of his master, even if that action is contrary to his master's expressed will.

This was not a new concept of the relationship between master and servant, ruler and ruled. Its appearance in English drama early in the seventeenth century reflects a growing acceptance of a potentially radical philosophy that had already been formulated in the sixteenth. As Angus's comment on Macbeth presupposes, commands were no longer an absolute in human relationships:

> Those he commands move only in command,
> Nothing in love.   (v. ii. 19–20)

Tyranny remained a problematic situation, for the tyrant still had power to abuse, sanctions against the disobedient: Pisanio still finds it necessary to supply his master with false evidence of his obedience. But now the ethical position was clear.

VI

The issue was dead by the 1630s. With the impeachment in 1626 of the Duke of Buckingham, Charles I's chief minister, it had been decisively established in law that a royal command did not indemnify the obedient subject: 'the laws of England teach us that Kings cannot command ill, or unlawful things. Whenever they speak, though by Letters Patent, if the thing be evil, those Letters Patent are void, and whatsoever ill event succeeds the executioner of such commands must ever answer for them.'[38] In Henry Glapthorne's *The Lady Mother*, written nine years later, an English court throws out the defence that orders shift the burden of guilt.

The subject's crisis of conscience had been a potent source of dramatic suspense, but now the tension had gone out of the situation. The dilemma did not detain Philip Massinger in *The Emperor of the East* (1631), in which the jealous title character orders his captain of the guard to murder the kinsman whom he believes, wrongly, to have cuckolded him. In *The Queen and Concubine* (1635), Richard Brome's recasting of *The Winter's Tale*, it is taken for granted that a subject should always act as his conscience dictates: to do otherwise is simply farcical. The courtier Horatio, whose catch-phrase is that he is 'true to th' Crown' (p.3, etc.), endeavours to have no opinions but the King's, and is forever being wrong-footed when the royal mind changes. When the general Petruccio is sent to execute an unjust sentence of death on his rival Sforza, the issue of obedience is not raised: it is a matter

---

[38] Holdsworth, *English Law*, i. 382; C. Roberts, *The Growth of Responsible Government in Stuart England* (Cambridge, 1966), 59.

of whether Sforza is truly guilty, and whether Petruccio can overcome his antipathy to the man and save him.[39]

Brome's treatment in particular shows how the moral imperatives have changed. There is no question of Petruccio's doing as he is told through an honest duteousness: he will be colluding in a crime out of personal enmity. The problem is no longer that the virtue of obedience entails the vice of murder: it is that to avoid committing murder entails disobedience. The distinction may seem factitious, but in the light of the dichotomy between possible responses to tyranny, there has been a significant shift towards political radicalism. Whereas earlier plays dealt with problems arising out of the duty of obedience, the situation now evoked the issue of the right of resistance; and in that debate, the assassin scenario had at best only a peripheral function.

[39] For a more detailed analysis of the play's rather antiseptic ideological structure, see M. Butler, *Theatre and Crisis* (Cambridge, 1984), 35–40.

6

THE FIRST HIRED ASSASSINS

I

WE have already seen that the success of *The Spanish Tragedy* was one of the factors behind the sudden popularity of episodes involving assassins in the late 1580s and early 1590s. The play's influence on the portrayal of such characters was no less decisive. As we saw in the last chapter, earlier plays— and many later ones—dealt with the stock figure of the tyrant, so that the assassin episode focused contemporary concerns about power and morality, authority and obedience. In contrast, Kyd's villain, Lorenzo, is a private individual, and his relationship with the assassin is correspondingly different.

The relevant thread of the plot traces the gradual process of corruption that leads Bel-Imperia's servant Pedringano to the gallows. That process sees Lorenzo seduce him away from his allegiance to his mistress, embroil him in murder, first as accomplice and then as assassin, and then drop him, fatally. In particular, the sequence stresses the medium of exchange which links the pair: Lorenzo uses his economic power to buy villainy, and Pedringano is the first hired assassin in English drama.

The dramatic pointing comes at the start of the sequence, when Lorenzo tries to wrest from the servant details about his mistress's love-life. He begins by reminding Pedringano of the protection and favours he has bestowed on him, and promises further reward—

> store of golden coin,
> And lands and living join'd with dignities,
> If thou but satisfy my just demand. (II. i. 52–4)

Anxious to show willing but concerned not to compromise himself, Pedringano makes excuses, so Lorenzo tries another tack and draws his sword:

> Nay, if thou dally then I am thy foe,
> And fear shall force what friendship cannot win. (67–8)

When it is clear to Pedringano that his interrogator will not stint to kill him, he hurriedly tells everything. At this, the promised reward is handed over and future loyalty pledged: 'your honour's liberality | Deserves my duteous service, even till death.' (96–7)

Once Pedringano has left the stage, Lorenzo sums up the incident:

> Where words prevail not, violence prevails:
> But gold doth more than either of them both.   (108–9)

What we have seen is not simply a change of loyalties: this is what Lorenzo hoped to effect with his words, playing on Pedringano's gratitude, and when it is not forthcoming, he threatens, 'Thou diest for more esteeming her than me.' (70) His action is to 'trump' Bel-Imperia by introducing new considerations and, in turn, a new mode of social relations. As a servant in a noble household, Pedringano's social role is based on mutual obligation, he to serve his mistress and she to maintain him. By threatening his life, Lorenzo places him in a position where he must choose between loyalty and self-interest. Once he has committed himself to the latter by saving his life, he is ready to consider Lorenzo's offer in different terms: 'Thou know'st that I can more advance thy state | Than she' (103–4), he is told. Worldly ambition and desire overrides simple loyalty, and Pedringano (whose name means, appropriately, both 'wandering' and 'morally errant') enters a dual allegiance. Later, when Hieronimo asks him, 'Where's thy lady?', he replies, as Lorenzo enters, 'I know not; here's my lord.' (III. ii. 54)

Pedringano does indeed serve two masters, but the second is not Lorenzo but Mammon. The point is signalled at each of the two murders he is involved in. The first is that of Horatio, hanged in the arbour of his assignation with Bel-Imperia. Pedringano is set to watch for intruders, being, Bel-Imperia believes, 'as trusty as my second self' (II. iv. 9). It is a mark of his true loyalties that he does exactly the opposite:

> Instead of watching, I'll deserve more gold
> By fetching Don Lorenzo to this match.   (12–13)

He does not speak again in the scene, but his actions underline his cupidity and his betrayal: he leads a party of armed men to the garden where they will be able to find his mistress. Judas Iscariot did much the same, we remember. The parallel is left delicately unstressed, almost subliminal, but it was clear enough to the author of the additions to the play that were first printed in 1602: commissioning a painting of the incident, Hieronimo asks that the murderers' beards should be 'of Judas his own colour' (Addition 4. 137).[1] There is no longer any value in singling out Pedringano here, for he is dead; but it seems that the author of the additions saw a similarity between the murder scene and the betrayal of Christ, a similarity which is centred on Judas. Like Pedringano, Judas accepted money, and his name was sometimes linked with that of Cain, the first murderer.[2] He is an apposite parallel for a character about to become a hired assassin.

---

[1] i.e. red, like that of the medieval stage Judas.
[2] e.g. R. Greene, *Complete Works*, ed. A. B. Grosart (1881–6), x. 39; cf. Hebrews 12: 24.

We see Pedringano paid in advance to commit the next murder, that of Serberine, and he inspects the money whilst awaiting his victim:

> Here is the gold, this is the gold propos'd:
> It is no dream that I adventure for,
> But Pedringano is possess'd thereof.   (III. iii. 5–7)

It is a speech of pure avarice: Pedringano is fascinated by the presence of the money which might, in another job, be no more than a proposition to be realized later. The repetition and broken rhythm of the first line makes it an excited stutter as he thrills to the opening of his purse. He has reached his moral nadir: we have watched him strain his conscience by degrees to the point where he can shrug off a murder. It is fitting that the agent of his degeneration should be a gleaming focus of attention as he does so.

From here, the logic of the situation is inescapable. Once Pedringano has betrayed his trust for money, the only thing he can be trusted to do is earn more money:

> They that for coin their souls endangered,
> To save my life, for coin shall venture theirs.   (III. ii. 113–14)

Even so, the full implications are not pursued in this play, largely because Lorenzo's mistrust is not shared by the murderers.

The little we hear from Serberine before he is shot down reveals a naïve loyalty which brings him dutifully to the place appointed for his murder. Pedringano is much the same: fixated on the person of his employer, he believes Lorenzo has deserved his service by the exercise of 'liberality' (II. i. 96). The notion persists in the second murder scene:

> And he that would not strain his conscience
> For him that thus his liberal purse hath stretch'd,
> Unworthy such a favour may he fail,
> And, wishing, want, when such as I prevail.   (III. iii. 8–11)

He presents the murder as a straining for a stretching—an exchange of congruent actions that the alliteration underlines. But the truth peeps out at the end when he contrasts his own imagined future of prosperity with the poverty that will be the lot of the hypothetical unfortunate without a flexible conscience; the bright presence of the gold itself reinforces the point. In other words, the assassin is trying to fit his relationship with Lorenzo into the terms he is used to: Lorenzo is his 'noble lord' (13) who will, in his benevolence, 'stand between me and ensuing harms' (14). He did the same, we remember, when Pedringano was to be punished for assisting Bel-Imperia in her liaison with Don Andrea: 'I stood betwixt thee and thy punishment' (II. i. 49). The recurrence of the figure of speech is revealing: clearly

Pedringano thinks that nothing has changed. We, and Lorenzo, know that this is not so.

II

Pedringano was a moderately memorable feature of *The Spanish Tragedy*: in 1610, referring especially to the hanging scene, Robert Daborne called it 'the play of *Pedringano*'.[3] Lines associated with him were not among those quoted in later works, however: Claude Dudrap's catalogue of allusions to the play yields only one instance, Jonson's parody of Lorenzo's threats in *The Poetaster* (1601).[4] In this case, Kyd's influence lay not in creating verbal clichés but in bringing a new type of character to the English stage. Although there were some previous examples in prose fiction, no extant play before *The Spanish Tragedy* had presented a hired murderer: stage assassins had hitherto been instruments of tyranny. As we have seen, the latter type continued well into the next century; but increasingly after Kyd, it was the carrot of a fee rather than the stick of authority that induced assassins to commit their murders. Of the seventeen plays featuring the character in the period 1587–92, ten explicitly state that he is working for money.

Probably the next stage assassins after Pedringano appeared in plays written in the shadow of *Tamburlaine* (1587–8): *The Wars of Cyrus* (1588) and *The Wounds of Civil War*. Narratively and dramatically, the episodes of the Assyrian Ctesiphon's mission to assassinate Cyrus, and of the abortive murder of Marius at Minturnum in Lodge's play, owe little to Kyd. Nonetheless, Ctesiphon, like Pedringano, is hired, not commanded to kill, and is named from the Greek for acquisitiveness, *ktesis*, though his behaviour does not altogether bear this out. It is likely, moreover, that Lodge had Pedringano in mind when creating his assassin, who is named Pedro, and who has a clumsily stressed concern for his fee.

Pedro's negotiations with his would-be employers take up about half of the episode. At first it seems that he is simply taking the opportunity for a revenge killing, for his parents have been among Marius' victims. One of the hirers, Favorinus, presses the point:

> The greater honor shall betide the deed;
> For to revenge on righteous estimate
> Beseems the honor of a Frenchman's name.   (III. ii. 72–4)

---

[3] R. Daborne, *A Christian Turned Turk*, i. 2074.

[4] C. Dudrap, in J. Jacquot (ed.), *Dramaturgie et société* (Paris, 1968), ii. 628–31; B. Jonson, *The Poetaster*, III. iv. 247–54, after *The Spanish Tragedy*, II. i. 67–75.

No sooner is this articulated, however, than Pedro unaccountably changes his position: the man who, moments before, was eagerly asking for his sword now declares, *'Mes messiers, de fault avoir argent, me no point de argent, no point kill Marius.'*[5] (75–6) He works for hire and salary, not revenge, so forty crowns satisfy him as the intangible rewards of personal honour do not.

The direct influence of *The Spanish Tragedy* is also evident in *Caesar's Revenge*, a Roman history play that may have premièred at the Rose in June 1595. The scene in question shows the murder of Pompey by Achillas and Sempronius, the latter a Roman who has served under him. This character's treachery is emphasized: Pompey dies telling him, 'O Villaine thou hast slayne thy Generall' (743), and Caesar later remembers him as 'Traytorous Sempronius' (799). He explains early on the reason he is determined to murder his old commander:

> But cause I see that now the world is changd:
> And like wise feele some of King *Ptolomeis* gould.
> Ile kill him were he twenty Generalls.   (651–3)

He is given a speech on the power of money which begins,

> Tis for no shadowes I adventure for:
> Heere are the Crownes, heere are the worldly goods.   (669–70)

The words are, of course, virtually Pedringano's. Clearly Kyd's character continued to be a classic exemplar of the hired assassin even after the proliferation of the type in the early 1590s.

It may be added that Appian, the source of *The Wounds of Civil War* and the relevant part of *Caesar's Revenge*, makes no mention of a fee in either case. This is true in most identifiable sources of the ten plays in question: monetary reward is something which playwrights deliberately introduced. For example, the author of *Woodstock* found in Holinshed's *Chronicles* a version of the murder of the central character by servants assigned to the task by their master, Thomas Mowbray, and turned them into outside contractors working for 'heaps of gold' (v. i. 5).[6] In this case, the change occurred in the process of expanding a far from detailed narrative for the stage. What is more remarkable is that in *James IV*, Greene took the trouble to transform a character that was already fully developed.

The play is based on a novella by Cinthio in which the Irish king Astatio has a captain from his retinue murder his wife Arenopia, as it turns out, unsuccessfully. The captain is presented as a man entirely devoted to his master: 'one of those who, provided they do what is pleasing to their lords, do not consider whether it is just or unjust, honest or dishonest'.[7] When the

---

[5] 'Gentlemen, for lack of money, if I have no money, I will not kill Marius.'
[6] R. Holinshed, *Chronicles of England, Scotland, and Ireland* (1807–8), ii. 837.
[7] R. Greene, *James IV*, appendix, 135.

Queen escapes for the first time, he pursues her with a persistence born of this loyalty: he assumes that she has discovered the plot and decided to flee to her father in Scotland, which could not harm him personally but would cause a major diplomatic crisis for Astatio. Finally, when he catches up with her she is rescued at the last moment; nonetheless he reports to the King that she is dead. Even this is presented as loyalty: when he left her, Arenopia was severely wounded and had lost a lot of blood, so he has cause to hope she died of her wounds; being ashamed to admit to his own failure, then, he takes a gamble and tells Astatio what he wants to hear.

Greene turns the captain into the comic Frenchman Jaques, a more independent and less thoughtful figure. He has two reasons for undertaking to kill Dorothea: he has been promised money and a potentially lucrative position at court; but there is also an element of directed aggression. No other character shares his fascination with acts of brutal violence, acts which are obsessively articulated in his dialogue. We first see him threatening a purveyor: 'I shall *étampe* your guts and thump your backa that you *ne point mange* this ten hours.' (III. ii. 37–8) When he receives his commission, it is the chance of violence as well as the hope of worldly reward that attracts him: 'Stabba the woman, *par ma foi! Monseigneur*, me thrusta my weapon into her belly, so me may be guard *par le roi*.' (128–9) These are the considerations which make him pursue Dorothea after the first attempt has failed, moreover: 'me will rama *pour la monnaie*' (IV. iii. 21). They also underlie his false report of the Queen's death. Greene eliminates the rescue and the assassin's calculated lie: Jaques simply tells the truth as he believes it to be. Once he has fought with Dorothea and wounded her, his attention shifts from the stroke to the reward, and, so eager is he to be made '*un chevalier* for this day's *travail*' (IV. iv. 58–9), he does not wait to see her die but merely takes it for granted that the wound is, as she has announced it to be, mortal. The emphasis on violence may be a result of the adaptation of the story for a different medium: the cunning and intellect of Cinthio's captain are well suited to prose fiction, whereas the bristling, explosive energy of Jaques would show up well on stage. The change from loyalty to a fixation on material reward, however, suggests an interest in that trait which Kyd was the first to focus.

Dramatists not only introduced the assassin's fee but emphasized it. In *The Massacre at Paris*, for example, the three murderers set to kill the Duke of Guise each have their own lines and concerns: the first brushes off a slur on their manhood, the second is bloodthirsty, and the third, who will shortly relent and warn the victim, just wants to get the murder over with. On one point, however, their voices are in unison: 'You will give us our money?' (xxi. 13), they ask their employer, the Captain of the Guard. Earlier in the play, Marlowe wryly makes the old Queen of Navarre tip the apothecary who has just poisoned her: our sense of the money relationship is heightened by our awareness that the murderer has the wrong partner in the transaction. Mosca makes the same joke in *Volpone* (1605–6) when he tells Corbaccio of his master's reluctance to employ a physician: the medical profession is rife with human vivisectionists, 'and he is loath | To hire his death so' (I. iv. 31–2); it would, the implication is, be like the victim paying his own assassin. Employer could also be contrasted with murderer to stress the latter's distinctive financial motives. In the 1591 pamphlet account of the case of Lincolne, who paid a labourer to kill his children, we are told that 'the devill entered so farre into his minde' that he thought of murder; but as for his hireling, 'the hope of the money . . . so wrought in his thought, that forgetting God and all godlynes, in the ende without anie greate delaie he consented to the fact'.[8]

A useful model for explaining the popularity of this type of assassin is the interest in the Machiavel who employs him. I argued in Chapter 3 that the Machiavel represented a reaction to an ideological change which threatened the traditional jurisdiction of morality; and that he therefore combined topical reference to a contemporary problem with an old form of villainy, intrigue. A similar combination occurs in the assassin.

Pedringano's sin of avarice had long been denounced by moralists and churchmen; in associating the character with Judas, Kyd gives it a pedigree of at least sixteen centuries. A considerable body of inherited ecclesiastical teaching condemned avarice and undue profit, and this had strong scriptural backing: no man could serve both God and Mammon, the love of money was the root of all evil, a rich man could get a camel through the eye of a needle more easily than himself into the kingdom of heaven, and Pauper was likely to be a soul in bliss while Dives lay howling.[9]   At the same time, however, money and its acquisition had become a subject of great interest: Old Fortunatus, that financial Faustus who rejects Fortune's gifts of health, wisdom, and the like in favour of an inexhaustible purse, was very much an anti-hero for the times. The power of money was a frequent topic in the folk-wisdom of the proverbs: the divine Thomas Becon commented ruefully on the number and truth of such sayings.[10] In modern times, it was thought, money ruled: 'All things are obedient to money.'[11] Richard Taverner included this saying in his redaction of the *Adagia* of Erasmus, but ignored his source's Tilley-like accumulation of classical authorities. For him, it was a piece of contemporary wisdom: 'This Proverbe was never better verified than at this

[8] *Sundrye strange and inhumaine Murthers, lately committed* (1591), A3ʳ.

[9] R. H. Tawney, *Religion and the Rise of Capitalism* (Harmondsworth, 1938), 17–74; Matthew 6: 24; 1 Timothy 6: 10; Matthew 19: 24; Luke 16: 19–31.

[10] T. Becon, *Early Works*, ed. J. Ayre (Cambridge, 1843), 222–3.

[11] Tilley, T. 163. For similar proverbs, see Tilley, L. 504, M. 1050, M. 1061, M. 1072, and M. 1102.

daye amonges Christen men, whiche nevertheles by theyr profession, ought to despise worldly goodes.'[12] The discrepancy between treasure on earth and treasure in heaven was not a new one, of course; the point is that it seemed new to contemporary commentators.

The crux of the problem, however, was not worldliness versus asceticism, but the ethics of worldly conduct. Conservative opinion held that economic and all other forms of activity were to be governed by moral and spiritual considerations: 'economic transactions were one department of ethical conduct, and to be judged, like other parts of it, by spiritual criteria'.[13] However, just as Machiavelli posed a challenge to the dominance of the church in the field of politics, so pragmatism was perceived to be a threat in financial activity: the two are explicitly linked in *The Jew of Malta*. Moralists responded as they had to Machiavelli, forcefully expounding the sinfulness and evil consequences of avarice:

> Howe many for money have bene robbed and murthered?
> Howe many false witnes and for money perjured?
> Howe many wyves from their husbands have bene enticed?
> Howe many maydens to folly for money allured?
> Howe many for money have spirites and devilles conjured?
> Howe many friends for money have bene mortall foes?
> Mo mischieves for money then I can disclose.
> Howe many Kings and Princes for money have bene poysoned,
> Howe many betrayers of their countrey for money every day[?][14]

At the same time, there was an interest in figures like the prostitute and the bribed judge, who transgressed the proper bounds of economic activity: sex and justice were not things of sale; and neither was death.

Being among the most serious of crimes, murder in particular was frequently named among the 'daughters of Covetousnes'.[15] For example, the protagonist of Wager's morality play *Enough is as Good as a Feast* (1560) falls under the spell of the Vice Covetous and says he will follow his teaching 'if it were mine own father to kill' (946). In the allegorical superplot of Robert Yarington's *Two Lamentable Tragedies*, Avarice and Homicide are presented as partners in crime. This was not a criminological explanation of murder; it was an appropriation of murder as a means of blackening avarice—guilt by association.

The hired assassin exemplified this association in concrete terms: he was a case in point that showed just how far some people might be prepared to go for money. In other words, the character's emergence as a recurrent figure

[12] R. Taverner, *Prouerbes or Adagies* (1569), B6ᵛ.
[13] Tawney, *Religion and the Rise of Capitalism*, 186.
[14] T. Lupton, *All for Money* (1578), A2ᵛ; cf. *Caesar's Revenge*, ii. 671–7.
[15] J. Manningham, *Diary*, ed. R. P. Sorlien (Hanover, NH, 1976), 198.

in English drama was a symptom of contemporary concern about the role of morality in economic activity, just as the stage Machiavel focused a broader worry about the limits of morality in general. In times of ideological upheaval such as this, villains were reassuring because they were easy to condemn. Pedringano and his descendants were highly topical figures in a period that saw its established concepts of good and evil under threat.

III

Though payment is the murderer's predominant concern, it is not of absolute importance in the context of the murder episode as a whole: rather it is one side of a transaction. *The Wounds of Civil War* presents it as a perverted equation: 'Great is the hire and little is the pain' (III. ii. 81), Favorinus tells Pedro. The line's power lies in its failure to specify: Favorinus could be referring to any task, so for a moment his words bypass our instinctive response and, following the rhetorical and conceptual structure of the line, we weigh up the elements involved, before uncomfortably remembering that the work in question is a killing.

The issue is presented with most acuteness in *King Leir*. Among the characteristics of the messenger hired to kill Leir and his councillor Perillus is acquisitiveness. In each of the four scenes in which he appears we see him taking money: the sum total of his earnings in the play is six purses, three from Ragan and one each from Gonorill, Leir, and Perillus. The last two he weighs in his hands, declares, 'Ile none of them, they are too light for me' (1527), and then, comically, pockets them anyway. Moreover, he is constantly on the look-out for extra business: 'Here will be more worke and more crownes for me' (1178), he says as Ragan opens Gonorill's letter; and, knowing from Gonorill that a commission to kill Leir is in the offing, he cannot resist putting another idea to Ragan—

> If you will have your husband or your father,
> Or both of them sent to another world,
> Do but commaund me doo't, it shall be done.   (1217–19)

At this point Ragan gives him a *pourboire*, and his thoughts turn to fantasies of multiplication:

> Oh, had I every day such customers,
> This were the gainefulst trade in Christendome!   (1224–5)

His ideas become positively grotesque later when he accepts his commission in detail and receives a purse in each hand, representing the two victims:

> Oh, that I had ten hands by myracle,
> I could teare ten in pieces with my teeth,
> So in my mouth yould put a purse of gold.   (1328–30)

Ten hands make for ten purses, and so ten victims; but with ten purses to carry he will have no hand free to execute the contract, so he thinks of using his teeth—only to realize that they too could hold a purse. The effect is not unlike the end of Rochester's poem 'The Mock Song', where Phyllis, imagining her every bodily orifice plugged with a phallus, nonetheless wishes her eyes fucked out. In each case the bizarre hypothesis gradually rises to an extreme that indicates the insatiability of the desire.

However fantastic his discourse, though, the Messenger is also a realist. Gold may be an end in itself for him, but he is well aware that it is also a stage in an ongoing process, and he repeatedly interprets it as a signifier of something else. When Gonorill flings him a purse 'In token of further imployment' (1017), he presents it as a contract: 'A strong Bond, a firme Obligation, good in law, good in law: if I keepe not the condition, let my necke be the forfeyture of my negligence.' (1019–21) Later he rebuts the usual hirer's concern about his resolution by referring to the money: no matter how eloquently the victims plead for their lives,

> Yet here are words so pleasing to my thoughts,
> As quite shall take away the sound of his.   (1350–1)

In the murder scene, there is a double displacement as he explains that Perillus is to die along with Leir:

> I have a Pasport for him in my pocket,
> Already seald, and he must needs ride Poste,   (1681–2)

he says, and shows a bag of money. We realize that a passport to heaven is a death warrant, but that document proves to be as metaphorical as the contract or the encouraging words into which the gold was transformed earlier. In each case money is presented as something which induces an act, by obligation, by persuasion, and by legitimation. It is, in other words, a medium of exchange which is traded for an act of murder. The point receives visual emphasis after Ragan gives the Messenger a bag of gold in each hand: when we see him again in the next scene but one, two daggers have been substituted for the purses.

'A purse of gold giv'n for a paltry stabbe!' (1226), exclaims the assassin in the second hiring scene. It is an inhuman exchange: in making it, he presupposes a world in which everything is for sale. As such, he presents an ideological threat to the conservative position that morality applies in economic affairs. There is, of course, no doubt as to his moral status: to murder is evil. But he is the more powerful as an image of evil because he is never explicitly labelled as such. Whereas Pedringano admits that he is acting immorally in the cause of worldly success (he is, as he says, straining his conscience), the Messenger never even considers the question as he cold-bloodedly agrees to kill. He lives not outside the bounds of morality, but without them, an exponent of an extreme form of the new pragmatism of the sixteenth century.

This abrogation of morality is made explicit by the play's use of ana-chronistic Christian references, the most straightforward of which come from 'good' characters such as Cordella. In the Messenger's scenes these allusions assume an ironic character. When first sounded out by Gonorill, he declares his willingness to make away Leir in a secular parody of swearing on the Bible: 'By this booke I will' (1057), he says, and kisses her letter to Ragan. The parody excludes the action parodied: clearly he takes more account of the words of his employer than of the Word of God. Later, commissioned by Ragan, he remarks that murder could be 'the gainefulst trade in Christendome' (1225), strikingly suppressing the word's religious connotations. In the act of referring to Christianity, he marks himself off from it.

However, there are grounds for a subtler and more psychological reading of these references: they may show the Messenger to be unchristian, but he is clearly not non-Christian, for it is he who makes them; Christianity must be a part of his frame of reference which, for money's sake, he suppresses. The matter becomes important in the murder scene itself. One of the first things he does when he enters to find the victims asleep, is to take away their books. It is an action that begs interpretation. He later speaks of the books as 'Halberds' (1510) and 'weapons of defence' (1512). Unless we are to imagine two old men using their light reading to beat off an armed and lethally minded ruffian, only one conclusion seems plausible: they are books of divinity, which can be used defensively by quotation.

If this interpretation is correct, then it is highly significant that the assassin himself sees it this way and so 'disarms' Leir and Perillus: he knows that a part of himself will respond to Christian persuasion and make him relent. This moral side is already at work, and his thoughts recoil persistently from the killing. At first, he leads himself to the matter almost unconsciously: 'Were it not a mad jest, if two or three of my profession should meet me, and lay me downe in a ditch, and play robbe thiefe with me, & perforce take my gold away from me, whilest I act this stratagem, and by this meanes the gray beards should escape?' (1455–9) Once introduced, the idea of not having to commit the murder is hard to shake off. Having taken their books, he prepares to strike, but talks himself out of it: 'feare of death is worse then death it selfe' (1470), he argues, and he must not spare them that by killing them in their sleep; anyway he has orders to show Leir Gonorill's letter proposing the murder. Yet when he reveals himself to the victims, it is not

as a murderer: 'Stand, Stand' (1503), he says, and 'Deliver, deliver' (1505)—
'the thiefes salutation'.[16] Not unnaturally, they co-operate and he has to
admit, circuitously, that he is not what he claimed to be. Even in doing so,
he tries to evade his task:

> The Queene hath tyed me by a solemne othe,
> Here in this place to see you both dispatcht:
> Now for the safegard of my conscience,
> Do me the pleasure for to kill your selves.   (1549–52)

Caught between oath-breaking and murder, it is the only conscientious way
out for him.

The Messenger's reference to his conscience is an important turning-
point: it is a hitherto unadmitted element of his character, which prompted
the series of evasions and false starts that has gone before. By bringing it
to the surface, he has turned the tables on himself: now it is his murderous
half which takes up the arts of self-persuasion, insisting what a 'vyle old
wretch, and full of heynous sin' (1596) is Leir, to the extent that even his
daughters wish him dead. Even then the reasoning is from a moral premise,
as his earlier argument for postponing the killing took murderous sadism as
its basis. Now conscience has the upper hand in him, and a final decision to
relent soon follows. When he affirms to Leir the identity of his employers,
he swears it to be true. However, the old man rejects as inappropriate his
oaths by heaven and earth, while hell, his third choice, 'stands gaping wide,
| To swallow thee, and if thou do this deed.' (1632–3) Thunder and lightning
confirms his statement, and the Murderer convulses:

> I would that word were in his belly agayne,
> It hath frighted me even to the very heart:
> This old man is some strong Magician:
> His words have turned my mind from this exployt.   (1635–8)

There are still about a hundred lines to go before, with another burst of
thunder, he drops the daggers and proceeds no further; but the vacillation
he undergoes in the interim serves mainly as an excuse for moralistic
injunctions from the victims, and involves no attempt at the murder as
before—indeed, when Leir prompts him, he retorts, 'But I am not prepared
for to strike.' (1662) It is with Leir's mention of hell that he crosses the
threshold; everything after that is an over-extended wait for the inevitable.

What is striking is the way the assassin misunderstands what has happened
to him: he wishes Leir had never spoken the word 'hell', but he himself used
it first, in his oath—'by hell, and all the devils I sweare' (1631). Persistently
he attributes his relenting to their persuasion: when Perillus remarks that he
has 'some sparke of grace' (1749), he replies,

[16] T. Dekker, Old Fortunatus, v. ii. 5–6.

> Beshrew you for it, you have put it in me:
> The parlosest old men, that ere I heard. (1750–1)

Having seen his behaviour earlier in the scene, we know better. He has a bifurcated personality, and the acquisitive, pragmatic half is grudging in its recognition that there is another side which can prevail as it has: it is far easier to blame Leir and Perillus. In a world where God and Mammon were incompatible masters, it is a tension that the play cannot resolve: the assassin makes his final exit here, still insisting that the victims have talked him into relenting; all we hear of him subsequently is that he has had the good sense to steer well clear of Ragan.

IV

Gonorill's Messenger was among the first of many assassins who find the mercenary and pragmatic qualities that make them agree to commit murder giving way to conscience when the time comes to do so: some relent at the last moment and decide not to kill, and others who do the deed regret it soon afterwards. What does not recur, however, is the division of the murderer's persona between God and Mammon, and his inability to recognize the reason for his failure. This is because the issue was ultimately a matter of ideological rather than psychological interest: it is not a case of a mental block, but of one world-view failing to comprehend the other; so dramatists found other ways of approaching the subject.

This is clear if we examine the different ways in which the adherents of pragmatism and Christianity understood the phenomenon of the relenting murderer. Machiavelli's brief remarks on the subject in *The Discourses* present the pragmatic view: 'Irresolution on the part of operatives in doing their job, is due either to human respect or to personal cowardice. Such is the majesty and the respect inspired by the presence of a prince that it may easily damp the resolution of an operative or terrify him.'[17] He goes on to give several examples of this majestic charisma, beginning with the attempted assassination of Marius at Minturnum. Several stage hirers share Machiavelli's interpretation: they take care to check the resolution of their instruments when briefing them, aware that the sight of the victim may induce cowardice—

> Think not your work contrived so easily
> As if you were to match some common man.
> Believe me sirs, his countenance is such,
> So full of dread and lordly majesty,
> Mixed with such mild and gentle haviour

[17] N. Machiavelli, *The Discourses*, tr. L. J. Walker. corr. edn. (Harmondsworth, 1974), 413.

As will (except you be resolved at full)
Strike you with fear even with his princely looks.[18]

In *The Massacre at Paris*, moreover, the Duke of Guise relies on that power when he walks knowingly into the clutches of his murderers, armed only with a stare: 'princes with their looks engender fear' (xxi. 70), he says.

The awe-inspiring majesty of the royal face was a commonplace notion, but it is notable that in only one sixteenth-century play, *The Wounds of Civil War*, does it deter an assassin. In most other cases, the killers suffer a resurgence of normal human feelings of pity and conscience. In *The True Tragedy of Richard III*, Denten responds to the touching presence of the victims: 'it greeves mee to see what mone these yoong Princes make, I had rather then fortie pounds I had nere tane it in hand, tis a dangerous matter to kill innocent princes, I like it not' (1295–8). The fit is momentary: his resolution returns when he is browbeaten by Black Will. In the Folio version of *Henry VI, Part 2*, the Second Murderer repents too late, apparently struck by the manner in which Duke Humphrey faced death:

> O that it were to do! What have we done?
> Didst ever hear a man so penitent?   (III. ii. 3–4)

If he is a coward, it is conscience that has made him so: what a Machiavel would take for craven fear is laudable from the Christian viewpoint that most plays presume.

King Leir was probably a direct influence on the murder scenes of three plays: Shakespeare's *Richard III*, Yarington's *Two Lamentable Tragedies*, and the anonymous *The Maid's Metamorphosis*. Each derives some elements of its narrative from *Leir*, and these elements are differently combined, suggesting a return to a common source rather than a chain of indebtedness. In *Richard III*, the murderers are warned not to listen to the victim's pleas (as distinct from quailing at the sight of him), come upon him sleeping, and discuss whether or not to stab him before he wakes; when he does, they reveal the lethal intentions of his brother, who, like Leir's daughters, professes to love him. In *Two Lamentable Tragedies*, the victim is taken to a thicket ten miles out of town, and again there is a discussion between the murderers while he sleeps, which turns on the fact that to neglect the murder will be to break their oath. Finally, in *The Maid's Metamorphosis*, the victim is again lured away from court, the murderers are again warned not to listen to her words, and the discussion again turns on the dilemma of oath-breaking. *Richard III* and *Two Lamentable Tragedies* also draw on the dialogue of *Leir*, the latter very obviously.[19] Each of the plays follows *Leir* in having a killer who is uncertain whether or not he should commit the murder; and each departs from *Leir* in featuring two murderers rather than one.

In Shakespeare's and Yarington's plays, this uncertainty addresses the same ideological theme as in *Leir*: the opposing arguments of conscience and pragmatism, morality and money. Shakespeare's treatment is playful, setting off the murderers' vacillations with one of the jokes that litter the quick-fire dialogue:

SECOND MURDERER
What, shall I stab him as he sleeps?
FIRST MURDERER
No. He'll say 'twas done cowardly, when he wakes.
SECOND MURDERER
Why, he shall never wake until the great judgement day.
FIRST MURDERER
Why, then he'll say we stabbed him sleeping.
SECOND MURDERER
The urging of that word 'judgement' hath bred a kind of remorse in me.

(i. iv. 97–105)

The First Murderer's objection to killing Clarence in his sleep is a gag which turns out to have serious implications: as his companion corrects the point, Christian eschatology creeps into his consciousness and, once there, takes hold. The last line makes the first of a number of striking changes of register in the scene: it begins without the monosyllabic ejaculations that start its precursors ('What', 'No', 'Why'), and it has a portentous rhythm close to verse.

This change of register signals the emergence of a serious issue, but it is through levity that that issue is pursued. In *King Leir*, the movement of the assassin from cupidity to conscience was a slow, suspenseful process. Here the Second Murderer flashes between them with comic speed:

SECOND MURDERER
Some certain dregs of conscience are yet within me.
FIRST MURDERER
Remember our reward, when the deed's done.
SECOND MURDERER
'Swounds, he dies. I had forgot the reward.
FIRST MURDERER
Where's thy conscience now?
SECOND MURDERER
O, in the Duke of Gloucester's purse.   (118–25)

Commentators have emphasized the theme of conscience in the murderers' repartee, but the purse is just as important: conscience may be the subject discussed, but the humour of the lines derives from the balance with worldliness. In an almost Falstaffian set-piece on conscience, the Second Murderer portrays it as an irritating encumbrance that forces him to do things against his will: ''Tis a blushing, shamefaced spirit, that mutinies in a man's bosom. It fills a man full of obstacles. It made me once restore a purse of gold that by chance I found.' (134–7) The grudging tone is that of a pragmatist out for the main chance; but conscience too may be speaking. He is a little too insistent that he found the purse, and by chance, but if he did, how could he know to whom to restore it? It seems that, even as he denounces conscience for hampering a theft, conscience makes him ashamed to admit that it was a theft. Conversely, even when in the grip of conscience he is predicting how long it will take him to get free: 'It was wont to hold me but while one tells twenty.' (115–16) The First Murderer, also afflicted, describes it as a diabolic tempter: ''tis even now at my elbow, persuading me not to kill the Duke' (142–3). It is an economical and funny articulation of inverted values: his devil tempts him to do good.

When Clarence awakes, the focus of the scene shifts to him, and the lines move into verse as the balance of serious and comic is reversed. Now the murderers' jokes become grimly ironic. Clarence calls for a cup of wine, and is told, 'You shall have wine enough, my lord, anon' (160). There is the same effect later when he tries to send them to his (as he thinks) loving brother Gloucester:

CLARENCE
Go you to him from me.
FIRST MURDERER   Ay, so we will.   (229)

But not in the sense that Clarence expects: they are under orders to report back to Richard once they have finished with him. The humour turns on Clarence's ignorance of the plans that have been made for him, and so serves to emphasize the futility of his attempts to talk himself clear. The jerky flow of the discussion adds to the effect: it is not simply a philosophical dialogue without dramatic function. Periodically Clarence tries new angles of persuasion until he is reduced to asking, desperately and pathetically, whether they would have acted differently in his position:

> Which of you, if you were a prince's son,
> Being pent from liberty as I am now,
> If two such murderers as yourselves came to you,
> Would not entreat for life?   (258–61)

It is a moment of despair, a last unconvincing plea, but even as he makes it the suspense is moving to a higher level. His lines have been the ineffectual struggles of a doomed man, but at a late stage he has hit on a fruitful approach:

> Have you that holy feeling in your souls
> To counsel me to make my peace with God,
> And are you yet to your own souls so blind
> That you will war with God by murd'ring me?   (245–8)

Hitherto he has stressed God's revenge against murderers, but this is his first appeal to conscience, strongly placed at a key point in the scene for maximum emphasis. It shakes the Second Murderer's resolution: 'What shall we do?' (251), he asks, and for the first time we glimpse a chance that the murder will not take place. Ironically, this change of heart is fatal for Clarence: seeing some pity in the relenter's looks, he concentrates his efforts in that direction, turns his back on the more dangerous man, and receives a knife in it.

So far, conscience and cupidity have been ambient issues, present in the scene's jokes and dialogue; but any sense of their being two distinct and opposing positions has been blurred by the way the two murderers shuttled from one to the other. It is the murder itself which crystallizes the serious concerns of the scene: the assassins each commit themselves, one to Christian conscientiousness and the other to mercenary pragmatism. The staging of the moment emblematizes their divergence one from another. Clarence interposes between them: on one side of him, the Second Murderer shouts a warning, on the other the First stabs.[20] They have become two individuals rather than a pair of murderers: as the First carries the body off to the malmsey-butt, the Second remains on stage, comparing himself to Pilate and wishing a little water could clear him of the deed. Their closing exchange underlines the issue: the Second leaves in penitence, refusing his share of the fee; whereas the First takes his conscience for cowardice, and goes to make arrangements for the disposal of the corpse. Neither wants any part in the other's world-view: it is a final moment of devastating clarity.

Yarington makes a similarly schematic division of the two assassins for the sequence in *Two Lamentable Tragedies* in which Fallerio hires two ruffians to kill his nephew and ward Pertillo. However, whereas in Shakespeare the division is a climactic moment the scene works up to, in Yarington the First Ruffian's conscientious streak appears, unadulterated, far earlier. In the murder scene itself, he and his companion argue over whether or not to do the deed in the manner of a debate, with none of the comic fluidity of Shakespeare's murderers. Indeed, throughout the sequence, Yarington studiously avoids *Richard III*'s bizarre mixture of levity and seriousness. What this means, however, is that he runs into difficulties regarding the plausibility of the characters.

The mercenary concerns of both ruffians are firmly established in the hiring scene:

---

[20] This is the only way of staging the incident without upstaging one or other of the murderers.

> we are they indeede,
> That would deprive our fathers of their lives,
> So we were sure to have a benefit,   (D1ʳ)

says the First, while the Second enthuses, after Gonorill's Messenger, 'Two hundreth markes to give a paltrie stab' (D1ᵛ). There is nothing to prepare us for the moment later in the scene when, told by Fallerio that the boy has no father, the First Ruffian turns 'To the people' and comments,

> Yes such a father, that doth see and know,
> How we do plot this little infants woe.   (D2ʳ)

Yet, incredibly, he still proceeds with arrangements for the murder, and voices his religious objections only at the last moment.[21] It seems that Christian emphasis, with moralistic intent, is more important to Yarington than a credible depiction of villainy; so plausibility of character is violated in setting up the First Ruffian as a mouthpiece for that emphasis. The earnest tone of the scenes (in contrast with *Richard III*) makes the violation the more obvious.

A corollary of this is that the argument between the assassins is very one-sided in conception. There is, it is true, one moment that appears finely judged, when the pragmatic Second Ruffian misunderstands his companion's tender-heartedness:

> I know this purenesse comes of pure deceit,
> To draw me from the murthering of the child,
> That you alone might have the benefit.   (E3ᵛ)

He can interpret mercy only in his own, mercenary terms; but the relenter belies him by offering his own share of the money in return for Pertillo's life. However, the character's position is not sufficiently clear or consistent to sustain the interpretation: he is little more than a compendium of negative traits, cupidity being one of them. He paints himself as a sadistic practical joker (not unlike Marlowe's Ithamore) whose pleasure is

> To chop folkes legges and armes off by the stumpes,
> To see what shift theile make to scramble home:
> Pick out mens eyes, and tell them thats the sport,
> Of hood-man-blinde, without all sportivenesse.   (E3ʳ)

Appropriately, another characteristic is impiety: 'I nam'd not God unleast 'twere with an othe' (E3ʳ). Whereas the First Ruffian functions as a positive exponent of Christianity, the Second represents only opposition, his only consistency lying in his ability to evoke moral disgust.

These two plays are notable, then, for the differing degrees of sensitivity

---

[21] The earlier religious line was given to '*1 Ruf.*', whereas the relenter in the murder scene itself is '*2 Mur.*'; but they are surely the same character. I have regularized accordingly.

and commitment with which they approach the question. Whereas Shakespeare, and the author of *Leir* before him, could see (though not approve of)
both sides of the argument, Yarington has no understanding for the willing
assassin, only condemnation; so in his hands the two murderers are no longer
presented as Christian and pragmatist, but, more basically, good and evil. In
the contrast between the ideological perceptiveness of one play and the
banal moralism of the other, we see the range of attitudes that might be
attracted by the hired murderer and the ethical issues he raised.

v

Another influential feature of *King Leir* was the Messenger's fantasy of
success and prosperity in the profession of murder: 'This were the gainefulst
trade in Christendome!' (1225) In *Arden of Faversham*, Black Will has a similar
daydream: 'Ah, that I might be set awork thus through the year and that
murder would grow into an occupation, that a man might without danger
of law—Zounds, I warrant I should be warden of the company!' (ii. 105–9)
In other words, he imagines murder as a recognized trade with its own livery
company. To an extent, this is a kind of twisted social aspiration: Black Will
wishes that, like Abhorson, he could call his unsavoury occupation a mystery.
But the line reveals attitude as well as aspiration: he is claiming for homicide
an equal status with the legitimate trades represented by the guilds.
    The attitude constantly underlies Will's behaviour: inhabiting a play much
concerned with deals and bargains, he is the most commercially minded of
the stage assassins.[22] One of his characteristics is a curious brand of business
ethics: there is honour among murderers as there is among thieves. After
Arden's first lucky escape, Black Will tells his employer Greene, 'were my
consent to give again, we would not do it under ten pound more. ... I have
had ten pound to steal a dog, and we have no more here to kill a man. But
that a bargain is a bargain and so forth, you should do it yourself.' (iii. 71–
6) Having made a contract, he will not attempt to wriggle out of it, however
inconvenient to himself. His attitude to money is distinctive, too: he sets a
value on his work, and has clearly decided that the asking-price for this job
was too low. Throughout the play he is discriminating about money.
Unsurprisingly, large sums tend to excite him. 'Such words would make one
kill a thousand men!' (xiv. 132), he says when Mrs Arden makes him an offer
that adds up to sixty pounds—twenty down and forty upon completion.
The totting-up is important. He is keen to take on the murder at first because
Greene's initial offer looks like thirty pounds; he has second thoughts when

___

[22] A. Leggatt, *Shakespeare Survey*, 36 (1983), 124–6.

the first attempt fails, because the fee begins to look more like the ten he has in hand, and that is not worth the effort.

He has, in other words, a price threshold, a characteristic which particularly informs his meeting with Lord Cheyne. Much to his annoyance, Cheyne's arrival at a crucial moment saves Arden once again. It happens that Cheyne already knows Black Will, and after a little tongue-clicking at his criminal activities, he gives the killer a crown. Will takes no pleasure in the money: 'I would his crown were molten down his throat' (ix. 132), he says, once the munificent Cheyne has gone. He weighs the trifling sum he has made from the encounter against the forty-angel value of the murder it prevented. In this, he is a far cry from the avaricious Messenger of *Leir*, for whom every little helped in the accumulation of gold; Black Will is a much more calculating businessman.

Another facet of the assassin's professionalism is memorably presented in *Edward II*. As we saw in Chapter 3, Lightborn is a specialist killer skilled in a range of murderous techniques, some of which he lists. As he rises to the climax of this speech, an account of the 'braver way' (v. iv. 37) that he will use to dispatch Edward, Mortimer interrupts, asking what it is. Realizing that his tongue has run away with him and revealed some trade secrets, the assassin clams up: 'Nay, you shall pardon me, none shall know my tricks.' (39) He has said too much out of a fascination, not with violence like Greene's brutal Jaques, but with the technical aspects of killing: 'I learned in Naples *how to* poison flowers' (31, my italics); grammatically and psychologically, the phrase governs the entire catalogue. Technical excellence is Lightborn's constant concern: as Roma Gill has said, he is the only character who does not respond emotionally to Edward.[23] All he wants is to see a job well done: 'ne'er was there any | So finely handled as this king shall be' (v. v. 38–9). His imaginative life, then, centres on the moment of completion, the point at which technique yields the desired result:

> So, lay the table down, and stamp on it,
> But not too hard, lest that you bruise his body,   (111–12)

he instructs Matrevis and Gurney, and we register the double meaning of 'body', living flesh that can bruise and a corpse that can exhibit bruises. What is missing is any sense of a human being who can feel pain: Lightborn is mentally focused on the finished task, so the dead body predominates and Edward is treated as nothing more than lifeless material for processing, material which must remain in good condition if the finished product is to turn out perfectly. Finally, when he reaches that moment of perfection, he expects appropriate congratulation: Matrevis urges a quick getaway, but he insists, 'Tell me first, was it not bravely done?' (115) Here is the reflective

---

[23] C. Marlowe, *Edward II*, ed. R. Gill (Oxford, 1967), introduction, 32.

self-satisfaction felt after completing a good piece of work; but in this case the work has been killing a man.

The murderers in *Woodstock* show similar traits. They too are presented as technically competent, albeit in more mundane methods: 'See my lord, here's first a towel with which we do intend to strangle him; but if he strive and this should chance to fail, I'll mall his old mazzard with this hammer — knock him down like an ox, and after cut's throat.' (v. i. 7–11) There is more relish here for the act of violence itself than there was in Lightborn, but also a stress on the tools of the trade, the 'instruments for death' (6). As with Lightborn, there is an artisanal quality to the assassins' expertise, clearest in the ensuing exchange with Lapoole: he insists that it should look like a natural death, and is promptly told, 'There is no way then, but to smother him' (16); he brings requirements, they the knowledge and skills to meet them. Like Lightborn, moreover, the First Murderer delights in having executed his talents: 'Never was murder done with such rare skill' (252), he tells Lapoole, and later remarks to his partner, 'the deed's done and all things performed rarely' (269–70). In both plays, it is noticeable, the killers have their own characteristic adjectives expressing their skill: 'brave' in *Edward II* and 'rare' in *Woodstock*.

It is worth adding that assassins were sometimes compared with artisans outside the drama. I have already quoted Henri Estienne's horror that people bargained with murderers as if with masons or carpenters.[24] In England, it was alleged that Mrs Turner, the procuress in the Overbury case, had taken the same line: she refused to pay the murderer Weston after the first attempts at poisoning had failed, telling him, 'The man is not yet dead. ... Perfect your work and you shall have your hire.'[25] It is as if he were a craftsman trying to sell her faulty merchandise.

The effect of these traits is to make the murder plots analogous to normal economic behaviour. This is especially clear in *Arden of Faversham*, which evokes the realities of Elizabethan commerce in Black Will's allusion to the guild system, and in Mrs Arden's use of the common business practice of splitting a fee into two parts, payable in earnest and upon completion of the job. The incongruity is shocking: we see ordinary human conduct horrifyingly estranged from ordinary human values. In other words, our shock is another device causing us to recognize the moral limits on economic activity: when Black Will speaks of the law as an occupational hazard, we realize how much more it is than that. However, there is another reason for the emphasis on the normality of these figures' behaviour.

[24] Above, p. 10.
[25] McElwee, 90.

124THE FIRST HIRED ASSASSINS

VI

So far we have concentrated on the ideological–moralistic elements in the conservative economic thinking of the sixteenth century; but these concerns produced a further anxiety about the social consequences of the new mercenary pragmatism. Medieval theories of social organization had emphasized the co-operation of the different orders of mankind: as R. H. Tawney puts it, 'Society was interpreted . . . not as the expression of economic self-interest, but as held together by a system of mutual, though varying, obligations. Social well-being exists, it was thought, in so far as each class performs its functions and enjoys the rights proportioned thereto.'[26] In the sixteenth century, this view was under threat: Tudor emphasis on the commonwealth of England is a sure sign of strain. In practice, the feudal system was long dead and money payments for labour were well-established. No doubt the late medieval period had had its fair share of untrustworthy, mercenary labourers; but the ideological emergence of pragmatism made the subject a matter of potent concern.

The hireling embodied character traits which made him inherently untrustworthy: for John Bale, 'wageling' was a term of abuse, used of 'the instruments of Satan'.[27] Such a man 'loves the work for the wages', said Francis Bacon, and behind him there was the authority of the Bible, which contrasted the hireling with the good shepherd.[28] Machiavelli in particular saw the relative unreliability of money relationships: the thought informs his strictures on mercenaries. They have, he says, 'no loyalty or inducement to keep them on the field apart from the little they are paid, and this is not enough to make them want to die for you'; so corrupt are they, indeed, that they may 'prey on those who have commissioned them in the same way as they prey on those against whom they have been commissioned to fight'.[29]

Nonetheless it was around these mistrusted money relationships that society was now organized: the old feudal bonds of mutual obligation and personal loyalty had largely been superseded by the cash nexus. Responding practically, thinkers sought to apply the moral law to such relationships: they branded as thieves both employers who withheld wages and employees who took them for negligent work; virtue, it was insisted, lay in fair dealing.[30]

[26] Tawney, *Religion and the Rise of Capitalism*, 37.

[27] J. Bale, *Select Works*, ed. H. Christmas (Cambridge, 1849), 439.

[28] Sir F. Bacon, *The Advancement of Learning*, ed. A. Johnston (Oxford, 1974), 14; John 10: 12–13.

[29] N. Machiavelli, *The Prince*, tr. G. Bull, rev. edn. (Harmondsworth, 1981), 77–8, and *The Discourses*, 340.

[30] H. Bullinger, *The Decades*, tr. H.I., ed. T. Harding (Cambridge, 1849–52), ii. 37–8; T. Becon, *The Catechism*, ed. J. Ayre (Cambridge, 1844), 105, 106–7; J. Pilkington, *Works*, ed. J. Scholefield (Cambridge, 1842), 446–7. There was also a body of proverbial lore on the subject: see Tilley, H. 69, L. 12, M. 718, W. 2.

This, as well as the ethical issue, is addressed by *The Spanish Tragedy*: Pedringano's career is a microcosm of perceived social change in the period. His bond with his mistress is a personal one: he is her trusty 'second self' (II. iv. 9), privy to the kind of secrets Lorenzo covets. But this link is subverted by a monetary relationship with Lorenzo: Pedringano changes from servant to employee. As a result, he becomes an untrustworthy hireling, to be disposed of once his usefulness is over—a different angle on the problem of trust discussed in Chapter 4. In practice, it is Lorenzo who sees this, not Pedringano: his naïvety means that here the untrustworthiness of the hired murderer is only potential.

A few later plays deal with the question more directly. The earliest surviving example, though probably not the first in view of its patchwork of ideologically incompatible imitations, is *Selimus*, whose Jewish poisoner Abraham 'will venture any thing for gold' (1688), and declares himself as willing to poison his employer Selimus as his victim (1727–9). The point was made again in several Jacobean plays:

> Who thinketh to buy villainy with gold,
> Shall ever find such faith so bought so sold.[31]

Frescobaldi, a murderer used by Caesar Borgia in *The Devil's Charter* (1606), makes it clear that betrayal is a function of his hireling independence: 'I will second my Lord in any slaughter for his wages, and if any man will give me better hiers (when I have serv'd the Cardinalls turne) I will present my pistoll upon his sacred person afterward for charities sake' (1507–11); 'what can golde not doe?' (IV. iv. 43), asks Dr Benedict, protesting his innocence of such an intent in *The Honest Whore, Part 1* (1604).

In general, however, it was the hirer, not the assassin, who illustrated the infidelity thought to be inherent in money relationships. If we leave aside the central immorality of murder and examine the activities of Black Will, Lightborn, and Thomas of Woodstock's killers solely in terms of economic ethics, their conduct is unexceptionable: they keep their contracts, they ask a just price for their labour, and they take care to do a good job. Of course, no one would have thought these characters admirable examples of private enterprise: their trade is immoral, emblematic of the lengths people were prepared to go to make money. But their fair dealing in that trade sets them in contrast with their employers' perfidy.

Among the many bargains struck in *Arden of Faversham* are numerous contracts for Arden's murder: in the course of the play, Michael, Clarke, Greene, and Black Will and Shakebag are all employed to this end, sometimes simultaneously. The play begins with two agreements made independently: Alice Arden has suborned Michael, and Mosby has suborned Clarke; both

---

[31] J. Marston, *Sophonisba*, II. iii. 28–9.

have been promised the same reward, the hand of Susan Mosby. Not surprisingly, Alice is determined that her own arrangements should stand and Clarke should not be used; but she soon capitulates and, by the end of the first scene, is helping Clarke with his wooing at Michael's expense. Moreover, when Clarke's attempt fails, she does not simply revert to Michael, but puts a new plan into effect through Greene. She develops a kind of hyperactivity in her determination to eliminate her husband, obsessed as much with the planning as the results, which it is up to the more level-headed Mosby to stress; when, after many failures, Mosby wants to give up, it is she who turns delightedly to a 'new device' (xii. 65).

The result is that the early part of the play swarms with assassins, all competing with one another to the same end. The point is that Alice has made a series of contracts without considering their compatibility: it is left up to the other contracting parties to fight it out over who gets to do the job. The most assertive of them, Black Will, acts swiftly to cut out the opposition, relegating Michael to a subsidiary role:

> I am the very man,
> Marked in my birth-hour by the Destinies,
> To give an end to Arden's life on earth;
> Thou but a member but to whet the knife
> Whose edge must search the closet of his breast.   (iii. 159–63)

Neither does Alice consider her own ability to fulfil her side of the bargain— two men cannot marry the same woman. She promises a sum of money to Black Will, but is never seen to pay it; Will apparently helps himself when he drags the body into the counting-house.[32] Alice is a woman passionately committed to procuring a death; how she uses others to achieve that death is a matter of little concern to her.

Even so, Alice's irresponsibility as a contractor is relatively venial in comparison with the behaviour of other, more calculating hirers. Mortimer in *Edward II* actively intends not to keep his part of the bargain: from the start, Lightborn carries a 'secret token' (v. iv. 19) that tells Matrevis and Gurney he is to be murdered afterwards.[33] This is of course a conventional expedient of the hirer, but Marlowe adds the twist that Lightborn's death is a substitution for his fee: 'See how he must be handled for his labour, | *Pereat iste*' (v. v. 23–4), observes Matrevis; and Gurney tells the assassin as he stabs him, 'take this for thy reward' (116). Lapoole in *Woodstock* is even more explicit: 'Give their reward there!' (v. i. 273) he tells the soldiers he has brought to the scene of the crime, and they cut down the murderers;

---

[32] His first statement upon re-entering is, 'We have our gold.' (xiv. 249); there is only one place they can have got it from.

[33] There is no evidence as to what this token might be; but some kind of badge or ornament, worn prominently throughout the murder scene, would maximize the dramatic irony.

'The black reward of death's a traitor's pay' (277), he observes. Underlying the point is a pun on 'hire', which could mean both a payment for service (which is what the murderers expect) and just deserts (which is what they get).[34] It is true that the substitution of death for a fee had already been implied by both Jaques and Black Will, both of whom worry about being caught and 'hanged for their labour'.[35] The point here is that death is meted out by the party who should be paying the fee, and who is therefore in breach of contract.

I do not wish to suggest that the development of the stage assassin in and after *The Spanish Tragedy* was a serious contribution to the economic debate of the time. Direct application to contemporary social change was out of the question: few men were hired murderers in reality, so the plays do not address a major human problem; they play on abstract contemporary fears. Already the stereotype of the assassin had drawn on a political bugbear of the time; Kyd and his successors simply changed the issue to an economic one. In more or less sophisticated form, their handling of the hired killer reflected the various concerns inculcated in their audience by thinkers and moralists. The plays did not contribute to the debate; rather the debate contributed to the effectiveness of the plays.

[34] *OED* sb. 2 for the first sense; the second, figurative sense is not specifically represented in *OED*, but is very common in sixteenth-century texts.

[35] Greene, *James IV*, III. ii. 130; *Arden of Faversham*, xiv. 4–5.

7

HONOURABLE MURDERERS

I

In a commercial theatre, one of the most important determinants of change is the audience. At the crudest level, the paying playgoer calls the tune, so success will be imitated and failure forgotten. We can take it for granted that skilled, professional players and playwrights understood this principle, so besides the actual audience, there was also a presumed audience affecting their output. The content of a single play reflects what the author and acting company thought would prove popular; recurrent features reflect what actually was popular as the players strove to please their patrons every day. Moreover, if we can assume, as the last line of *Twelfth Night* (1601) suggests, that playgoers were regular rather than occasional in their attendance, then plays also reveal by implication the different states of the audience's acquaintance with those features.

By 1600, the assassin needed no introduction to playgoers: allusions in early seventeenth-century plays tell us that he was a stock character, whose participation in murder plots could be taken for granted, and whose behaviour followed familiar patterns. In *Antony and Cleopatra*, for example, Decretas reports Antony's death to Caesar, and takes care to disabuse him of the idea that the killing was done 'by a hired knife' (v. i. 21); evidently this is a reasonable assumption to make. Another reasonable assumption was that a contract to kill would involve money changing hands: there is no mention of a fee in *Volpone* when Corbaccio proposes that Mosca should give his master 'a dram' (III. ix. 14), but Mosca assumes it when he later says that the old man 'would have hired | Me to the pois'ning of my patron' (v. iii. 70–1).

We saw in Chapter 3 that audience familiarity with the conventional content of the assassin episode was presumed in 1592, when Marlowe played off audience expectations formed by those conventions against an increasingly unconventional enactment. What has changed in the intervening decade is the extent to which the conventions have been digested, and so the speed with which inferences are drawn: whereas Marlowe works out his effect slowly through a series of references and then a developing narrative, the later allusions require instant recognition and response. In particular, Shakespeare calls for this speed of reaction in *Hamlet* and *Macbeth*. In both these plays, he presents a twisted variant on a stock assassin situation, to powerful effect. In each case, the stock situation itself is barely signalled, so that the full effect requires an audience already familiar with the figure of the assassin.

When Hamlet decides not to kill Claudius at his prayers and so send his soul to heaven, he declares, 'O, this is hire and salary, not revenge!' (III. iii. 79) The line posits an improper model of the relationship between them. As a revenger, Hamlet should act as an executioner, to punish a murderer beyond the reach of legal process. To consign the man to everlasting bliss, however, would be not a punishment but a reward, albeit an unexpected one. Vindictive propriety at once reasserts itself as he ponders on the disproportion between his unaneled father's fate and the one he has projected for his uncle; but in the moment of realization, guilt flickers and the role-model changes. To reward Claudius for the murder would be to enter into a relationship with him of hirer and assassin, the more so in that the reward entails killing him: instead of a perfidious substitution of death for payment, the two are ironically equated. In giving that reward, therefore, Hamlet will take on moral responsibility for the murder. The fact that his father's death released a crown which Hamlet aspires to and which, after the usurper's death, he will wear, adds plausibility to that sense of guilt: in the act of paying the assassin, he will make himself the beneficiary of the crime. As he realizes what killing Claudius will entail, he feels, momentarily, that irrational sense of his own culpability that is common among victims of crime.

The murder of Duncan's grooms in *Macbeth* also plays on the hirer–assassin relationship, but this time to create moral repugnance rather than a psychological point. Like all murderers, Macbeth must reshape reality after killing Duncan, to establish his own innocence. In doing this he not only removes his own name from the list of suspects, but fastens the blame on the grooms: his wife smears them with blood, and the following morning he kills them in a feigned fit of righteous indignation; without their protestations of innocence, the presumption readily emerges that they were suborned by Malcolm and Donalbain. This is unsettling because Macbeth's action, killing them to stop their mouths, is like that of the hirer at the end of a conventional assassin sequence: figures like Pedringano and Lightborn die because they are hired murderers, the grooms because they are not. The juxtaposition with the guilty sets their innocence into horrifyingly sharp relief.

The import of these references is that an audience could be expected to recognize even an indirect allusion to the assassin; and some of the plays which include the character provide corroborative evidence. The murder plot in Act III of George Chapman's *The Gentleman Usher* (1602) is virtually undeveloped: there is a thirteen-line conversation between the hirer Medice and his servant, we see but do not hear another whispered exchange in the following scene, and that is all; we see the result when the victim Strozza is brought on injured, but the incident is never mentioned again. This is surprising because it is important to the play in two ways. First, it is narratively significant: it provides Strozza with the wound that dominates the latter part of the story. Secondly, it reflects on Medice's relation with his environment: it parallels the use that Prince Vincentio makes of Bassiolo as a pander immediately afterwards, and as such it is one of a number of elements which suggest that Medice is as much an embodiment of evils that are endemic in the court as he is an intruding gipsy who can simply be expelled at the conclusion; as such, the murder plot is one factor helping to create a bitter sub-text for the happy ending. Yet it is given only the barest of emphasis: presumably the audience would be able to fill in for itself the process of hiring an assassin.

Minimalist treatments of assassin episodes are quite common in plays written around the turn of the century. For example, when Iago takes order to kill Cassio in *Othello* (1603–4), the contract is all a matter of implication, in contrast with the explicit arrangements that Shakespeare read about in Cinthio's *Hecatommithi* (1565), his source.[1] Similarly, in Chapman's *Bussy D'Ambois* (1604), it is not spelled out that Monsieur has brought Bussy to court as an assassin until Bussy infuriates his patron in the third Act by refusing point-blank to countenance regicide. Lygdus, the eunuch engaged to kill Drusus in Jonson's *Sejanus* (1603), never even appears on stage: there seems to be no need to take the audience through the business of getting the slave hired, the victim poisoned, and the murderer dealt with.

However, this is not the only conclusion we can draw from these *fin de siècle* treatments of the assassin. If we accept that playgoers did not need to have the conventions relating to the character made explicit, then it follows that a fuller portrayal would have been found boring. Certainly these episodes are not primary centres of appeal and interest, even when they are given more stage time. In *Henry V* (1598–9), for instance, the Cambridge conspiracy has been discovered before we even learn of it, and when the assassins speak their own condemnations in urging severe treatment of the Southampton roisterer who has drunkenly traduced the King, the irony is so heavily weighted against them that their plot can never have its own substantive interest for the audience: it is simply a means to an auspicious start for the invasion of France.

A slightly different case is Shakespeare's transformation of the murder plot of Thomas Lodge's prose romance *Rosalynde* (1590), his source for *As You Like It* (1600). Lodge has an early sequence in which a Norman wrestler, 'desirous of pelfe', is 'procured . . . with rich rewards' by the Oliver-character

[1] Bullough, vii. 249.

Saladyne to kill his younger brother in a tournament.[2] Shakespeare does not cut or understress this part of the story; he develops the straightforward murder contract into something more subtle. Oliver is characterized by parsimony: he withholds from Orlando the 'poor a thousand crowns' (I. i. 2) bequeathed him, and refuses to spend money on his education. When he determines to teach Orlando a lesson, his first thought is to turn him out with those thousand crowns and let him see how far they get him; but having him murdered soon comes to mind as a cheaper alternative—'I will physic your rankness, and yet give no thousand crowns neither.' (81–3) True to his parsimony, he finds a way to have it done without paying: he would spend nothing on Orlando alive, and will spend nothing to see him dead.

Charles the wrestler, moreover, is too good-natured to be an assassin: Oliver merely uses him as one. He comes to Oliver worried that, for his own honour, he will have to injure Orlando if he insists on entering the ring. Oliver manipulates that good nature, first by inculcating righteous anger against 'one so young and so villainous' (144–5), and then by putting Charles in fear of reprisals if he lets Orlando live. He never explicitly states his intentions beyond an off-hand remark that he would not mind if Charles were to break his brother's neck: it is left to the audience to infer what he is up to. Again this implies acquaintance with the basic scenario, and the reason why Shakespeare should wish to vary it.

It is possible, then, that the assassin type was becoming barren of its former appeal in the second half of the 1590s; it is true that the period saw fewer plays featuring hired murderers, though this may simply reflect the fact that fewer plays have survived than from earlier in the decade. What adds weight to the speculation is the evidence of changes in theatrical taste in the later 1590s. *Tamburlaine*, *The Spanish Tragedy*, and their kind, which had been highly successful ten years earlier, were now derided as antediluvian bombast. A new type of comic character emerged, who quoted continually from such plays: Shakespeare's Pistol is only the best-known example. Andrew Gurr associates these changes with a divergence he sees in the repertoires of the Burbage and Henslowe companies from the late 1590s onwards.[3] It is certainly the case that the latter continued to stage Marlowe and Kyd into the following century; but we may also recall that the version of *The Spanish Tragedy* which held the stage after 1602 was a revision by Ben Jonson, which may have been commissioned to make the play more up-to-date.[4] Whether the shift in taste was local or general, however, it is possible that one of its consequences was an avoidance of assassin plots. We have seen that the character burgeoned in the late 1580s and early

[2] Bullough, ii. 168.
[3] A. Gurr, *Playgoing in Shakespeare's London* (Cambridge, 1987), 147–53.
[4] A. Barton, *Ben Jonson, Dramatist* (Cambridge, 1984), 15.

1590s in the wake of *The Spanish Tragedy*: could he have been done to death? We have also seen that in two plays of 1601, *The Poetaster* and *Satiromastix*, lines associated with him were quoted derisively. If that scorn was typical, then it is unsurprising that playwrights should have approached assassin scenarios with either sophistication, like Shakespeare, or minimalism, like Chapman: the character was not merely conventional, but clichéd, and the audience's familiarity brought with it contempt.

II

That the assassin became an unfashionable character type in the later 1590s is a hypothesis; but it is a fact that he was used more sparingly and more sparely in new plays written in those years. However, the character did not simply dwindle out of existence in the early Jacobean period: instead, we see a remarkable revival of interest from about 1600, especially after 1603 in plays given by the King's and the boy companies, the troupes which in Gurr's theory initiated the original turn of fashion away from *The Spanish Tragedy* and its ilk. An unlikely driving force behind this recrudescence was the development of a taste for the new genre of tragicomedy.

The best-known of the many characteristics of tragicomedy identified by its first theorist, Giambattista Guarini, is its presentation of 'the danger not the death'. There would seem to be little work for a murderer here; but though the phrase referred primarily to physical danger, it was also inflected in moral terms, in the somewhat legalistic sense of '*mens rea* not *actus reus*' — intention without commission. An assassin could provide the danger, and also come between the hirer's *mens rea* and the murder itself, so serving as the agent of both the 'feigned crisis' and the 'unexpected happy ending' required by Guarini.[5]

In the early seventeenth century, then, there emerged an interest (not confined to formal tragicomedies) in assassins who do not complete their mission. Of course, murder plots had failed in some earlier plays, but this was more often than not because the intended victim was the central character; a peripheral figure's chances of survival were better on the Jacobean stage. In consequence, the narrative importance of the assassin grew, and a number of new versions of the scenario came into being. One of the seminal plays in this development, though not the first, was John Marston's satirical tragicomedy of Italian court corruption, *The Malcontent* (1603), which flirts self-consciously with the established conventions of tragedy before subverting them. Among those conventions is the figure of the hired murderer. The form of the assassin plot established in *The Spanish Tragedy* made the

[5] D. L. Hirst, *Tragicomedy* (1984), 4.

character a victim of dramatic irony: he goes faithfully about his business, while we see his employer plotting to double-cross him. A corollary is that, no matter how much he engages our attention with comedy, with ideological interest, or with moral shock, he remains a minor character, a functionary in a more important villain's plots. Marston's innovation in *The Malcontent* was to alter the disposition of the episode's dramatic irony, and so to alter the dynamics of audience response.

The key element enabling this change is disguise: the malcontent Malevole is really Altofronto, the banished Duke of Genoa, so the villainous courtier Mendoza acts on partial knowledge in selecting him for use as an assassin. The first product of this situation, however, is not dramatic irony but suspense. Mendoza's attempt to murder Pietro, the present Duke, is a turning-point in the play: it changes the emphasis from the sexual vice of the first movement to the political intrigue of the second; and it gives Malevole his first opportunity to become embroiled in the corruption he censures. Some critics, such as T. F. Wharton, find indications in the earlier part of the play to suggest that Altofronto is rather more engaged than is healthy with his role of Malevole; it is a weakness of the play, Wharton suggests, that Marston does not exploit that ambiguity more fully to undercut the concluding restoration of order.[6] But to argue like this that the play is broken-backed is to miss the point of transition, the murder plot. The bitterness of Malevole's detraction certainly makes us unsure of him: does he rail at the things he wants? His involvement in Mendoza's stratagem will tell us: if deposition has made him genuinely malcontented, then he has a plausible reason for killing Pietro, his deposer. By acting or not acting in this episode, Altofronto will show his true moral status.

Marston maximizes our uncertainty by making Altofronto continue the performance to the last moment. Malevole responds to Mendoza's proposal with delight: 'My heart's wish, my soul's desire, my fantasy's dream, my blood's longing, the only height of my hopes!' (III. iii. 75–6) Moreover, as soon as Mendoza explains his designs, he begins active co-operation by suggesting an improvement. When left alone with his eavesdropping friend Celso, he closes the scene with moral commentary; but we remain uncertain which is the act and which the reality. Marston activates a final burst of suspicion in his next appearance, approaching the sleeping Pietro carrying a crossbow and pistol; but then he warns the victim and sets about preparing a murder story to take back to his employer.

As the audience achieves moral certainty, so the play achieves dramatic irony. Now that we are sure Altofronto has merely been playing along with the villain, his ability to out-think Mendoza comes to the fore. 'I'll hoist ye, ye shall mount,' Mendoza tells Malevole and the disguised Pietro; 'To the

⁶ T. F. Wharton, *Essays in Criticism*, 24 (1974), 261–74.

gallows, say ye?' (IV. iii. 85–6), responds the assassin. We have heard the joke before, in *The Spanish Tragedy*, but this time the victim understands it as well as the villain. Altofronto's intuition is swiftly confirmed: by the end of the scene, Mendoza has made arrangements for his two accomplices to poison one another. Again, this is a sophistication of *The Spanish Tragedy*: poison is a more certain way of eliminating both men mutually—but in the event, the plan fails and Mendoza, like Lorenzo, is left with a loose end. Both plays use an empty box in this situation, the pardon-box in one and the poison-box in the other. Again, the irony cuts different ways: in Kyd's play the joke is on Pedringano in that he does not know the box is empty; but in Marston's it is Mendoza who is ignorant. The presumed assassin is in control of the situation, using the same tricks to survive that an earlier hirer used against his instrument.

Marston had been toying with the assassin scenario, on a smaller scale, for some time before he wrote *The Malcontent*. He uses the relenting assassin of earlier plays in a one-scene incident in *Jack Drum's Entertainment* (1600), in which the man is re-hired by the intended victim to report the murder a success, but this is no more than a means to the discomfiture of the hirer: it puts the laugh on him when he sees the 'corpse' get up and thinks he is seeing a ghost. Humour is again the outcome in *Antonio's Revenge* (1600–1), when the villain Piero asks his accomplice Strotzo,

> Dear, hast thou steeled the point of thy resolve?
> Will't not turn edge in execution?   (II. v. 3–4)

The references to resolution and execution, and the metaphor of the sword blade, all imply the hiring of a murderer; but it turns out that Strotzo is not to kill anyone but only to pretend to be an assassin, 'fee'd' (11) by Piero's enemy Antonio. Strotzo plays the part to the hilt: 'I do not use to speak, but execute' (38), he says, echoing the assassin in *Richard III* who declared that 'Talkers are no good doers' (I. iii. 349). He underlines the point by the overblown gesture of drawing his dagger and laying his finger on his lips; the joke is that he will not need his dagger at all.

If these incidents show Marston indulging the fashion for laughing at plays like *The Spanish Tragedy*, then *The Malcontent* brings the trend to a culmination with a sustained and sophisticated parody, in which familiar situations are manipulated into unexpected forms. Nonetheless, he still works to the same end of 'wily beguiled': his Mendoza shows himself wilier than Kyd's Lorenzo, but Altofronto is wilier still. The difference is that whereas the ironies of *The Spanish Tragedy* are organized around a set of concentric circles, those of *The Malcontent* operate through three tiers, corresponding to the three central characters: Altofronto, Pietro, and Mendoza. This is a political hierarchy: each character claims the dukedom, but those on the lower rungs can achieve it only by eliminating those who are above them. But it is also a moral hierarchy, reflecting successive degrees of depravity in Pietro and Mendoza. These two interpretations give us correspondingly different views of the situation. On the one hand, Mendoza ascends to become Duke in a schematic version of the Richard III story; on the other, the office descends to his moral level. Since Mendoza himself is amoral, he can see only the political paradigm; we place more emphasis on the moral because, deprived of their titles, Altofronto and Pietro will not go away. Mendoza believes that he has reached the top of the political ladder after murdering Pietro, but this is because, unlike us, he cannot see through the disguises of Malevole and the Hermit of the Rock.

Like Lorenzo, then, Mendoza is a victim of dramatic irony in that, unbeknown to him, his crimes have been witnessed. However, the emphasis of the two plays is different, and so, accordingly, is the structure on which the irony is based. In the concentric world of *The Spanish Tragedy*, it is the fact of being overheard that matters, whereas in the hierarchy of *The Malcontent*, it is more a question of the identity of the witness. This is because Marston's Genoa is a more corrupt environment than Kyd's Spain. Lorenzo destroys Pedringano because he needs to keep his murders secret, but secrecy is not what Mendoza has in mind in planning the same:

> They shall die both, for their deserts craves more
> Than we can recompense; their presence still
> Imbraids our fortunes with beholdingness,
> Which we abhor; like deed, not doer. Then conclude,
> They live not to cry out ingratitude.   (IV. iii. 138–42)

He fears the name of ingrate more than that of murderer—a very Machiavellian trait.[7] Being Duke, he assumes, none can call his power to account; the irony is that his assassins are in fact the very men who can.

Marston's use of a disguise-plot, then, moves the assassin to the centre of the play, albeit as role rather than character. In speaking of this as an innovation, I am making an assumption about dating. It has long been recognized that *The Malcontent* is one of a group of early Jacobean plays which include the motif of a disguised prince: *Measure for Measure* and *The Fawn* (1605) are other important examples. The fashion is most plausibly accounted for by a chain of influence leading from a single play. This is not the place to construct a full *stemma*; but to demonstrate the originality of Marston's treatment of the assassin scenario, it is necessary to consider its relationship with another 'disguised prince' play, Thomas Middleton's *The Phoenix* (1603–4).

---

[7] Cf. N. Machiavelli, *The Discourses*, tr. L. J. Walker, corr. edn. (Harmondsworth, 1974), 179–89.

Like *The Malcontent*, Middleton's play has its disguised prince, Phoenix, discovering hidden corruption in the state, particularly sexual vice which will not stay in its proper place—'City and suburbs wear one livery!' (v. i. 239) There is also a political intrigue plot in which the conspirator Proditor hires Phoenix to murder the Duke, unaware that the victim is the assassin's father. The similarities suggest that the two plays are linked in some way, the major differences that Middleton was the debtor.

First, Phoenix adopts his disguise not as a victim of circumstance like Altofronto, but as a means of seeing abuses that would pass unnoticed from a prince's lofty viewpoint. This emphasizes, somewhat heavy-handedly, the moral theme that is only implicit in *The Malcontent*, at the expense of the audience's uncertainty about the hero. If Middleton is imitating Marston, it is a fair exchange, for an audience would have seen the trick before and know the prince would turn out virtuous in the end—a point which conversely argues against an imitative Marston. Moreover, suspense was disposable because the murder plot seems to have held little interest for Middleton anyway: it is only lightly sketched, whereas the sexual themes have his full attention. Such lack of enthusiasm suggests this part of the story is included out of obligation rather than originality—something most understandable in a play cashing in on an earlier success.

Perhaps the same logic explains the fate of Proditor, which has been found puzzling: he has not only plotted the death of the rightful ruler of Ferrara, but introduced an assassin into the presence-chamber itself; yet he is punished only with 'everlasting banishment' (v. i. 197), not death. Mendoza, too, is merely ejected at the end of *The Malcontent*, but this is a carefully judged gesture of contempt, the fate of an incompetent; imitation by Middleton, it would seem, turns it into a risky act of clemency towards a dangerous traitor.

All this is subjective hypothesis: the case must finally rest on external evidence. *The Malcontent* had a far longer and more eventful stage history than *The Phoenix*: our only primary evidence about the latter is the 1607 quarto's title-page assertion that it 'hath beene sundrye times Acted by the Children of Paules, And presented before his Majestie'; whereas we know that Marston's, originally staged by the Blackfriars boys, was soon stolen by the King's Men and adapted for the Globe, and that it remained in the adult company's repertory until at least 1635.[8] The theft is presumptive evidence of Marston's originality: why should Shakespeare's company steal a derivative play—especially when they already had at least one of their own in the same genre? For positive proof, however, we must date the two plays.

The evidence for dating *The Phoenix* is relatively straightforward: topical allusions suggest that it was written in the summer of 1603, and it may have

---

[8] Bentley, i. 123.

een given before the King on 20 February the following year.[9] For *The Malcontent*, we have a longer range, from the publication in early 1602 of the translation of Guarini's *Il Pastor Fido* that influenced Marston, to the play's entry in the Stationers' Register on 5 July 1604—a somewhat early publication for a play first staged in that year. Another factor we must bear in mind is the closure of the theatres from 19 March 1603 until 9 April 1604. This is important because, whichever dramatist was the debtor, his company was probably seeking to emulate the theatrical success of the earlier play. If we accept this assumption, it is most likely that *The Malcontent* came first. Otherwise we should have to find time in the three months between the reopening of the theatres and the registering of the play for publication, for Marston to see *The Phoenix* at Paul's and write his own version, and for the Blackfriars company to rehearse and stage it. It is an impossibly cramped schedule. The latest plausible time for the original Blackfriars staging of *The Malcontent*, then, is early in 1603.[10]

If this conclusion is correct, then a possible scenario might be the following. The Blackfriars boys staged *The Malcontent* shortly before the playhouses closed, and it proved successful. During the closure period, writers for other companies reworked aspects of the play, perhaps because the theatres needed to reopen, after a long absence, with new plays of assured popularity—it was not a time to take risks. Therefore Shakespeare, for the King's Men, took the 'disguised ruler' plot and produced *Measure for Measure*. At about the same time the young Middleton produced a more slavish imitation of *The Malcontent* for the Paul's boys. Probably a few months after the reopening, another, anonymous playwright produced *The Fair Maid of Bristol*, which not only adds a disguised hero employed as an assassin to the plot it takes over from the ballad *Constance of Cleveland* (1603), but also repeats the device in its second plot, exploiting its popularity to the point of overkill. As we can see from this three-play spectrum, Marston's imitators separated his play into component parts almost immediately; so this development of the assassin proceeded largely independently of the disguised ruler play.

The virtuous character disguised as an assassin was a plot device that saw service well into the reign of Charles I, with the disguises becoming increasingly criminal: Strange takes on the role of a soldier in Nathan Field's *A Woman is a Weathercock* (1609), Medina becomes 'Doctor Devil' in Thomas Dekker's *The Noble Spanish Soldier* (1622), and in Shakerley Marmion's *The Antiquary* (1635) the disguise is actually a bravo. By 1638, the scenario's well-worn familiarity is apparent from John Ford's attempt at a variation of

[9] B. Maxwell, in J. G. McManaway, G. E. Dawson, and E. E. Willoughby (eds.), *Joseph Quincy Adams Memorial Studies* (Washington, DC, 1948), 743–53; P. Yachnin, *N&Q* 231 (1986), 375–7; E. K. Chambers, *The Elizabethan Stage* (Oxford, 1923), iii. 439.

[10] For further evidence, see T. A. Pendleton, in J. W. Mahon and T. A. Pendleton (eds.), *'Fanned and Winnowed Opinions': Shakespearean Essays Presented to Harold Jenkins*, (1987), 84–5.

it in *The Lady's Trial*. The sub-plot deals with the sexual misadventures of the wanton Levidolche, who hires Parado, a ruffian, to murder two of her ex-lovers. In fact, Parado is her ex-husband Benatzi in disguise. Contrary to expectations, however, dramatic irony works with, not against the hirer this time: Levidolche sees through the disguise, while Benatzi tries to go through with the scheme. The situation is unconvincing: there is no good reason for Benatzi's adopting a disguise at all, nor for his failure to recognize Levidolche; and her hopes of remarrying him could hardly be served if he were caught executing her orders. Ford seems less interested in plausibility than in playing games with convention, in reversing expected norms; so the play's main value to us is as evidence of those expectations.

A more powerful variation occurred far earlier, in *The Revenger's Tragedy*. If *The Phoenix* was Middleton's initial, somewhat imitative response to *The Malcontent*, the later play effects a more assured transformation of Marston. It has debts to *The Phoenix* at its peripheries, such as the names Lussurioso and Castiza, but Middleton adapted actual incidents from *The Malcontent*. Both plays, in particular, have scenes in which a man disguised as a malcontent is hired to commit a murder; but Middleton introduces a twist. Malevole spares Pietro because he is not the man Mendoza takes him for, and he has a different set of values. Values do not come into Vindice's case. He cannot kill his target Piato because Piato is himself wearing a different disguise. It is not an incident that Middleton makes much of: it draws its power from the contrast with the earlier play. In *The Malcontent* and its tragicomic successors, the assassin is a moral centre in a corrupt society, ready to restore order once the disguise is off; his refusal to co-operate in murder gives the audience, true to Guarini's requirements, the illusion of danger without the death to follow. But without its moral element, the situation helps to define a tragic world of the blackest opportunism and depravity.

III

The individual form of murder which gave most scope for adaptation to tragicomedy was poisoning. It was accepted that to dispatch one's enemies in this manner required specialist assistance, particularly from corrupt members of the medical profession. There were a number of archetypes of such experts. Great men, for instance, might keep a professional poisoner on their payroll. An example was Giulio Borgarucci (*fl.* 1564–79), known as 'Dr Julio', who was physician to Robert Dudley, the much-libelled Elizabethan Earl of Leicester.[11] Reputedly Borgarucci

[11] *Calendar of State Papers, Domestic Series, 1547–1580*, ed. R. Lemon (1856), 272.

> could rid mens lives yet noe blood spill,
> Yea with such great dexteritie and skill
> Could give a dramme of poyson that should slay,
> At end of th' yeare, the month, the weeke or day.[12]

The name 'Dr Julio' seems to have become a stock epithet for a physician moonlighting as a professional poisoner: such characters bear that name in *The Fair Maid of Bristol* and *The White Devil* (1612).[13] Contributing to its currency, perhaps, was its assonance with 'Jew', another archetypal poisoner. The Jews' superior medical knowledge, which made them so attractive as court physicians, was often thought to extend to toxicology: a celebrated example was Dr Lopez, allegedly suborned by Spain to poison Queen Elizabeth in 1594.

There were a few court physicians and Jews among the drama's hired poisoners, but the most common type of specialist accomplice was the apothecary who sold the poison in the first place. Known to contain poisons as well as medicine, the apothecary's shop was an image for things of both good and evil consequence. The apothecaries themselves had been mistrusted since at least the time of Henry VIII, when legal powers to search their premises were established by Parliament: the principal aim was to root out bad medicines, but the rumour was also abroad that 'potycaries kyll men'.[14] Stage apothecaries were far from universally malignant, but one undertakes a poisoning for the Duke of Guise in *The Massacre at Paris*, and another supplies poison to a murderess in William Haughton's *The Devil and his Dame* (1600).[15] Perhaps most revealing is Edward Sharpham's *The Fleer* (1606), not for the apothecary's actual behaviour but an attitude shown towards him: there is nothing particularly rascally about him, yet the villain takes it for granted that he will sell poison—as if all members of the profession traffic in murder under the counter. It was a piece of folklore that bore little relation to reality. Few real-life poisoning cases involved apothecaries, and by far the commonest substance used was ratsbane (i.e. arsenic), a readily available household rat poison.[16] The notion that it took an expert to sell or administer poison was entirely mythical.[17]

[12] T. Rogers, *Leicester's Ghost*, ed. F. B. Williams, jun. (Chicago, 1972), ll. 221–4.

[13] See also *Pathomachia* (1630), E1ʳ.

[14] 32 Henry VIII c. 40 s. 2; J. Heywood, *The Four PP*, l. 366, in J. Q. Adams (ed.), *Chief Pre-Shakespearean Dramas* (1924).

[15] For the argument for identifying *The Devil and his Dame* with the play published in 1662 under the title *Grim, the Collier of Croydon*, see W. M. Baillie (ed.), *A Choice Ternary of English Plays* (Binghamton, NY, 1984), 173–80.

[16] F. T. Bowers, *Journal of English and Germanic Philology*, 36 (1937), 492. It should be added that, since the law has no respect of poisons, the type was not always specified in contemporary accounts of cases.

[17] Which is not to say that some people did not act upon it—the Overbury murder being a case in point.

The problem with poisoners, as with other accomplices, was that they were not necessarily reliable; and as specialists they had their own peculiarly devious way of double-crossing their employers. Narcotic drugs, thought to be opiate in character, had long been a useful plot device (in Chaucer's 'Knight's Tale', for instance), and as early as Boccaccio's time they were credited with soporific effects so strong that they were indistinguishable from death.[18] By the time they entered the English imagination via the *novelle*, these potions had three separate narrative uses (which then shaded into one another on the stage). They could be taken by accident and produce comic complications, as in the Latin comedy *Hymenaeus* (1579). They could be administered or taken knowingly to achieve the appearance of death without causing death itself, as in *The Jew of Malta* and *Romeo and Juliet* (1595–6). Finally, they could be substituted for poison in order to prevent a murder or, occasionally, a suicide. A popular incidental feature was a scene showing the victim waking up, unexpectedly or otherwise, in the tomb, or later, in a cunning twist probably introduced by Middleton in *The Puritan* (1606), on the way to his own funeral.

By far the commonest use of the sleeping potion in plays was in murder plots. One reason for this was that it made so clear a contrast with poison. The sixteenth-century imagination conceived of poison served in a golden cup or 'sweetned with suger', outward attractiveness concealing its lethal effects; but the initial effects of a sleeping potion themselves concealed its true, harmless nature.[19] The two substances therefore made a pair, and one was a ready substitute for the other. It is clear, for example, how Shakespeare's imagination shuttles between poison and potion in Act IV of *Romeo and Juliet*: Juliet is suicidal, but it is not poison that Friar Lawrence gives her; and later she worries that it may not be potion after all. It was an uncertainty that proved ideal for tragicomic murder plots.

On one level, the appeal of tragicomedy was akin to that of the twentieth-century 'cliffhanger' serial: an audience, knowing the convention that the hero cannot be killed, wonders how he can possibly escape, how the play can possibly live up to the generic requirement of 'the danger not the death'. A poisoning plot could take the play into the most extreme situation possible, death, and still remain within bounds, provided that the use of a sleeping draught was concealed from the audience. In practice, as with the disguise plot, playwrights could not attempt the same trick twice: the casualness with which we are told of the device in John Day's *Law Tricks* (c.1604) suggests how quickly the surprise must have worn off.[20]

[18] For a fuller account of the sleeping potion in history and drama, see T. P. Harrison, jun., *Texas University Studies in English*, 27 (1948), 54–67.

[19] Tilley, P. 458; A. Arnauld, *The Arrainement of the whole societie of Iesuites in Fraunce* (1594), D2ʳ.

[20] J. Day, *Law Tricks*, ll. 1818–21.

Nonetheless, as with the disguise plot again, the substitution of potion for poison continued in use as a dramatic device until the 1630s, with some plays introducing new variations and complications. In William Cartwright's *The Siege* (1638), for example, the 'poison' goes astray and 'kills' the wrong person; and two plays, *The Honest Lawyer* (1615) and *The Lost Lady* (1637–8) use a simple non-toxic substance rather than a potion, with the victims feigning the symptoms. In particular, some dramatists did not bother trying to deceive the audience, but made the substitution clear from the start, and sought their appeal in other ways: that of *Cymbeline* comes from the layering of irony upon irony as the potion changes hands, each time with different ideas about its nature; and *The Honest Lawyer* achieves a tense moment when the parsimonious murderer decides to use 'Two peny-woorth of Rats-bane', and his son has to talk him into accepting something else.[21]

Plays in which the potion is used to simulate murder, but no character has actual murderous intent, need not concern us here. When there is murder intended, the switch is made by a third party, usually the vendor of the poison. In a few plays, however, including the first dramatic use of the sleeping draught to avert murder, in *The Devil and his Dame*, the assassin is responsible for the swap. In Haughton's play, the poison is supplied by Ralph Harvey, the barely seen and wholly unmemorable apothecary, but the would-be murderess makes the mistake of asking her husband, Dr Castiliano, to administer it. He tells the audience in a tone of injured self-esteem,

> Well, I have promis'd her to kill the Earle,
> And yet, I hope, ye will not think I'le do it.   (IV. iii. 115–16)

This is surprising for two reasons. First, Castiliano is a Spaniard, and certain national characteristics, such as jealousy, have been attributed to him; one might expect the use of poison to be another. Secondly, Castiliano is, nationality and all, really an identity assumed by a devil incarnate, Belphagor. Anticipating *The Devil is an Ass* by sixteen years, Belphagor returns to hell asking not to be sent back to earth, 'For there dwells dread, and horror more then here' (v. iii. 12). The play seems to be a deliberate subversion of stock evil types; the averted assassination serves that theme.

Another assassin who uses sleeping potion to fake a murder is the servant Blunt in *The Fair Maid of Bristol*. The play is important in that, in the wake of *The Malcontent*, it hybridizes the device with a disguise plot: 'Blunt' is in fact the victim's friend Harbart. What is striking is that though the author is within a whisker of a satisfactory combination, he fails to take the opportunity and leaves the plot full of holes. Blunt is not a specialist, so it is questionable whether he would have the knowledge or access to materials required to pull off the trick; and his commission is not to poison his victim,

[21] S.S., *The Honest Lavvyer* (1616), H2ᵛ.

so besides faking death he also has to smear the body with his own blood
to simulate violence. Yet in the other plot, another character is disguised as
a physician, 'Dr Julio', and is hired to poison two people—and his response
is only to leak the conspiracy to one of the victims. It was left to Edward
Sharpham in *The Fleer* and Robert Armin in *The Two Maids of Mortlake*
(1608) to combine the two elements in the obvious way and have the heroes
disguise themselves as apothecaries.

Again, however, the sleeping draught was used most powerfully when
transplanted to tragedy, in John Mason's *The Turk* (1607). The play's villain
is Borgias, Governor of Florence, and his principal instrument is Muleasses,
the Turk. From the first the dynamics of their relationship is suspicious.
Muleasses is giving Borgias a lot: not only his services in murder but also
military support for his scheme to make himself king of Italy. His return on
the investment seems remarkably small: whereas Borgias expects great
power, all Muleasses can look forward to is marriage to his ally's daughter. In
contrast with Borgias' straightforward relationship with the slave Eunuchus,
whom he uses for lesser killings, this is problematic.

It is therefore no great surprise when, in his first scene, Muleasses
comments on Borgias' incompetence in villainy: it was an unwise move 'To
lay another in thy bosome' (753), and the Turk has rewarded the Italian with
treachery—the 'murder' has been effected by 'a sleepy juyce' (789), not
poison. But here saving a life denotes evil, not good intent: Muleasses
emerges from the shadow of Borgias as a second villain with his own motives
and his own political cunning, and the rest of the play deals with their cross-
purposes in plotting. It is an extension of the innovations of *The Malcontent*:
again the assassin moves from a subsidiary role to being a character in his
own right; but this time he acts not for virtue but vice.

IV

Disguises and sleeping draughts made slick plot devices; but Dekker and
Middleton chose to do without them when they wrote to the new taste for
unfulfilled murders in *The Honest Whore, Part 1*. This may have been merely
fortuitous: a sleeping potion has already been used for other purposes before
the murderous commission is given, so it avoids repetition if Dr Benedict is
content simply to lie about the victim's death. At face value this looks like
just another case of an honest physician; but the point is the change of
emphasis. Now honesty is itself the focus of the play's reverse. In the hiring
scene, he and the Duke (who has given out false news of a death) dovetail
so perfectly that it is impossible to tell who is corrupting whom:

DUKE   O would t'were true.
DOCTOR
  It may my Lord.
DUKE   May? how? I wish his death.
DOCTOR
  And you may have your wish.   (I. iii. 91–3)

Later, we hear the Doctor's lie before we know it to be one. The surprise is
that he has been virtuous all along: instead of a poison that is not a poison,
we are shown a poisoner who is not a poisoner.

Dekker went further with the uncooperative assassin in his tragicomedy
Match Me in London (?1611). The play opposes citizen morality to court
corruption, figured most obviously in the King's lust and the political
ambition of his underlings; but it is the courtiers' acceptance of murder both
to promote and to oppose these overt signs of corruption that indicates how
endemic the problem truly is. The Queen, for example, is chaste and not
unnaturally aggrieved by her husband's eye for the citizen wife Tormiella,
but her readiness to kill her rival, possibly by hired 'slaves' (III. iii. 5), taints
her also. Assassins abound, but they double-cross their employers every
time; both the sleeping potion and the disguise plot are used, the latter, it
appears, imitated directly from *The Malcontent*.[22]

The cases of Tormiella and the Doctor, procured to kill the King and
Admiral Valasco respectively, are straightforward. When the Doctor is
approached, he protests at first, but Prince John's sword at his throat makes
him change his tune. He becomes almost excessively accommodating:

JOHN
  When?
DOCTOR
  When you please.
JOHN
  This day?
DOCTOR
  This hower.   (III. i. 45–8)

Once the threat is removed, he underlines the duress involved: 'I am beaten
to these things.' (63) Tormiella is the same, forced into a regicidal vow by
the malcontent Gazetto's threat of violence; neither of them has any intention
of performing the murders they undertake.

Cordolente, Tormiella's husband, is another matter. Set on, Othello-like,
by Gazetto to murder his wife, he comes to the point of commission before
he finds he cannot do it. Significantly, the action moves swiftly up to this
moment, with a dumb show serving for abbreviation: we see him sweep to

----

[22] Dekker re-uses the joke of the assassin's understanding the implications of 'mounting' as
his reward for the crime (IV. vi. 66).

his revenge, only to stop sharply at the eleventh hour. Also significant is
the fact that his subsequent explanation of the incident is confused and
contradictory:

> I had no power to kill her,
> Charmes of Divinity pull'd backe mine Arme,
> She had Armor of proofe on, (reverence of the place).
>
> (v. iv. 10–12)

If the blow was prevented by divine intervention, then Tormiella had no
need of metaphorical armour to protect her from it; finally he discards
external inhibitions and admits that he could not, for reverence, bring himself
to kill in a church. We have been watching a man in the grip of the murderous
but evanescent passion of wrath, brought back to self-control on realizing
where he is. Psychologically less static than Tormiella or the Doctor, he
shares with them a character defined by citizen honesty: as with them, it is
his involvement in murder that is out of character, induced by Gazetto.

All this is run-of-the-mill tragicomic material. So is the device whereby
the King seems to have ordered the privy murder of Prince John, when in
fact the ambitious brother has been kept on the brink of death in a demonstration of royal power and mercy. The case of Gazetto, Tormiella's
rejected suitor, is more problematic.

In his disguise of Lupo Vindicado, Gazetto is hired by the King to kill
the Queen and Cordolente, whom he figures allegorically as a scorpion and
an ox. Once alone after receiving his orders, Gazetto declares his intent:

> I scorne to be thy bloud hound,
> Why should I vexe a Soule did never greeve me?
> The Queenes an honest Lady: should I kill her
> It were as if I pull'd a Temple downe
> And from the ruines of that built up a stewes,
> She lives, but Butcher like the Oxe Ile use.   (iv. vi. 67–72)

Whatever impression of probity we may have built up in the course of
the speech is blown away by the closing statement that he will fulfil the
other half of the contract. The point is made more starkly when he
reveals that the Queen is still alive: 'I had no reason to kill her' (v. v. 33),
he says.

Instead of someone of higher moral standing than his employer, then, the
guise of hired killer hides a man who will readily commit murder: the assassin
turns out to be a revenger. Quickly transcending his role, he becomes a
procurer himself, setting on Tormiella and Cordolente as murderers; in the
dumb show, he is seen at one side, laughing at the chaos his activities are
causing. It is a development that more resembles the independence of
Muleasses in *The Turk* than anything from Dekker's genre here, so it is

unsurprising that the dramatist should fight shy of it at the last moment. Gazetto's final remark in the play is presumably intended to redeem him: 'I had not the heart to hurt a woman, if I had, your little face had beene mall'd ere this, but my Angers out, forgive me.' (78–9) The implications of this line directly contradict what we already know: instead of being able but unwilling to kill her, he is willing but, in his heart of hearts, unable. He turns out, implausibly, to be, like Cordolente, a good man who gave in to wrath for a time, but has now returned to moral rationality.

The weakness of this ending reflects a weakness of Jacobean tragicomedy as a whole in dealing with human evil as exemplified in the assassin. Clearly the character type provided dramatists with a useful device: he was a weak link in the murder process, a component which might perform unpredictably; but the resultant plots stress narrative complications at the expense of the character itself. In disguise plots, the character is a fiction anyway, and benevolent poisoners are emphasized first as the possessors of specialist knowledge and only secondarily as men chosen to kill. They are uncomplicated figures in themselves who are placed in an unusual position; the interest lies in the strategies by which they seek to maintain their personal integrity in that position. They achieve centrality, that is, by transcending the role of hired murderer that is thrust upon them; the role itself remains at the margins. Dekker's achievement was to strip away the elaborations of other playwrights, to reveal this basic point: the stereotype is invoked only to be discarded, and instead of a hired murderer, we find a character with his own, not necessarily pure motives for action.

This simple form of the murderer's double-cross went on to become a stock situation: it is treated with no great ceremony in *The Honest Man's Fortune* (1613), which implies that it is already familiar ground. Robert Gomersall's tragedy *Lodovick Sforza* (1628) is organized around the untrustworthiness of hired instruments:

> I was betraid, betraid, and by those men
> By whom I conquer'd,   (2310–11)

laments Sforza's ghost at the end of the play. Three times he uses others: to seize power by poisoning Duke Galeazzo, to consolidate his regime by murdering the widow, Isabella, and later to regain power by the 'civill murther' (2228) of war. Each time his employees play him false: the professional assassin Vitellio kills Galeazzo, but then accepts Isabella's offer to ply his trade against Sforza; Caiazzo, set to kill Isabella, falls for her, spares her, and finally defects to France; and the Swiss mercenaries hired to attack Milan renege when they hear their paymaster is a murderer.

The danger of an instrument's treachery had always been implicit: it was the foundation of the hirer's usual caution in first speaking of murder. A corollary of the realization of these fears in tragicomedy is that hirers in such plays tend to be less suspicious. Mendoza reveals his mind to Malevole after nothing more than a hyperbolical mercenary promise to be 'thy slave beyond death and hell' (III. iii. 73); the Duke in *The Honest Whore, Part 1* is even more candid. In *Match Me in London*, Prince John trusts a man whose only incentive to kill has been a threat, and though the King takes the precaution of wrapping his proposal in a cryptic story, he goes on to expound the conundrum himself. Recklessness like this is quite at odds with the caution of earlier hirers: it is a mark of ineptitude that disables them from being a major threat, making it all the easier to establish a secure happy ending.

In other words, most Jacobean tragicomedy flirts with evil, but cannot portray it seriously: it is a genre of hedonistic entertainment that sports with human crimes, and not with follies. Its assumptions about crime may be summed up in the words of Anabell in *The Fair Maid of Bristol* when she tries to save her hirer husband from the gallows: 'Intents are nothing till they come to acts' (D4ᵛ). According to this dubious principle, characters can plot murder and escape the consequences, so long as something goes wrong with the process of commission, and they are benevolently inclined by the end. Since it is not this (generally painless) change of heart but the intervention of the assassin that averts the crime, the burden of moral action is disingenuously shifted from author to instrument, when it should be carried equally by both. The assassin, then, serves to shield his employer from our censure. This is why Dekker endangers the stability of his conclusion when he grants Gazetto criminal characteristics: if the victim's escape is fortuitous, engineered by no one, then the assassin joins the hirer among the guilty, there is nobody to draw our fire, and so the happy ending overtly validates immorality. In this genre, then, assassins can be safely introduced only so long as they are not really assassins at all. At every turn, the plays duck the serious issues raised by their material: they are theatrically exciting, but morally bankrupt.

An instructive contrast is with the plays Shakespeare wrote under the influence of the vogue for tragicomedy and abortive assassinations. In *Pericles*, both Antiochus and Dionyza, hirers of unsuccessful murderers among their other crimes, die in flames sent either directly or indirectly from heaven:

> The gods for murder seemed so content
> To punish; although not done, but meant. (Epilogue. 15–16)

In *The Winter's Tale*, the punishment for obeying immoral orders is to be eaten alive by a wild bear. There can be scope for redemption, but it is never easy: Leontes, like Posthumus in *Cymbeline*, has to undergo bitter remorse for his murderous jealousy before he has earned reconciliation and a happy ending. Other tragicomedies are trivial in comparison: their sin is the sin of forgiveness.

8

THE SOPHISTICATION OF THE STEREOTYPE

I

In general, early Jacobean dramatists were less explicitly moralistic than their Elizabethan predecessors. Their plays deal with villainy not in order to brand as unethical certain forms of political and social behaviour, but as a human experience: in *Macbeth* and plays like it, for instance, characters are shown in states of premeditation, and dramatic tension comes as much from the decision to commit murder as from the murder itself.[1] In this period, then, the assassin type acquired new attributes and addressed new concerns. The starting-point for this development was the limitations of earlier treatments of the character.

As we saw in Chapter 6, the playwrights and audiences of the late 1580s and early 1590s were interested in hired assassins as embodiments of the sixteenth century's concern about the moral and social implications of the unrestrained pursuit of money. The plays dealt with abstract issues that might have been addressed using the techniques of the recently outmoded morality drama, accommodating them instead in realistic scenarios: ten years earlier, Pedringano might have been named Covetise. This means that character is secondary to ideology in Kyd's portrayal: Pedringano may be understood, in E. M. Forster's terms, as a 'flat' character, 'constructed round a single idea or quality'—in his case, avarice.[2] In so far as such figures have them, their character traits serve this theme: there is a psychological element in the portrayal of the Messenger in *King Leir*, for example, but it is primarily a kind of inverted psychomachia, a conflict between two value-systems, not a representation of actual human behaviour; the character's descendants in plays like *Richard III* reflect more clearly the dramatists' schematically ethical concerns.

These characters are not personified abstractions, neither are they complex representations of human beings. Their limitations may be conceived as a 'lack', which subsequent playwrights supplied; in line with the interests of the early Jacobeans, this entailed a move from conceptual to human interest, and from an ethical to a social problem. The late Elizabethan assassin was a murderer through avarice, but avarice was (for the sake of moral emphasis)

[1] M. Wiggins, in A. Marwick (ed.), *The Arts, Literature, and Society* (1990), 23–47.
[2] E. M. Forster, *Aspects of the Novel*, ed. O. Stallybrass (Harmondsworth, 1976), 73.

treated as *sui generis*. This begged an obvious question; and conditions in the 1590s made its answer equally obvious.

II

The years 1594–7 saw four bad harvests in succession: the price of food rose to levels so high that John Stow thought them worthy of note in his *Annals*.[3] John King surveyed the situation from his pulpit in York: 'Behold! what a famine God hath brought upon our land; and making it to persevere yet hitherto, doth increase it. One year there hath been hunger: the second there was a dearth: and a third there was great cleanness of teeth.'[4] There were food riots in London in 1595, and insurrections in Norfolk and Oxfordshire the following year. Always a social problem in Elizabethan England, poverty and unemployment were at crisis level: the Parliament of 1597–8 enacted several new measures for the relief of the poor.[5]

In this context, the emaciated Mantuan apothecary in *Romeo and Juliet* was a figure of some topical interest.[6] Romeo's words underline the physical signs of the man's penury:

> Famine is in thy cheeks,
> Need and oppression starveth in thy eyes,
> Contempt and beggary hangs upon thy back   (v. i. 70–2)

—hangs, that is, like the 'tattered weeds' (40) in which the wretch clothes himself. It is to buy food that, reluctantly, he commits the capital crime of selling poison.

The apothecary was an element that accrued to the Romeo and Juliet story on its journey north from Italy in the later sixteenth century. In the Italian versions by Luigi da Porto (*c.*1530) and Matteo Bandello (1554), Romeo already has the poison when he hears of Juliet's 'death', but the blasé Mediterranean attitude to murder implicit in this detail was evidently unacceptable to Pierre Boaistuau, who adapted the story into French in 1559. In order to explain Romeo's acquisition of this essential element in the plot, he invented a poor but avaricious apothecary who sells the hero poison for fifty ducats.[7] The character then passed, essentially unchanged, into the English versions by Arthur Brooke (1562) and William Painter (1567); the first was Shakespeare's source, and he almost certainly knew the second too.

[3] A. B. Appleby, *Famine in Tudor and Stuart England* (Liverpool, 1978), 112–13; J. Stow, *The Annales of England* (1601), 4P1ʳ, 4P2ʳ, 4Q3ʳ, 4Q3ᵛ, 4Q5ᵛ, 4Q6ᵛ.

[4] J. Strype, *Annals of the Reformation*, new edn. (Oxford, 1824), vii. 294.

[5] 39 Elizabeth I cc. 3, 5.

[6] The role was probably written for John Sincklo, a grotesquely thin small-part actor: A. Gaw, *Anglia*, 49 (1925–6), 289–303.

[7] F. Belleforest and P. Boaistuau, *Histoires Tragiqves* (Paris, 1568), i. F3ʳ.

It was not Shakespeare's decision, then, to represent the apothecary as a victim of poverty; what is important is the attitude to poverty revealed by the changes he makes. In Brooke, the character is a villain. Romeus asks him for

> Somme poyson strong, that may, in lesse then halfe an howre,
> Kill him whose wretched hap shalbe the potion to devowre. (2579–80)

The apothecary, conquered by 'covetise' (2581), hands over a poison powerful enough 'To kill the strongest man alive' (2588). Evidently he believes Romeus intends to use it on a third party, so (Romeus' actual intentions notwithstanding) he is morally an accessory to murder, and is duly hanged at the end. The transaction also has a clandestine element made more explicit by Painter: the shop is open, so other customers must not see or hear anything illicit cross the counter.[8]

It is notable that Shakespeare eliminates everything that works to the apothecary's discredit. The shop is closed, so the characters do not have to whisper in a corner—which was not feasible on stage anyway. Romeo admits that the poison is for suicide—the taker is to be 'life-weary' (63)—and the apothecary's dialogue (78–80) shows that he believes this. Finally, there is no reference to his being hanged. Instead of Brooke's avaricious villain, we have a man who is loath to break the law, even in penury: 'My poverty but not my will consents.' (76) Indeed, Romeo insists as he pays that, whatever the law may say, the man has done nothing unethical:

> There is thy gold—worse poison to men's souls,
> Doing more murder in this loathsome world,
> Than these poor compounds that thou mayst not sell.
> I sell thee poison; thou hast sold me none.   (81–4)

If we are disposed to find his reasoning factitious, we may also recall that we have already heard Lady Capulet refer to another 'one in Mantua' (III. v. 88) who administers poison, and who must be a more terrible individual than this poor creature who has merely supplied it, once, and unwillingly at that. In this case, comparisons are far from odious.[9]

Shakespeare's sympathetic treatment of the apothecary would have been surprising for a sixteenth-century audience, for it was at odds with the associations that audience would have brought to the character. We have already seen, for example, that apothecaries in general had long been suspected as purveyors of poison: this man's reluctance must have seemed striking. Moreover, his lean countenance indicated more than just hunger: it also had more sinister associations.

---

[8] Painter, *The Palace of Pleasure*, ed. J. Jacobs (1890), iii. 115.

[9] The comparison is Shakespeare's invention: Lady Capulet does not propose to have Romeo poisoned in the sources.

For one thing, it marks him out as the figure of Death, portrayed as an animated skeleton in sixteenth-century iconography. This serves to complete a thematic pattern in the play. Friar Lawrence has used chemical means to simulate death in Juliet, with the result that Death is invoked as a surrogate bridegroom for her.[10] With the bony apothecary, however, Death enters the action in person, to supply Romeo with a more lethal drug. It is the point at which the Friar's plans go decisively wrong, and it is marked with iconography which casts a shadow over the rest of the tragedy: having bargained with Death, Romeo will never leave the tomb he enters.

More importantly for our purposes, however, leanness was associated with members of the underworld and others scraping a living in the penumbra of the law: the thief Jack Fitten in *Arden of Faversham* (ii. 47) and the mountebank Pinch in *The Comedy of Errors* (?1591; v. i. 238) are both said to be 'lean-faced'; in *The Jew of Malta*, Barabas gains an accomplice in Ithamore when he asks, parsimoniously, for an especially lean slave; and one of the assassins in *Two Lamentable Tragedies* has a 'hollow discontented looke' (E1ʳ).[11] It is understandable that Caesar should have thought such men dangerous, and surprising that the apothecary is not.

We, in our turn, are surprised by an emphasis of Brooke's: although the episode begins with Romeus' reasoning that the man's 'nedy lacke' (2573) will make him a ready retailer, when this proves so he is deprecated for covetousness. It is Shakespeare, however, who is out of line with sixteenth-century criminology. Poverty was not commonly considered *per se* to be corrupting: 'As riches for the most part engendreth idlenesse, and contempt of learning, and learned men: So Povertie causeth sobrietie, and maketh men vertuous and discreet.'[12] It would not be strictly true to suggest that the link between poverty and crime was unknown to contemporary commentators, but most thought on the subject had a limitation. Social theorists drew a distinction between the deserving poor, destitute 'by impotency' or 'by casualty' (and doubtless far more sober, virtuous, and discreet as a result), and the 'thriftless poor' who were victims of nothing more than their own idleness.[13] Accordingly, the 1597–8 Parliament which passed Acts for poor relief also instituted laws for the punishment of rogues, vagabonds, and sturdy beggars.[14] Since idleness was reckoned to be 'the moder [i.e. mother] of al vices', poverty was only a stage in the development of criminality, which grew ultimately from the evil nature of one class of poor.[15] Brooke's apparent double standards over his apothecary simply indicate that the

[10] See M. M. Mahood, *Shakespeare's Wordplay* (1957), 57–8.
[11] 'Hollow' implies either leanness (*OED*. adj. 3) or sunken cheeks (*OED* adj. 2b).
[12] R. Cawdrey, *A Treasvrie or Store-Hovse of Similies* (1600), 4C3ʳ.
[13] W. Harrison, *The Description of England*, ed. G. Edelen (Ithaca, NY, 1968), 180.
[14] 39 Elizabeth I cc. 4, 17.
[15] Lord Berners, *The Boke of Duke Huon of Burdeux*, ed. S. L. Lee (1882–3), vol. i, p. xliii.

proposition was reversible: if evil nature produces the criminal poor, then all criminal poor are evil-natured. Shakespeare's portrayal of a man forced by indigence into crime, however, shows a humanity perhaps born of actual observation of poverty and hunger during England's lean years.

III

The apothecary is not an assassin, but Shakespeare's presentation of him, radical in its time, heralded new attitudes to criminality that gave a further dimension to the type. Subsequently crime was increasingly understood as primarily a social phenomenon: Robert Burton alleged in *The Anatomy of Melancholy* (1621) that 'poverty alone makes men thieves, rebels, murderers, traitors, assassinates'.[16] Dramatists were developing such ideas from the turn of the century onwards: instead of a character with a sinful desire for money, some Jacobean plays portrayed the hired murderer as a man with a genuine need for it.

One aspect of this development was the assimilation of the assassin to the common early seventeenth-century figure of the malcontent. The latter is not, strictly speaking, a distinct character type. If we attempt to define him as such, we are faced with a bewildering variety of exemplars: it is a long way from the railing of Shakespeare's Jaques to the villainy of his Iago. Malcontents prove to be a very mixed bag who share only the condition of being malcontented. Moreover, that condition could arise for many reasons: Edmund is a bastard, Iago has had his promotion blocked, Malevole has been dethroned; foreign travel, melancholy, and political disaffection could also produce such men.[17]

The best way to understand the Jacobean concept of the malcontent is as a loose set of characteristics, only some of which needed to be assembled in any individual exemplar. One factor, however, was common to them all, abstraction or alienation from society: they are characters on the fringes who do not partake of or contribute to human intercourse and the body politic. The portrayal is distinct from that of underworld figures in earlier drama: the Elizabethan criminal was a man preying on society, the Jacobean malcontent one excluded from it. Whether its cause was social or psychological, the consequence of this exclusion is a vindictiveness which could express itself as either satire or crime. Obviously such a man held attractions to those seeking the services of a murderer: 'discontent and want | Is the

[16] R. Burton, *The Anatomy of Melancholy*, ed. F. Dell and P. Jordan-Smith (New York, 1948), 302; see also 296, 300–1.
[17] See Z. S. Fink, *Philological Quarterly*, 14 (1935), 237–52; T. Spencer, in J. G. McManaway, G. E. Dawson, and E. E. Willoughby (eds.), *Joseph Quincy Adams Memorial Studies* (Washington, DC, 1948), 523–35; T. McAlindon, *English Renaissance Tragedy* (1986), 34–5.

clay to mould a villain of' (IV. i. 47–8), observes the hirer Lussurioso in *The Revenger's Tragedy*.

Of the malcontent's subsidiary traits, it is melancholy that is most often a feature of the early seventeenth-century assassin: it afflicts a variety of killers and potential killers such as Middleton's Vindice and Webster's Bosola; by the 1630s, it had become a traditional attribute of 'hired slaves, that murther at a price'.[18] The trait was open to two interpretations. It could be understood as a natural response to neglect, but a more old-fashioned view presented it as a physiological phenomenon: the melancholy man suffered from an excess of the humour black bile, which induced psychological peculiarities that could, in certain circumstances, include murderousness.[19] Either way, melancholy was another useful signpost for a would-be hirer.

The malcontent assassin is important to us here because it is often poverty that has made him malcontented. The emergence of this figure begins with Lazarotto in *The First Part of Hieronimo*, 'A melancholy, discontented courtier' (i. 114) whom Lorenzo engages to kill his sister's fiancé. He represents a transitional stage between the criminal and the malcontent, in that Lorenzo chooses him for his prior criminality: his 'hands are wash'd in rape, and murders bold' (117). It is relevant that his career should include rape as well as homicide, for allusions to lust define the overall tone of the sequence in which he appears: through recurrent reference to sexuality, the dramatist develops an image of the perversion of crime that contrasts with the normal emotion Lorenzo hopes to frustrate—an emotion we see in the following scene when the two lovers take their leave of one another. Lorenzo, however, loves his villainy, and his instruments of villainy: 'Oh sweet, sweet policy, I hug thee' (123). Night, setting for murder, becomes his bride, a 'yawning beldam with her jetty skin' (110); and Lazarotto, his assassin, is wooed as 'my soul's spaniel, my life's jetty substance' (iii. 1), and later 'my sweet mischief . . . | Honey damnation' (14–15). The scene is not homoerotic: its horror derives from the inappropriateness of the sexual metaphor. Lazarotto adopts a woman's role, with an image of pregnancy; but the child of their union is to be a murder. Moreover, Lazarotto is no beauty: he is, in fact, a walking skeleton.

Emaciation here has the same literal and symbolic connotations as in *Romeo and Juliet*: the assassin's 'famish'd jaws look like the chap of death' (i. 115). Less efficient than his metaphysical counterpart, he ends up killing the wrong man: his identification as Death contributes mainly to the comic-grotesque tone of the sequence. Poverty is more important: there is still a strong thematic concern with money. Lazarotto shares characteristics with a number of previous assassins: he 'will do anything for gold' (119); he prides

[18] T. Rawlins, *The Rebellion* (1640), D4^v.

[19] L. Babb, *The Elizabethan Malady* (East Lansing, Mich., 1951), 84.

himself (mistakenly) on his skill, criticizing Lorenzo at one point for being 'slack in murder' (vii. 60); and like *Arden of Faversham*'s Black Will he has his own professional ethics—

> Gold, I am true;
> I had my hire, and thou shalt have thy due.   (62–3)

Moreover, when he accepts his part in Lorenzo's quasi-erotic role play, he introduces his own qualification. He conceives sexuality in mercenary terms, casting himself as a prostitute: 'for gold and chink | Makes the punk wanton and the bawd to wink.' (iii. 31–2) His terms of endearment are reserved for his 'dainty ducks' (30), the ducats he is to receive.[20] However, the play differs from previous treatments of the economic theme in that Lazarotto is not simply avaricious: beneath his passion for money there is privation. He is certainly starving; the reason, it appears, is that he is a younger son with no expectations to borrow on. The consequence is desperation: 'What dares not he do that ne'er hopes to inherit?' (58)

Stage hirers were quick to take the point. Men like Chapman's Bussy D'Ambois and Dekker's Gazetto are earmarked (mistakenly) as potential assassins because they are poor: Monsieur believes Bussy will 'take | Fire at advancement' (I. i. 49–50), and the King finds Gazetto 'crafty, envious, poore, and bold' (III. ii. 88). Macbeth's first pair of murderers, too, are poverty-stricken: Banquo, he tells them, has 'bowed you to the grave | And beggared yours for ever' (III. i. 91–2)—brought them to such penury, that is, that they cannot support themselves nor leave their descendants any patrimony.

In *The Malcontent*, there is a further twist: Mendoza first shows an interest in Malevole on hearing he has been banished from the court. If we take Malevole as a kind of court fool, then he has suffered the fate that was a constant threat to Feste in *Twelfth Night*: dismissal. Mendoza offers a job to a man whose alternative is unemployment. Similarly, the anonymous play *Charlemagne* (1604) opens with Didier, a courtier who has been cheated of his wealth, proposing to 'rayse a broken state by service' (115) to the villain, Ganelon; the service in question happens to be a poisoning. The prospect of poverty proves to be as corrupting as the prolonged experience of it.

The hiring of a man who has just lost his source of income became a recurrent situation: it is how the Duke of Orleans procures the murderous services of Dubois in *The Honest Man's Fortune*, for example. This enabled, in particular, a fresh approach to the problem of the discharged soldier. We saw in Chapter 4 that murder was a natural profession for a trained man of violence to take on; but with more emphasis on the moment of discharge, the economic pressures on such men loom larger. In *King Lear*, the war ends, and an officer considers his options when Edmund offers him a job:

[20] 'Duck' was a common term of endearment at the time (*OED* sb.[1] 3a).

> I cannot draw a cart,
> Nor eat dried oats. If it be man's work, I'll do't. (Q: xxiv. 37–8)

There is a touch of desperation here: he will take any work if it keeps him from the animal life of unaccommodated man. In John Fletcher's *Valentinian*, the issue is treated at greater length. The cashiered soldier Pontius cannot find other employment because he has only one skill to sell:

> Could you not leave this killing way a little,
> (You must if here you would plant your selfe)[?] (III. ii. 14–15)

Seen from afar by Valentinian, he seems a suitable murderer; but since his initial cashiering, and his subsequent difficulties, stem also from his honesty, peacetime killing is no option for him and his only escape from the situation is by suicide.

That poverty made a man an assassin was a myth: the commonest crime of the Elizabethan pauper seems to have been theft, whereas murder was rare.[21] The groundwork for that myth was laid in Shakespeare's apothecary: traders in poisons and hired murderers belong to a similar milieu. However, the direct influence of *Romeo and Juliet* is traceable in only one, rather late play, Thomas May's *The Heir* (1620), which borrows the plot of lovers from rival families, amongst other situations from Shakespeare.[22] The play also includes a disguise scenario in which the character of Eugenio is hired, like Vindice, to murder his *alter ego*. His disguised persona is a needy man named Irus, after the beggar in the *Odyssey* who had become proverbial for poverty.[23] Willingness to take on work, of whatever kind, is part of the act: he admits, 'I was poore, | And want made me be hir'd.' (I1ʳ) His statement upon accepting the job derives directly from the words of the apothecary, transformed into an evasion of personal responsibility: ''tis poverty that does it, and not I' (E3ᵛ).

There was one key difference between the apothecary and an assassin, however. Shakespeare goes to great lengths to exonerate his character, as we have seen, but this was not possible with a murderer. Audiences were faced with an emotional oxymoron: the man's poverty evoked sympathy, his crime, condemnation. Jacobean and Caroline dramatists repeatedly try to wriggle out of this quandary by insisting that poverty does not in itself deprave a man. Some use the tragicomic device of the uncooperative assassin: Pontius in *Valentinian* is an obvious case in point. Others avoid the issue by making the character inherently evil-natured. The depraved Lazarotto, for example, is a villain who finds that 'this lazy age | . . . yields me no

---

[21] A. L. Beier, *Past and Present*, 64 (1974), 15–16; J. Samaha, *Law and Order in Historical Perspective* (1974), 22, 36.

[22] A. G. Chester, *Thomas May: Man of Letters* (Philadelphia, 1932), 87–8.

[23] Tilley, I. 101.

employments' (iii. 5–6). His very name is significant, and is stressed by multiple repetition when he first appears: derived from 'lazaretto', it suggests moral disease and putrefaction.

Some plays also suggest that the assassin's poverty is his own fault. For example, the bravo in *The Antiquary* claims to have 'no other means, nor way of living'; but when told that 'There are a thousand courses to subsist by', he insists,

> I; but a free and daring spirit scornes
> To stoope to servile waies, but will choose rather
> To purchase his revenew from his sword.   (F1ʳ)

Pressed, he proves driven by pride, not real necessity. Moreover, he shares Lazarotto's desire for 'employment to set wickednesse awork' (E3ʳ): he is not a bravo perforce through unemployment, but an unemployed bravo. (Of course, he is not really a bravo at all; but it is a good act.)

In *The Virgin Martyr* (1620), a tragedy of early Christian persecution by Thomas Dekker and Philip Massinger, the need for money itself is called into question. Among the notable characters of Dekker's scenes are Spungius and Hircius, the household servants of the title-character Dorothea. They are supported at her charge, so they want gold only to serve their vices at the tavern and the brothel: it is for these purposes that they misappropriate money given by their mistress for charitable distribution. Their destitution is their own doing, moreover: in betraying Dorothea for money, they cut off their long-term regular supply, as well as their means of living. The result is that they have to enter the employ of the villain's evil genius Harpax: 'Will any of you kill a man?' he asks them, 'Or stab a woman?' (III. iii. 197, 200); answering in the affirmative fits them to be the torturers of their former mistress.

None of this embodies a new approach to the relation of poverty and crime. Like the Elizabethan social theorists before them, the dramatists insist on good and evil character as determinants of men's actions in conditions of poverty, so they present their assassins as members of the thriftless poor. They are, in short, seeking to avoid radical social comment.

In *The Whore of Babylon* (1606), Dekker's Spenserian allegory of Elizabethan foreign affairs, the nettle is grasped: the figure of Campeius (representing Edmund Campion) elicits both pity and judgement by turns. Refused patronage by Titania (Queen Elizabeth), he develops a grudge against his country for 'not rewarding merit' (II. ii. 127) that makes him ripe for recruitment as an assassin by King Satyrane (Philip II). On his last appearance, the choric figure of Time ruefully sums up his career: 'A scholler makes a ruffian' (IV. i. 13). It is with that transformation that Dekker effects a change in our attitude.

Campeius is a victim of academic penury, a theme Dekker had already addressed sympathetically in an earlier play.[24] As such, he is representative of a genuine early Stuart social problem, the 'alienated intellectual' trained to occupy a station in life above that he was able to achieve in a time of full employment in high office.[25] His learning should have brought him better fortunes, he complains:

> I was not borne to this, not school'd to this,
> My parents spent not wealth on me to this.   (II. ii. 123–4)

Yet he is so 'nail'd downe by wilfull beggerie' (114) that he cannot even afford to travel in search of more lucrative employment. With Satyrane's assistance, he travels to Babylon (Rome), there to receive 'showers of gold' (III. i. 134). With his change of fortune comes the objective correlative of a change of clothes: we first see him dressed in a 'thred-bare gowne' (II. ii. 134), but Satyrane gives him 'rich attires' (149 s.d.) which are 'to be worne in Babylon' (163).

It seems a reasonable exchange: if we had sympathy for his poverty, we can also understand the attractions of patronage. But the scene in Babylon functions through dramatic irony, so we can see beyond Campeius' viewpoint. We have heard, as he has not, the Empress (the Pope) state at length her contempt for her instruments and her intention to betray them: we know that he is living in a fool's paradise. It is the thin end of the wedge: our sympathy has been qualified. Dekker soon changes it to judgement: by the time Campeius leaves the stage, he has consented to murder. The scholar has turned ruffian, and our pity has turned to condemnation.

The difference here from earlier treatments of the poverty-stricken killer (and from some later ones) is that moral judgement is contingent upon the action, not the action contingent upon moral judgement. In earlier cases, our assessment of the assassin's character was constant, determined by whether or not he was finally to go through with the murder. In contrast, we can change our mind about Campeius when necessary: we can feel pity for him, yet equally legitimately condemn him when his actions warrant it. He is a developing character who makes an existential choice which determines our subsequent attitude to him; but, unlike previous assassins such as Hubert, he chooses evil. With this, we have moved on to a new stage of the character's development.

[24] *Patient Grissil* (written in 1600), I. ii. 133–48.
[25] See M. H. Curtis, *Past and Present*, 23 (1962), 25–43.

IV

Once the assassin had become a figure of human as much as of moral interest, it was possible for individual dramatists to endow the character with internal processes. The earliest attempt to portray the psychology of a hired murderer was made by Thomas Heywood in a scene of his history play, *If You Know Not Me, You Know Nobody, Part 2* (1605); he was followed by Dekker in *The Whore of Babylon*, which covers some of the same events allegorically. Campeius is a somewhat spare example in the later play, but the centre of attention in both is the killer William Parry, a man who has committed himself to murder but finds that, in the end, he cannot do it. The focus of interest reflects the material: instead of a decision to commit a murder, we watch the inhibitions at work, the process of guilt.

Parry was among the earliest and most famous of the Roman Catholic traitors who undertook Elizabeth I's assassination. After being pardoned by the Queen for attempted murder, he had travelled on the Continent, where he was converted to Catholicism and persuaded to return to England and kill his benefactress; but though he maintained the pose of a loyal informer throughout 1584, his exposure early the next year brought him to a traitor's death.[26] The official account of his treason painted a black picture of a wicked malcontent since childhood; the two plays, however, are notable for the human qualities they attribute to Parry.

The case gave difficulty to contemporary commentators because Elizabeth's continuing patronage of the miscreant appeared dangerously rash. The official account takes on a curiously equivocal quality in its presentation of her behaviour. When Parry admits to involvement in a conspiracy, it is said,

any other Prince but her Majestie ... would rather have proceeded to the punishment of a subject that had waded so farre, as by othe and vowe to promise the taking away of her life . . . yet such was her goodnes, as in steade of punishing, she did deale so gratiously with him, as she suffered him not onely to have accesse unto her presence: but also many times to have private conference with her.[27]

Even after his exposure, 'her Majestie continued her singular and most Princely magnanimitie'.[28] She is princely, but singular among princes: anxiety over her recklessness is stifled in panegyric, but the contradiction reveals it presence nonetheless.

This tension is the greater in Heywood's play because the Earl of Leicester and the Queen appear as exponents of opposing opinions on Parry's fate.

[26] For a fuller account, see L. B. Smith, *Treason in Tudor England* (1986), 11–19.

[27] *A Trve and plaine declaration of the horrible Treasons, practised by William Parry the Traitor against the Queenes Maiestie* (1585), A2ᵛ–A3ʳ.

[28] Ibid. A3ᵛ.

There is no clear indication of a preferred view. Parry goes to the gallows as Leicester wishes, and at one point the Earl strikes a note of exasperation at his Queen's clemency:

> Let her alone, sheele pardon him againe:
> Good Queene we know you are too mercifull,
> To deale with Traitours of this monstrous kinde. (2370–2)

It is he, too, who has the last word on the subject: 'Good Queene you must be rul'd.' (2377) In a play which ostensibly celebrates Elizabeth's virtue, however, her views merit our serious consideration. Her remarks to herself on statecraft, picking up *Richard II*'s gardening analogy, give us an early indication of the gentler approach she is to take:

> Weedes must bee weeded out, yet weeded so,
> Till they doe hurt, let them a Gods name grow. (2329–30)

At this point the political 'weed' Parry 'offers to shoote' (2331 s.d.), but does not pull the trigger. It is a significant juxtaposition, raising the question of how far Parry has actually done harm—a question Elizabeth seeks to answer by assuring him that, if he repents, her clemency may be exercised again.

This clash between Leicester and Elizabeth is important because it crystallizes the tensions in the portrayal of Parry himself. The man's crime is horrifying—pointing a loaded pistol at an anointed monarch with intent to kill. To a degree, the scene supports the view of him as a villain:

> Heaven blesse our Soveraigne from her foes intent,
> The peace we have, is by her government, (2226–7)

remarks an anonymous courtier at the start; enter Parry in another significant juxtaposition. After some gossip about his background—attempted murder, conviction for burglary, royal pardon—the three lords leave Parry alone, and the scene takes a turn.

The assassin's soliloquy reveals him as a man torn with guilt over his intention. At one level, his problem is the same as the Messenger's in *King Leir*, the force of his vow to kill: he must be damned for murder or damned for forswearing. But there is a more personal dimension: his Catholic instigators have assured him that 'The deed is just and meritorious' (2291), and he has received papal absolution; but he is also intensely aware of his debt to the Queen for his pardon. This is a more human Parry than emerged from the government propaganda of 1585, and one more commensurate with Elizabeth's attitude: a man whose conscience finally retards him from murder. For all that he himself attributes his quaking to her supernatural protection, the action tells us otherwise. When he tries to shoot her, it is in the back, and when she turns to face him he tries to hide his weapon.[29] He is ashamed to let her see him repay her kindness with treason.

Heywood's main interest seems to be in the human qualities of Parry which disable him as an assassin: as we might expect, he takes the Queen's part. Had he wished to portray a straightforward villain, he could have laid more emphasis on how he got into the situation, perhaps extending the episode to include scenes of his conversion and recruitment. It is true that Parry begins and ends the scene as such a figure, simplistically branded 'a Traitour' (2374), but in the interim we have seen the human being that term obscures, psychologically plausible in his sense of personal obligation. This is what Elizabeth too can see: it is she who gives him the opportunity to resolve his dilemma by falling on one side or the other, penitent sinner or obdurate villain. Leicester merely refuses to make such fine discriminations; and the result is the wicked William Parry of official Tudor history.

Dekker's is a subtler and less sympathetic, but equally human portrayal of Parry—or Paridell, as he is called. On his first appearance he receives his original pardon for murder, but unlike Heywood's version he is far from grateful:

> To run in debt thus basely for a life,
> To spend which, had beene glory! O most vile!   (II. i. 169–70)

Dekker underlines the ingratitude by juxtaposing him with Campeius, who is refused favour in the same scene. Both men go on to turn assassin, but at least Campeius has a reason for his grudge; his presence serves to set Paridell's depravity into relief.

Paridell's resolve to kill the Queen is left to our inference: we know that he has already attempted a murder, and that he resents being beholden to her for his pardon; when he next appears, the forces of Babylon have already recruited him as a killer. But his course is far from straightforward. It is a *donné* of the play that guilt comes inevitably and indelibly with murder: Paridell himself admits that he is 'Deservedly' (II. i. 155) sentenced to death; and guilt is always the most sensitive spot in Babylon's various assassins. Titania has an uncanny ability to play on this sensitivity for her own defence. In a scene where the court proves to be devoid of armed guards, she commends an assassin on his sword and remarks what a good murder weapon it would make; he departs silently, 'with shame' (IV. ii. 57). Moments later, she cows Ropus (Lopez) in the same manner: when he tells her she will never taste the like of his 'new extraction', she replies, 'Why, shall that be my last?' (76–7) Faced with knowingness like this, the murderers simply do not have the gall to go through with it.

---

[29] This is clear from the fact that she takes 18 lines to notice it: she sees him at l. 2332, sees the pistol at l. 2350.

These are sketches: Paridell's guilt is fully developed. On arrival on the Continent, he first discusses his intent with a number of his Babylonian confederates. Two things are striking: his search for conviction in legality, morality, and high motives, and his shying from the deed itself. His interlocutors are very sensitive to the latter: when he states his intention to go to Babylon, not Fairyland (England), he is asked, 'You change not byas[?]' (III. ii. 58); and his statement that, having sworn to do it, he has no choice, is met with 'Do you stagger?' (90) If his vow provides a crutch for his staggering, then so does his high-mindedness: he wants to root his murder in something more than ingratitude. The matter comes to a head in discussion with an Albanois (Scotsman): Paridell tries to wrest moral assurance from him, but the answer is not the one he wanted. According to observers, they are 'hard at it', but in the next line Paridell disengages: 'the time, | Doe's pull me from your sweet societie' (168–9). The lameness of the excuse is revealing: he is desperate to get away because, if he pursues the issue any further, he will be forced to question his own lofty motives.

Paridell's return to Fairyland is marked by a further stage in his self-doubt: by confessing to Titania and posing as an *agent provocateur* he hopes to leave himself another option. But the gambit fails: the Queen's response is non-committal, and she has arranged for his admission to be overheard by her councillor Florimell. Learning this disconcerts the traitor, and he worries that he has undone himself: in trying to keep his options open he has merely closed them. On course for assassination, he has to take an uncertain refuge in the purity of his motives. When a kinsman questions these once again, his response is to divert attention to pragmatic concerns: Titania is ill-guarded, and his escape will be an easy one.

If Heywood's Parry was a man with a moral dilemma, Dekker's is a man trying to avoid one. He is in the grip of an evil obsession and does not want to face the fact: adopting the role of Babylonian assassin is a means of denying depravity; but the repressed returns. Whether or not he kills the Queen is ultimately a matter of his conscious choice.

His final scene, alone with Titania, is written for suspense: we have had hints that his kinsman will inform on him, and we wait to see if he can bring himself to do the deed before this happens. He finds the situation intolerable, and craves release from it: 'O unhappie man; | That thou shouldst breathe thus long' (v. ii. 69–70). When he makes a move to stab her in the back, he bungles it and has to claim, significantly, that it was a suicide attempt. Further agonies ensue over his vow:

> For not dooing am I damde: how are my spirits
> Halde, tortured, and growne wilde?   (110–11)

Re-reading his warrant from Babylon prompts him to another attempt, but then at last the courtiers arrive with his kinsman: 'As he offers to step to her, he staies sodainly' (139 s.d.). It is significant that he should stop himself without restraint: it is still his decision. Recourse to the warrant was simply another attempt to pull legality around him, another desperate evasion. He meets exposure and execution not with fear or fortitude but relief: 'Tis welcome, a blacke life, ends in blacke fame.' (162) It is a final release of tension, a final admission of the man he truly is.

Dekker's treatment of Paridell made an important advance in the history of the stage assassin. The character, among the most individualized in the play, carries one of the main threads of the action. He appears in five scenes, as many as Titania and one more than his employer the Empress; his part, at roughly 275 lines, is one of the longest, with only Titania, the Empress, and Como having more to say. It is, moreover, longer than any previous assassin's, except for characters like Malevole who transcend the role. Like earlier assassins with substantial parts, he is independent of his employer, but unlike them, he has passed beyond a stereotype: the principal purpose of two of his five scenes is to develop his internal processes. Dekker has taken a character type that was usually secondary and made it a principal centre of attention and interest.

This revolutionary and original move may seem a surprising departure in Dekker. Not only has he been called 'the most traditional of Elizabethan writers', he is also a dramatist noted for his strongly Protestant allegiances: he is an unexpected author to find in the *avant garde* of Jacobean drama, and an unlikely one to be giving serious consideration to the human predicament of a Roman Catholic hireling, especially in the wake of the Gunpowder Plot of 1605, a time when traitors' ends were to be smiled at.[30]   However, it is worth recalling his similarly unorthodox portrayal of Campeius in the same play, and, later, his unconventional approach to another assassin scenario in the Gazetto episode of *Match Me in London*, discussed in the last chapter. All three characters are given a greater degree of independence and consciousness than was usual for assassins. This will seem less anomalous in the light of other aspects of his work.

Critical estimates of Dekker are twofold: he has been portrayed as a stern moralist, who condemns the underworld more vigorously than other writers on the subject; but other commentators have stressed 'his humanitarian spirit' and his 'boundless charity' towards his characters.[31] Each view privileges one half of a divided artistic personality: Campeius has the attention of each

[30] M. C. Bradbrook, *The Growth and Structure of Elizabethan Comedy*, new edn. (Cambridge, 1973), 121; J. Gasper, *The Dragon and the Dove* (Oxford, 1990), *passim*.
[31] N. Berlin, *SEL* 6 (1966), 263–77; F. S. Boas, *An Introduction to Stuart Drama* (Oxford, 1946), 147; Bradbrook, *Elizabethan Comedy*, 128.

side in turn as he transforms from poor scholar to vicious traitor. These two halves imply different approaches to characterization. Dekker is evidently in judgemental mode in the portrayal of Spungius and Hircius in *The Virgin Martyr*, who are simply worthless and unmitigated villains; but in creating more complex figures, he draws on resources of fellow-feeling to enter, provisionally, into their mental world.

This is not to say that we exonerate Paridell and Gazetto: Dekker has enough human sympathy to allow them autonomy of thought and action, but he does not necessarily approve the action they take; as in a Browning dramatic monologue, sympathy and judgement are in tension. In this respect, these characters appeal to the early Jacobeans' interest in premeditation and the experience of evil: we respond in much the same way to Macbeth. There is a signal difference, however: Dekker does not allow murderous intent to lead to murderous action. Moreover, both Paridell and Gazetto are reformed (though, in Paridell's case, not reprieved) at the end of the play: Paridell admits that his life has been 'blacke' (v. ii. 162), and Gazetto turns from murderousness to sheepish benignity. The tension between the two sides of Dekker has been unstable, and dominance ultimately rests with the moralist: one side can allow the other to dabble in criminal psychology only if, in the end, the prospective assassin does not make himself a murderer; and even then, the characters must be neatly pigeon-holed into the appropriate moral stereotype, at some cost to plausibility in the case of Gazetto.

Dekker opened up a new way of portraying the assassin, but he lacked the artistic courage to lay aside morality for long enough to exploit his own innovation effectively. In his *œuvre*, the assassin who kills cuts himself off from sympathy and centrality: Dekker never gave serious treatment to such a figure. For that we must turn to the work of one of his associates: John Webster.

9

WEBSTER'S KILLERS

I

The Renaissance courts of John Webster's tragedies swarm with assassins. The plays depict a society in which aristocratic lust and honour pursues its intrigues through murder. Hired killers are the skilled technicians of such a society, the men who do the essential but dirty job of putting inconvenient people out of the way. Such men appear not only in a number of cameo parts, but also as major characters: Flamineo and Lodovico in *The White Devil*, and Daniel de Bosola in *The Duchess of Malfi* (1614).

The critical fortunes of these figures have been variable. In recent decades, their importance has been rated very highly: in 1957, a case was even made for Bosola as the central tragic figure of *The Duchess of Malfi*.[1] Yet only half a century before, E. E. Stoll dismissed the same character as an empty device: 'Really, he is like the Messengers, the Prologues or Epilogues, or the person last on the stage at the end of the scene, who has to drag the bodies off,— a dramaturgic puppet, a fine sort of stage-property.'[2] The evidence is against Stoll. Webster created Bosola much as Shakespeare created the witches in *Macbeth*, by combining a series of minor figures in his source. Had he simply wanted machinery to do Duke Ferdinand's bidding, he need not have bothered. Bosola and Flamineo are among the longest parts in their respective plays: the question is not whether, but why, they are major characters.

This is a question because, as we have seen in the foregoing chapters, hired murderers do not make natural leading roles—hence, presumably, Stoll's assumption. From its earliest beginnings in *Cambises*, the type had been a cat's-paw for a more important character. When such a figure became the centre of attention, as in *Bussy D'Ambois*, it was by seizing control of his destiny and refusing to be another man's instrument—in effect, by ceasing to be an assassin at all. Webster's characters, in contrast, are manipulated to the end by their aristocratic employers.

In several respects, Webster was influenced by recent trends in the portrayal of the assassin: Flamineo's poverty and Bosola's melancholy are standard traits of early Jacobean killers, as we saw in the last chapter. Webster may also have had in mind Cyril Tourneur's Borachio in *The Atheist's Tragedy*

[1] C. G. Thayer, *Studies in Philology*, 54 (1957), 162–71.

[2] E. E. Stoll, *John Webster* (Boston, 1905), 126.

(1609): like Bosola, he is a scholar, 'read | In Nature and her large philosophy' (I. i. 3–4).[3] Perhaps most influential of all, though, was Webster's friendship with Thomas Dekker, one of the first dramatists to make the assassin a centre of human interest.

Webster began his career as a playwright working in collaboration with Dekker between 1602 and 1605, but since the work of Stoll—who did for Webster what Dowden did for Shakespeare—it has been generally assumed that with *The White Devil* he broke free from Dekker's influence to enter a new phase of his artistic career.[4] Evidence in the play, however, suggests that he kept up the connection. Given his known habits of composition, it need not be significant that he quotes a phrase almost verbatim from *The Whore of Babylon*.[5] What is more revealing is that he alludes several times to aspects of Dutch society, references which have not all been traced to printed sources.[6] This is suggestive because the Low Countries were a particular interest of Dekker's, who may have been of Dutch extraction; and because Webster does not make similar allusions in *The Duchess of Malfi*, written in 1614 after Dekker had been imprisoned for debt. It is plausible, then, that Dekker was taking an interest in his former protégé's work at the time he was writing *The White Devil*, and perhaps influenced the decision to première the play with the Queen's Men, the company for which he was working at the time—auspices that Webster was later to regret.[7]

Whatever the validity of this hypothesis, Webster certainly knew his former collaborator's ground-breaking portrayal of Paridell in *The Whore of Babylon*, and this probably influenced his own innovative treatment of the assassin type. His predecessors had been interested in the people who act and are acted upon: the go-betweens were primarily functional. Dekker had broken out of that mould, and this would have been congenial to Webster. His tragedies deal with people who cannot direct their own lives, cannot make their own choices. His theme is, so to speak, the subjectivity of the subjected, so the central characters of his plays are 'the people that things are done to', as Muriel Bradbrook has put it.[8] He is fascinated, for example, by the restricted social lot of women, unable to marry without the consent of a father or brother or even, like Leonora in *The Devil's Law-Case* (1617),

---

[3] Webster probably knew the play: he seems to have imitated a passage from it (I. iv. 128) in *The White Devil* (III. ii. 274).

[4] Stoll, *John Webster*, 43–4, 83.

[5] *The White Devil*, III. ii. 80, from T. Dekker, *The Whore of Babylon*, v. i. 81; on Webster's composition, see R. W. Dent, *John Webster's Borrowing* (Berkeley and Los Angeles, 1960).

[6] *The White Devil*, I. ii. 33, II. i. 321–2, III. ii. 6, 86, and the notes to these passages in the Revels edition.

[7] For further possible links between the two authors at the time of *The White Devil's* composition, see Stoll, *John Webster*, 20–2, and J. R. Brown, *Philological Quarterly*, 31 (1952), 353–8.

[8] M. C. Bradbrook, *John Webster: Citizen and Dramatist* (1980), 119.

a son. Assassins, then, are of interest for the very condition of instrumentality
that earlier characters had to transcend if they were to take centre stage: it
is their inability to break free of that condition that makes them Webster's
tragic heroes.

II

Many roads lead to Flamineo: he amalgamates such diverse character types
as pander, satirist, counterfeit madman, Machiavellian politician, and assassin.
But it is not helpful to try to break him down into these constituents: he
takes the roles by turns, but they are all within his personal capability. He
is a complex individual, not a stereotype, so to see him clearly, we must see
him whole.

The relationship between Flamineo and his master, the Duke of Bracciano,
is delineated at once:

BRACCIANO
   Flamineo.
FLAMINEO   My lord.
BRACCIANO   Quite lost Flamineo.
FLAMINEO
   Pursue your noble wishes, I am prompt
   As lightning to your service.   (I. ii. 3–5)

The Duke has the power to command the Secretary's attention, but all that
follows is an expression of despairing infatuation: his love for Flamineo's
married sister Vittoria is a hopeless one. In such intimacy lies dependence:
Flamineo is the man who will take steps to see that he is not 'quite lost'.

It is Flamineo, then, who dominates the scene: the climax may be the
liaison of Bracciano and Vittoria, but it is Flamineo's triumph, and he watches
voyeuristically as it proceeds. The foregoing action has concentrated on his
arrangements for this moment, while Bracciano was shunted off into a closet
at an early stage. He acts as 'fixer' in the affair; if he has any individual
antecedent at this point, it is not a hired assassin, but Mosca. The manipulation of his brother-in-law Camillo underlines the role: he pretends to fix
Camillo's marital problems even as he fixes Vittoria's adultery. By the end
of the scene, it is clear that he will be called upon to fix a murder.

There is more to the scene than a consummate display of stage-manage-
ment, though. At the moment towards which all Flamineo's efforts have
been geared, the wooing of his sister, a discordant note is struck, and we
are shown how very fragile is his control of the situation. That discord is
his mother, Cornelia, who also watches the seduction, with a response quite
opposite to Flamineo's relish. At the moment Bracciano shows his hand—

'you shall to me at once | Be dukedom, health, wife, children, friends and all' (267–8)—she intervenes, and her reproaches send Vittoria scurrying shamefacedly away.

The effect of the incident on the future development of the plot is slight: it demonstrates how Vittoria is apt to crack under pressure (as she is later to do at the House of Convertites and at her death), but neither the adultery nor the proposed murders of Camillo and Isabella, the two lovers' inconvenient spouses, are averted. Cornelia's importance lies not in her influence on events, which is minimal, but in the fact that she is someone whom Flamineo cannot manipulate: whereas he talked Bracciano and Camillo off the stage with ease, his efforts to get rid of her are conspicuously ineffective. For the first time, he meets resistance; so for the first time Webster has the opportunity to explore his character.

His response to his mother's intervention is revealing: after a rather spiteful gibe at her sense of honour, he asks, ironically,

> I would fain know where lies the mass of wealth
> Which you have hoarded for my maintenance. (311–12)

Maintenance is a concern which crops up frequently with him, when his guard is down, and when he is feigning madness: he inhabits a 'world which life of means deprives' (III. iii. 97). His father, it appears, sold all his land, put money in his purse, 'and like a fortunate fellow, | Died ere the money was spent' (I. ii. 318–19)—but not long before, we infer. In other words, he converted a source of regular but modest income into a lump sum, a common expedient of the early Jacobean social climber out to raise money quickly in order to finance conspicuous consumption.[9] In effect, he cheated his eldest son of the patrimony that, in seventeenth-century terms, he might legitimately expect. In consequence, Flamineo explains in an affective passage, he had to support himself at university by performing menial tasks for his tutor, and only secured a degree by underhand means, 'conspiring with a beard' (323).[10] Still conscious of the discomforts of privation, Bracciano's service is his alternative option.

There is a significant dislocation in Flamineo's discourse here: Cornelia's forestalling of his sister's adultery seems discontinuous with the forceful account of his financial situation that it brings forth. The two subjects are linked in his mind: he sees his hopes of future advancement—bearing his beard 'out of the level | Of my lord's stirrup' (313–14)—dashed by his mother's subversion of his efforts. This calls into question the nature of his

---

[9] L. Stone, *The Crisis of the Aristocracy* (Oxford, 1965), 37, 164–5, 184–8.

[10] The phrase is obscure. It is possible that Webster wrote 'beadle'—the officer responsible for collecting graduation fees—and that 'beard' was printed in error (by attraction from 'beard' ten lines earlier).

agency in the seduction, which was stressed so heavily earlier in the scene. His relationship with Bracciano is not a conventional one of master and servant: we have seen that Bracciano's initial assertion of authority, summoning his secretary, breaks down at once into a kind of complicity. Flamineo actively encourages his desire for Vittoria, because he hopes to gain by it: 'I made a kind of path | To her and mine own preferment' (III. i. 36–7), he tells his brother Marcello later. Such expectations account for the engagement with which he watches the tryst, and his fury when it goes wrong.

Nothing we learn of Bracciano in the course of the play gives us reason to doubt that the situation is primarily of Flamineo's making. The Duke is a natural aristocrat, a man of poise and *sprezzatura* in verbal encounters. Such is his self-confidence that he can even incriminate himself in court and get away with it.[11] But he is not a man of action. We see him engage in physical violence only once, and that is in the (as he thinks) controlled circumstances of a fencing display; it is far more his style to watch the murders he has commissioned at long range, courtesy of a conjurer. Moreover, only once do we see him make a decision, to engineer Vittoria's escape from the House of Convertites where the court confines her after Camillo's murder. Even this is a sign of practical ineptitude: he takes the idea from a letter written to her by his former brother-in-law, Francisco de Medici, which is what Francisco intended in sending it in the first place. This is simply an extension of an already established characteristic: he needs people to make his decisions for him. It is Vittoria who proposes the murders; and it is Flamineo who decides that he shall pursue his interest in Vittoria, whom he, 'Quite lost', had thought inaccessible.

Arranging adultery must proceed to arranging murder if Flamineo is to achieve the advancement he seeks. Should Vittoria turn out to be just a sexual diversion for Bracciano, his beard will remain at stirrup-level; but if Bracciano marries her, he will become the brother-in-law of a Duke, and entitled to ride with him. From the start, then, his scheme includes the murder of Camillo and Isabella: the assassin himself sets up the situation in which his services are required. His hopes for promotion are stressed again, then, when he introduces Bracciano to the professional poisoner, Dr Julio, who is to undertake Isabella's death. Totally in control of events, Flamineo explains, 'when knaves come to preferment they rise as gallowses are raised i' th' Low Countries, one upon another's shoulders' (II. i. 320–2). The poisoner is being raised by Flamineo to the Duke's service, but like the criminal in the impromptu Dutch hanging, he will be left dangling while the secretary walks off to his reward.

It is the tragedy of Flamineo that things do not go according to plan. He

---

[11] Because Vittoria has said that she did not know of her husband's death before being told at her arraignment, he incriminates them both when he tells the court that he was at her house on the night of the murder to extend his charity to her as a widow (III. ii. 161–3).

is arrested after murdering Camillo, and Bracciano shows no obvious interest in protecting him. Throughout the second half of the play he is less confident and less in control: events have passed out of his hands, so all he can do is hope, and fear. When he meets Bracciano at the House of Convertites, he is afraid that he will suffer the usual fate of hired assassins, 'a Spanish fig, or an Italian sallet' (IV. ii. 61) from his employer. At the same time, he still has expectations of reward. Again Mosca-like, he raises the subject peri- phrastically in a fable, but denies the application when Bracciano makes it: it is humiliating to have to ask.[12] And because he will not ask, and so receive a straight answer, he lives in constant uncertainty about his future: a state, by turns, of hope and rancour.

It is his constant capacity to see hope that keeps him in anxiety. The marriage of Vittoria and Bracciano 'Confirms me happy' (v. i. 3), and even the Duke's death, his obligations unfulfilled, has 'some good luck' (v. iii. 80) in it, since it results in Vittoria's becoming regent during the minority of Giovanni, Bracciano's son. But throughout Act v Flamineo mistrusts uncertain odds: he advises Mulinassar not to accept Bracciano's 'bare promise' (v. i. 134) of a pension, and he chooses to murder Marcello rather than risk an evenly matched duel. Finally he determines to 'be resolv'd what my rich sister means | T'assign me for my service' (v. iv. 117–18), and then, conversely, whether she intends his death. This is the purpose of his ruse with the suicide pact and unloaded pistols. That Vittoria shoots him and proposes to break her side of the bargain confirms his suspicions:

> I knew
> One time or other you would find a way
> To give me a strong potion.   (v. vi. 152–4)

When he rises unharmed, he rises dispossessed of hope: all that is left to him is her murder, and his own death.

III

The White Devil is not formless, as some critics would have us believe.[13] Its structure is an elegant *chiasmus* of plot and counter-plot: the first two Acts rise to the murders of Isabella and Camillo, the last two to the revenge of the Medici faction for these murders. The two sections are parallel: each has, early on, a set-piece wooing scene between Bracciano and Vittoria, watched by Flamineo; and each ends with violence. But between the two there occurs a shift in the balance of power. In the first half, Francisco and Cardinal

[12] Cf. B. Jonson, *Volpone*, I. i. 53–66.
[13] This viewpoint is summarized by Robert Ornstein in *The Moral Vision of Jacobean Tragedy* (Madison and Milwaukee, 1960), 128–9.

Monticelso engineer Camillo's absence from Rome in order to facilitate Bracciano's affair and so draw him into 'notorious scandal' (II. i. 388), but they are outplayed because the Duke has plans of his own: Francisco remarks that he would rather have given his sister to death than to marriage with Bracciano, but we have seen murder plotted, and know that the two alternatives are no longer distinct. In the second half, however, it is Bracciano who is outplayed by Francisco, in arranging Vittoria's flight from Rome; and his wedding, too, turns out to be fatal. Act III, then, is the fulcrum: the two sides face off, secretary against secretary, instigators against bereaved, and assassin against assassin.

Flamineo's opposite number in the Medici faction, his brother aside, is Count Lodovico. Each man is the inverse of the other: Lodovico is a fallen aristocrat, Flamineo an aspirant commoner; and whereas Flamineo's career spirals downwards to tragedy, Lodovico's takes an upward path to the consummation of his revenge. When they first meet in Act III, one is a suspect in a murder case, the other a criminal returned unlawfully to Rome. They are equals in standing as they are equals in discontent, a position expressed in the grotesque compact of melancholy they make with one another. The agreement is soon broken because the equality it is based on is the equality of men passing one another. By the end of the scene, it is a thing of the past: Lodovico has been pardoned, and he swaggers over his erstwhile, downwardly mobile partner, provoking a quarrel. Their temporary equilibrium has served only to show the opposite developments of their careers.

Where Flamineo has a position in Bracciano's service, Lodovico begins as an outcast, 'Banish'd' (I. i. 1) from Rome. His ejaculation is the first thing we hear in the play; the opening scene continues by developing and explaining it. Two versions of Count Lodovico quickly emerge: according to him, he is a victim of the machinations of others, both Fortune and 'great enemies' (7); but Gasparo and Antonelli, his interlocutors, insist that he is 'justly doom'd' (13) for a career of riot and excess that ended in murder. The killings are the crimes for which he has been banished, and again there are two points of view: to Gasparo, they are 'Bloody and full of horror', to Lodovico, 'flea-bitings' (32). Antonelli encourages stoical acceptance of his lot, but Lodovico insists on seeing himself as a man wronged, and wronged in particular by Vittoria and Bracciano, to whom it seems he has sued unsuccessfully for help.

His recourse, then, is revenge:

> I'll make Italian cut-works in their guts
> If ever I return.   (52–3)

This may seem nothing more than pique, but his grudge against Bracciano soon develops. In the course of Acts II and III, he gravitates towards the opposing faction, suing to Monticelso for repeal, entering Isabella's household at Padua, and finally returning to Rome as young Giovanni's escort. Since, we are told, he is emotionally and sexually attracted to the Duchess of Bracciano, her murder seals his enmity for the Duke: her total fidelity to wedlock is a cause for jealousy, and this turns to fury when she is killed—the anger of a man who sees something he values destroyed by a less appreciative owner. Revenge for lost honour becomes revenge for lost life.

We saw in Chapter 4 that, although the revenger and the assassin were distinct in the contemporary mind, the one might be a good choice to be the other. So it is with Lodovico: he has sworn to avenge Isabella's murder, but Francisco hopes a thousand ducats will strengthen his resolution—

> 'Tis gold must such an instrument procure,
> With empty fist no man doth falcons lure.   (IV. i. 134–5)

With money reinforcing revenge, Lodovico himself says, he is 'doubly arm'd' (IV. iii. 151).

To a degree, Lodovico has always been Francisco's instrument: in one respect it is his utility to the Medici faction that generates the rise in his fortunes during the play. In the first half, it suits Francisco for him to be an outcast and a pirate, for it supplies a pretext for getting Camillo out of Rome. In the second half, however, he is more directly useful, as chief assassin, no doubt in part because of the prior experience which caused him to be banished in the first place; so he is brought back into society under Francisco's patronage. The problem is that he could be caught in a circular process: he could end up being banished for murder again, or worse; so he needs to be assured that he has a patron powerful enough to pervert the course of justice for him. Monticelso, newly elected Pope, is the obvious choice: the knowledge that the murder has papal approval, Francisco thinks, 'will confirm more than all the rest' (134). It does not matter that Monticelso himself is not in Francisco's confidence: he simply sends the assassin gold with a lie about its origins. Making Lodovico believe himself protected is more important than arranging protection itself.

The ruse portends the usual double-cross; but it never comes to this, because Francisco has misunderstood Lodovico. His behaviour is not what might be expected from a professional killer. He never invokes his papal protection, and he seems more solicitous for his employer's safety than his own: he counsels Francisco to leave Padua before the final murders are enacted, and he has settled his own affairs in case he 'should chance to fall' (V. v. 4). In the end, it is true, he names Francisco as the instigator of the killings:

GIOVANNI
By what authority have you committed
This massacre?
LODOVICO   By thine.
GIOVANNI   Mine?
LODOVICO   Yes, thy uncle,
Which is a part of thee, enjoin'd us to't.   (v. vi. 284–6)

But this is not the betrayal of a frightened man, nor does it endanger
Francisco: for all his hopes that everyone involved 'shall taste our justice'
(292), the boy Duke of Bracciano has no power to try the ruler of an
independent state. Rather Lodovico's revelation is a taunt. The joke serves
to disorientate Giovanni in his first moment of ducal grandeur. The follow-
up then tells the child that a man he loved and took as a pattern of virtue
has 'turn'd murderer' (290). Gleefully exposing the boy's innocence, the killer
steals the judge's thunder.

Lodovico can do this because he has achieved a satisfaction that transcends
personal survival: neither the prospect of execution nor the restoration of
order can disconcert him, so he dominates the final moments of the play, as
he did its first scene.[14] Throughout, his approach to murder has shown the
marks of the aesthete and connoisseur: it is he who speaks of stab-wounds
as openwork embroidery, 'Italian cut-works' (I. i. 52), and he who complains
of Francisco's dullness in rejecting an inventive method of killing Bracciano,
one that will be 'recorded for example' (v. i. 76), in favour of one of tried
and tested efficiency. When captured, he shows the artist's total absorption
in his work, irrespective of its consequences:

                    I do glory yet,
          That I can call this act mine own:—for my part,
          The rack, the gallows, and the torturing wheel
          Shall be but sound sleeps to me,—here's my rest—
          I limb'd this night-piece and it was my best.   (v. vi. 293–7)

It is the absorption, too, of the revenger: in this lies Francisco's misunderstanding and the most fundamental contrast with Flamineo.

Flamineo undertakes panderism and murder in the expectation of a reward
which he never receives: 'Why here's an end of all my harvest, he has given
me nothing' (v. iii. 187). He attempts to better himself in society, but all he
achieves is degradation and rejection; all that is left to him is naked self-
determination—'at myself I will begin and end' (v. vi. 258). This is the point

---

[14] I suggest, then, that it was as Lodovico, not Flamineo as is usually supposed, that, as
Webster put it, the worth of Richard Perkins's acting crowned the beginning and end of the
play: he mentions Perkins as a friend, not a principal actor, and Perkins is not known to have
played another leading role until after 1626. (*The White Devil*, ed. J. R. Brown [1960], introduction,
p. xxiii.)

at which Lodovico begins the play. Antonelli counsels him in his banishment to 'Have a full man within you' (I. i. 45); and the self-sufficiency he discovers is in the consuming passion of revenge. Revenge is his reason for wanting to return to Rome, not reintegration into society; so there is ultimately no need for Francisco to give him assurance of safety after he has committed the murders. Whereas Flamineo kills for advancement, the killing itself is Lodovico's *raison d'être*—Francisco's gold is welcome, but incidental to him. At the conclusion, then, Flamineo's talk is of extinction and nothingness, whereas Lodovico has achieved fulfilment: the play presents the triumph of a man hired to be the assassin he is not, and the tragedy of an assassin without hire.

IV

Flamineo and Bosola are often treated as a pair, subject to generalizations that apply equally well to either. It is true that there are similarities between them: we hear of Bosola's university career at Padua, for example, and he too kills in the hope of a pension only to be disappointed. But if we press these similarities too far, all three of Webster's major assassins lose out: the part of Lodovico, counterpointing Flamineo, is marginalized, and so are the clear differences between the two university men.

We can begin to appreciate these differences if we examine a trait common to both. Each character takes the role of a satirical commentator, a dramatically alienated intellectual anatomizing the behaviour of his social betters; but each plays the role with an individual voice. Flamineo speaks with a kind of acute, sardonic knowingness: whatever his subject, he is constantly engaged, relishing the act of observation. Moreover, he has a sense of humour: his metaphors characteristically make witty application of one situation to another. In Bosola's mouth, however, tropes express bitterness: 'Thou art a box of worm-seed, at best, but a salvatory of green mummy' (IV. ii. 124–5). Commentary spills over into railing, and his remarks are not always occasioned by particular situations: his attack on the midwife's use of cosmetics, for example, is quite uncalled-for. Antonio's statement that he 'rails at those things which he wants' (I. i. 25) is wide of the mark, though it could apply to Flamineo: Bosola's caustic satire is not a sign of ambition but of a fundamentally life-hating nature.

Unlike Flamineo, moreover, Bosola is given no particular social background. At the time of the action, he is already a displaced person, an ex-convict who has been a *forzado* in the galleys. The fact is insisted upon in the first scene (it is mentioned three times), though the exact circumstances are never made clear: Bosola speaks of a two-year period (34–5), Delio of

seven years (70). What is important is that, for however long, he has been
through an experience that was a by-word for the depths of misery.[15] In the
galleys, a later commentator remarked, were to be found 'people ... who
are so weary of themselves and their lives that they are not terrified by any
danger'.[16]

Like most elements of the character, Bosola's background in penal ser-
vitude was Webster's invention. Perhaps he had in mind the case of Scoto
of Mantua, sentenced to the galleys for poisoning the Cardinal Bembo's
cook and impersonated by Volpone during this enforced absence.[17] A
cardinal is also involved in Bosola's crime, though this time as its suborner.
The relationship between the two men is central to Bosola's situation at the
start of the play, which is not unlike that of the later Flamineo: both live in
hopeful uncertainty. The position is an impossible one. An ex-convict is not
a suitable recipient of ecclesiastical patronage, so though the Cardinal has a
use for him, he 'would not be seen' (225) to be associated with his preferment.
Bosola in turn knows that his service has deserved well (several years in the
galleys is a lot to go through for another man), and he haunts the Cardinal,
chafing at his own neglect while lesser men, 'crows, pies, and caterpillars'
(51), are advanced instead.

Where the central fact of Flamineo's world was the ever-present danger
of economic ruin, that of Bosola's is ingratitude. It is the vice of which he is
the victim at each end of the play, and from which he is anxious to keep
himself free. His efforts to maintain that integrity propel him into Ferdinand's
service as a spy in the court of the Duchess of Malfi. He has a strong
antipathy to the job, calling it devilish, treacherous, and villainous by turns;
later he speaks of 'this base quality | Of intelligencer' (III. ii. 327–8). But
Ferdinand has trapped him by procuring his reward, preferment at Malfi,
before recruiting him. It is literally an offer he cannot refuse:

> to avoid ingratitude
> For the good deed you have done me, I must do
> All the ill man can invent!   (I. i. 273–5)

It is not simply that it will seem churlish to turn down the advancement he
has been badgering for; to do so would be to implicate himself in the vice
he has most suffered from in others.

The oddity of Bosola's statement here is compounded by its context. It
is remarkable enough to hear anyone say that he must commit an ultimate
human evil (be it spying or no) in order to avoid the sin of ingratitude, but
the line is the more surprising in that it is spoken by a hired murderer whose

---

[15] Conditions on the galleys are described by G. Ives, *A History of Penal Methods* (1914),
104–5.

[16] J. Nohl, *The Black Death*, tr. C. H. Clarke (1926), 166.

[17] Jonson, *Volpone*, II. ii. 45–6.

first response when given money is the phlegmatic question, 'Whose throat must I cut?' (249) The exchange with Ferdinand brings to a culmination the audience's moral disorientation over Bosola. At his first confrontation with the Cardinal, he is an enigma: mystery is developed around what he has done for the Cardinal that entitles him to a reward. The Cardinal's wish that he would 'become honest' (40) sorts with the information that he has been in the galleys, but not with the facts of how he got there, in the Cardinal's service. Bosola himself implies that the deed was moral when he complains that virtue is its own reward—'only the reward | Of doing well, is the doing of it' (31–2).[18] We soon learn that the deed was a murder, that the Cardinal suborned it, and that his ingratitude is politic, for appearances' sake; but Bosola's attitude to the crime continues to puzzle us. The incident with Ferdinand makes things clear: Bosola has an inverted hierarchy of values. Murder impinges on his conscience less than espionage, and (for all that he vilifies spying as 'All the ill man can invent') ingratitude is still more opprobrious. In these positions lies the groundwork for his later development.

That development is from an assassin who disdains the role of spy to a spy who cannot find it in him to be an assassin. He does his work as an informer faithfully, if truculently; his break with Ferdinand comes in Act IV, over the torture and murder of the Duchess. The change is best understood in terms of Bosola's personal system of values. For him, the greatest sins are those of dishonesty in personal relationships: the hypocrisy of spying on his mistress, and the ingratitude of withholding a *quid pro quo*. The same trait explains why he accepted his term in the galleys without, so it seems, attempting to incriminate the Cardinal as many another assassin would have done. Even his railing might be understood as a kind of gauche honesty in the manner of Coriolanus. As for his attitude to murder, it is pertinent to recall Muriel Bradbrook's distinction between an act of violence and an atrocity: 'Violence implies the rupture of an existing relationship, with one partner seeking the absolute domination of the other. ... An atrocity is a gratuitously criminal act between two without previous relationships; it is strictly a meaningless act.'[19] Bosola is a man of atrocity, not of violence: an assassin does not usually have a prior relationship with his target, nor the chance to develop one; cutting a throat is an act best done quickly, and from behind.

Killing the Duchess is different: it is the culmination of a relationship with someone he has known, served, and betrayed for years. In theory, the murder merely consolidates a rupture between them that has already occurred, when he was revealed to her as Ferdinand's agent: he takes on no significantly

---

[18] Cf. Tilley, V. 81.
[19] M. C. Bradbrook, *The Artist and Society in Shakespeare's England* (Brighton and Totowa, NJ, 1982), 164.

different function in arranging her death. In practice, he chooses to do this not as Daniel de Bosola but in the guise of the common bellman; but this is not simply because he cannot face her in his own person. The rupture of their former relationship institutes another in which he can act as her assassin; but it debars him from undertaking another, less expected role.

His overt function in the first of the two torture scenes that make up Act IV is to stage-manage Ferdinand's visit to the Duchess, and to show her the bodies of her husband Antonio and her children. The effect of this incident on stage is important: reading the stage direction, we know that these are 'artificial figures' (IV. i. 55 s.d.), but in the theatre there is nothing to tell us that they are not corpses. At the end of the previous Act, we saw Antonio take flight to Milan with a price on his head; this is our first news of him since. The straightforward inference is that Ferdinand has had him killed. Literary tradition supports it: murdered lovers are often used to torment their surviving partners. For example, the husband is indeed dead in the Cinthio story that may have been Webster's source for this moment.[20] The corpse hand belongs to the same genre: the gift of a part of the lover's body, such as Guishard's heart in *Gismond of Salerne*, is often made to women guilty of sexual transgression. Bosola's behaviour gives colour to the assumption: Ferdinand has shown her the bodies, he tells the Duchess,

> That now you know directly they are dead,
> Hereafter you may wisely cease to grieve
> For that which cannot be recovered.[21]   (58–60)

For the rest of the scene, his words to her are in the same vein: words of comfort, cajoling her from despair and 'vain sorrow' (76).

Then Ferdinand tells us it has all been a trick:

> These presentations are but fram'd in wax,
> By the curious master in that quality,
> Vincentio Lauriola, and she takes them
> For true substantial bodies.   (112–15)

The news does not materially alter the Duchess's torture, of course, but it brings a new dimension to our sense of that torture. Showing her the bodies would have been a brutal way of telling her the truth; but since they are not the bodies, and since Antonio is still alive, the action is not only brutal but gratuitous. It is most cruel in so far as it is a lie.

To understand Bosola at this point in the play, we must understand the nature of his involvement in Ferdinand's scheme. He says that he pities the

---

[20] G. Boklund, *The Duchess of Malfi: Sources, Themes, Characters* (Cambridge, Mass., 1962), 51–2.

[21] I revert here to the quarto punctuation of line 58, altered by the Revels editor; I take 'now you know directly they are dead' to be a subordinate clause.

Duchess, an important development if it is true; but if he knows the bodies are just dummies, he is consciously participating in her torment and so must be lying. The indications are that, as we might expect, he is telling the truth. When Ferdinand tells us of his ruse, it seems that he tells Bosola too: 'Why do you do this?' the spy asks, shocked; 'To bring her to despair' (116), comes the reply. Bosola has spent much of the scene so far trying to bring her out of the despair that the sight of the corpses occasioned; Ferdinand's aim, he has assumed, is that she should come to terms with her loss as an irrecoverable one. Now, in rapid succession, he learns that he has been inveigled into promoting a lie, and that his actions so far have worked against his master's plans: to one who so values honesty and loyalty, no revelation could be more shocking.

His reaction to the knowledge is assertive: 'Faith, end here: | And go no farther in your cruelty' (117–18). Instead of bowing to Ferdinand's will, he tries to change it, to suit his own feelings of compassion: 'when you send me next, | The business shall be comfort' (136-7). The business turns out to be murder, of course, but if she must die, he will not kill her soul: before having her strangled, he brings her by degrees to mortification—fits her for death. But this is not a part he could undertake himself. Though he advises Ferdinand to end her despair, he shrinks at first from seeing her again personally. Or at least:

> Never in mine own shape,
> That's forfeited by my intelligence,
> And this last cruel lie.   (134–6)

Bosola the courtier who turned out to be a spy, Bosola who unwittingly tortured the Duchess with the lie of her husband's death, Bosola who has been the agent of all her misery, is not the man to offer solace. If the business is to be comfort, whether for life or death, he must undertake it in another person; and so he does.

Bosola's pity would be scanned: it is a surprising trait in a hard-bitten cynic who has been used to make his living at murder; but it is not a change which Webster sketches in any detail. Psychological explanation is less important, though, in that it is not a conversion: it is a local emotion called forth by a single individual, the Duchess. Killing her, he probes her stoicism and fortitude to the heart, then stands by and lets the executioners get on with it. With her waiting-woman Cariola, he behaves differently: as she struggles and tries pretext after pretext to save herself, he issues irritated orders to 'throttle her' (IV. ii. 251), seeing her off with a sardonic joke—if she is, as she says, with child, 'Why then, | Your credit's saved' (254–5). There is no pity here. What he has experienced is a sudden and unexpected flare of humane feeling in a particular situation; it changes his later actions, but not his attitude to life. It has a precedent in Flamineo:

> I have a strange thing in me, to th' which
> I cannot give a name, without it be
> Compassion.   (v. iv. 113–15)

What was a perplexing moment for the earlier assassin becomes narratively important when it happens to Bosola.

If we seek for more explanation than this, the discovery in himself of a long-neglected streak of benevolence, we must speculate; but the material is there to speculate upon. Bosola's railing and cynicism are not disinterested or detached: if he hates life, it is the hatred of a disappointed man— disappointed not in personal ambition, as Antonio would have it, nor in simple love of piety, but in a more existential idealism. He is a man who has experienced the worst life has to offer: in the galleys he plumbed the depths of the human condition. It has equipped him to reproach life, but also to see the pity of it: the underside of his railing is compassion. Cariola does not merit it: biting and scratching at her executioners, she is a fool making vain keeping of life. But the Duchess, who describes her misery in terms of the galleys and who endures it with nobility, excites a fellow-feeling that wishes her release, not through death but comfort.

Whether or not this speculative conclusion is a valid one, there is a central contradiction in Bosola's behaviour to the Duchess: he pities her, and he murders her. Later he articulates the problem himself when he says he 'was an actor in the main of all | Much 'gainst mine own good nature' (v. v. 85–6). He was an unwilling murderer, he says, much as he was an unwilling spy: the parallel is important. He took the job of spy because fidelity to his patron was more important than fidelity to himself, and so it is with murder:

> though I loath'd the evil, yet I lov'd
> You that did counsel it; and rather sought
> To appear a true servant, than an honest man.   (IV. ii. 331–3)

Again we see his twisted moral position expressed in an inverted proverb: he hates the treason and loves the traitor.[22] He counts the authenticity of a personal relationship for more than the authenticity of his own 'good nature': that is his tragedy.

Webster wrote *The Duchess of Malfi* during a period when tragicomedy was in fashion; more specifically, at a time when the genre had become familiar, and a sophisticated audience could be expected to second-guess the surprise *dénouement*. For example, *The Honest Man's Fortune*, staged the year before *The Duchess*, leads us to believe that the faithful page Veramour is really a girl, like Bellario in Beaumont and Fletcher's *Philaster* (1609), and the true surprise is that he is really no more than he seems. The same sophis-

---

[22] Cf. Tilley, K. 64.

tication has a bearing on Webster's play, and on Bosola. The nature of tragicomedy is averted tragedy; but *The Duchess of Malfi* is averted tragicomedy. That is why Act ɪv is so important. In a formal tragicomedy, Act ɪv is the point of greatest tension: 'everyone is brought to the height of suffering: the "danger" is most extreme, the threats of "death" most intense.'[23] As we saw in Chapter 7, that danger could include seeming death, provided the character could be brought back to life in time for the Act v resolution: for all its dark tone, the supposed death of Antonio is a characteristically tragicomic incident. But in this Act ɪv, the Duchess undergoes both danger and death, despite the teasing coda in which, Desdemona-like, she recovers only to die again. In his remorse, moreover, Ferdinand wishes Bosola had behaved like an assassin in a tragicomedy:

> Why didst thou not pity her? what an excellent
> Honest man mightst thou have been
> If thou hadst borne her to some sanctuary!
> Or, bold in a good cause, oppos'd thyself
> With thy advanced sword above thy head,
> Between her innocence and my revenge!   (273–8)

They are the words of a man who earlier remarked that pity was 'nothing of kin' (ɪv. i. 138) to Bosola. The irony is that he did pity her; but he lacked the moral perspicacity, and the independence, to act on it. And that is the play's tragedy.

v

What these three murderers have in common is that they are all, in some way, victims: victims of society or victims of their superiors. Lodovico insists on the fact in his first scene, pointing out the inequalities of the legal system that has condemned him: 'I wonder then some great men scape | This banishment' (ɪ. i. 38–9). Our response is a divided one: justly doomed he may have been, but the sentence is fortuitous in a society where prosecution goes by rank. Flamineo and Bosola, too, are established early on as victims, the former of his father's ruinous excesses, the latter of a broken contract. In each case the wrong strikes the keynote for the man's preoccupation: revenge, poverty, ingratitude. At the root of each character lies the fact that he has been sinned against.

The result is that all three are constrained by circumstances: it is as victims that they become subjected. Without absolute freedom to direct their lives, they have to pander to the whims of powerful patrons: they are dependent on those patrons to make their living, and, in Lodovico's case, for help in

---

[23] D. L. Hirst, *Tragicomedy* (1984), 19.

securing a pardon. Webster's interest is in the different ways in which they respond to this condition. Lodovico's career is the most personally successful of the three because he makes the necessary mental adjustment to enable him to find his own satisfaction in his master's work: it is a sign of his freedom that Francisco cannot predict his behaviour. Of course, this has meant casting off materialist concerns with his own comfort and safety; and it is in this that Flamineo and Bosola fail.

Flamineo's commitment to material values is established in his altercation with his mother at the end of his first scene:

CORNELIA   What? because we are poor,
Shall we be vicious?
FLAMINEO   Pray what means have you
To keep me from the galleys, or the gallows?   (I. ii. 314–16)

The force of his rejoinder lies in the double sense of 'means'. He asks how ('by what means') she can save him from such a fate: he is poor in a world of graduate unemployment, and poverty will necessarily drive him to crime, and so to the risk of punishment—only means (financial support) can prevent it. It follows that virtue is a luxury he cannot afford; and if he must offend, he may as well do it for high stakes. Pandering his sister to Bracciano is an obvious course to take in a society where the family controls female sexuality. It is little more than his father did before him: we learn from Monticelso that Corombona Senior, Volpone-like, held out for twelve thousand ducats from Camillo over a six-month period, before he would consent to Vittoria's marriage—without dowry. Flamineo is his successor as head of the family, and is exercising the same rights over the commodity of his sister's body. However autonomous he appears in his scheme for preferment, then, he is acting within constraint, with economic pressure at his back and common practice marking out his course: even in struggling against his subordinate position, his actions are determined by his circumstances.

Bosola is more obviously not the maker of his actions and situation. Throughout the first four Acts, he is a strangely passive figure: the other characters manipulate him as if he were a convenience for their benefit, not a person in his own right. Ferdinand and the Cardinal treat him as an all-purpose villain, useful for whatever spying, torture, or murder they happen to need. Even Antonio's friend Delio cynically proposes to cover up the Duchess's child-bed pangs by framing him on a poisoning charge: the consequences for an innocent man seem not to matter. Bosola responds like Patience on a monument:

It needs must follow
That I must be committed on pretence
Of poisoning her; which I'll endure, and laugh at.   (II. iii. 68–70)

He is a man who accepts the lot his betters have planned for him, just as he obeys orders, with stoical resignation: he sublimates his personal feelings to the deeds required of him, because action without responsibility is the safest course to take. By the time he decides to initiate action himself, it is too late.

Bosola grows in moral sensibility in the last two Acts, with two results: it makes him a much more conscious commentator on his own condition, and it turns him from assassin to revenger. He explains the action of the last scene as

> Revenge, for the Duchess of Malfi, murdered
> By th' Arragonian brethren; for Antonio,
> Slain by this hand; for lustful Julia,
> Poison'd by this man; and lastly, for myself,
> That was an actor in the main of all
> Much 'gainst mine own good nature, yet i' th' end
> Neglected. (v. v. 81–7)

Besides the bizarre twist of the killer avenging two of his own victims, there is a risk of bathos here: after listing three murders, there is an anticlimax when he cites his own neglect as the fourth occasion for revenge. No doubt it still rankles, but this is more than a case of a contract broken, justly revenged. Bosola stands with the Duchess, Antonio, and Julia because all four have been destroyed as a direct or indirect result of the actions of Ferdinand and the Cardinal: three have been killed, the fourth has suffered moral annihilation.

In 1612, Sir Henry Yelverton's condemnation of Lord Sanquhar suggested that in such cases as these the killer was as much a victim as the person killed: the hirer procured not only the death of one person, but the damnation of another.[24] By making his assassins major, individualized figures who have functions beyond killing, Webster is able to dramatize the point. We get to know Flamineo in his first scene, and probably develop a sneaking admiration for the quality of his intellect as, witty and urbane, he runs rings around a foolish cuckold like a city comedy trickster. Then, in a terrible contrast, we watch a dumb show in which he snaps the same man's neck. The scene is the more horrifying because we have seen that the killer is capable of more than brutality: because we know the man, we have a sharper sense of the depths to which he has sunk.

In *The Duchess of Malfi*, the issue is paradoxically both more blurred, because we know from the start that Bosola is a killer, and more explicit, because Bosola himself provides a commentary:

> What would I do, were this to do again?
> I would not change my peace of conscience

[24] Above, p. 15.

For all the wealth of Europe.   (IV. ii. 339–41)

By invoking and frustrating the audience's tragicomic expectations of the Duchess's revival at this point, Webster underlines the fact that Bosola's deed is final, cannot be undone. Both men, in their different responses to dependency, come sooner or later to brand themselves with the mark of Cain.

Moreover, accepting the task of murder destroys them in more than a moral sense. They are placing themselves in a specific role, assassin, which attracts very varied responses from different characters. To some sections of Malfi society, it seems that moral considerations are irrelevant: Antonio, who usually tries to find something positive to say about people, will look for 'goodness' (I. i. 77) in Bosola even when told he is a hired murderer, and the Duchess does not demur at accepting a servant who has been in the galleys. With public morality to uphold, the churchmen are more ambivalent: the Cardinal needs Bosola's talents but will not admit it, and it is at least plausible that Monticelso should behave similarly towards Lodovico, as Francisco's ruse shows. But the Dukes, the all-important patrons, show an aristocratic contempt for their instruments: to them assassins are base men doing a useful job, like dustmen; and a relationship with them involves exploitation without commitment.

Characters who choose the trade of murderer, then, are blind to their own best interests. Bosola and Flamineo both know that, as the former puts it, 'the consequence of murder' (v. iv. 39) is the elimination of the murderer: both allude to the fact in the manner of a general principle.[25] Yet neither thinks to apply that principle to his own case until he has become a killer. More fundamentally, both men delude themselves that they can rise through degrading employment. Even in moments of moral consciousness, Bosola clings to the idea:

> There are a many ways that conduct to seeming
> Honour, and some of them very dirty ones.   (v. ii. 305–6)

Even when he is manipulating Bracciano, then, Flamineo is making it possible for Bracciano to manipulate him. For such as him and Bosola, the dirty ways lead only to destruction.

---

[25] *The White Devil*, IV. ii. 60–1; J. Webster, *The Duchess of Malfi*, v. ii. 299–301.

10

THE ASSASSIN IN DECLINE

I

In the period of nearly three decades between *The Duchess of Malfi* and the closure of the theatres in 1642, only one play made important and original use of the assassin: Thomas Middleton and William Rowley's *The Changeling*. It is a treatment very different from Webster's. Beatrice and De Flores are, if anything, even more central than Flamineo and Bosola: the murder of Beatrice's fiancé Piracquo is the subject of the play. But whereas Webster was interested in the human experience of being a hired murderer, this play deals with the situation of using one. Moreover, the 'realism' of the narrative is of a very different order from Webster's.

Robert Jordan has suggested that the story operates not through the psychological subtlety of the two main characters, but as a trope on folk tales of the 'beauty and the beast' variety: the maiden is forced into a liaison with a loathsome creature, but here the twist is not that the beast is a prince, but that the beauty is a beast.[1] Jordan underestimates the complexity of the characterization, but throws important light on the working of the plot, which is built from familiar materials and consciously invokes their familiarity. But the similarities never run true: the authors vary their story from its originals at crucial moments, creating a sudden, sharp particularity. For instance, with its recurrent references to creation and to De Flores as a serpent, the play is a version of the Fall in which that event is averted: Adam refuses the apple and Eve alone is damned. The plot renders itself distinctive by going against its archetypes.

This raises questions about how we should view the characters. Let us begin by considering the most vivid, from whose actions the entire story flows: Beatrice. The use of that name is itself contentious. The character is called Beatrice throughout the stage directions, but only once in the dialogue, at a late stage in the action. This could be confusing to an audience, since speakers otherwise name her Joanna, eight times in the course of the play. The equivalent character in the source is called Beatrice-Joanna, and many editors import this combination, entirely without textual authority, as a way round the difficulty.[2] Certainly they have a point: the original Beatrice-

---

[1] R. Jordan, *RenD* NS 3 (1970), 162–5.
[2] i.e. they emend the 1653 quarto's *'Joanna, Beatrice, Joanna'* (I2ʳ; V. iii. 148) to 'Joanna, Beatrice-Joanna'.

Joanna clearly provided both the names given to the character, but to efface the gap between source and play by conflating those two names into one is to bypass evidence of the authors' insouciance as to what their leading lady should be called.

The most frequent term of address for Beatrice, used twenty times, is 'lady', and in this lies the key to the problem. 'Lady' is an impersonal term with connotations of purity and chastity, evident in the character of the Lady in Middleton's *The Second Maiden's Tragedy* (1611).[3] This play illustrates Middleton's ambivalence over realistic names: besides its Govianus, Sophonirus, and the like, it has generic figures like the Lady, the Tyrant, and the Wife. Other plays, such as *The Phoenix* and *The Revenger's Tragedy*, use names which confer moral qualities or plot functions upon the bearer. The dramatist's naming of parts became more subtle as his career went on, but the names of his later characters continued to be suggestive.[4] De Flores, as many commentators have recognized, is a case in point: it is he who deflowers Beatrice. Accordingly, his name is mentioned twenty-nine times in the play: we are not allowed to forget it. It matters much less whether the heroine is Beatrice, Joanna, or Beatrice-Joanna, because the names convey nothing more than particularity: it is in the general role of 'the Lady' that we are invited to view her.

The difficulty is that Beatrice is not a 'lady' in the sense in which Middleton used the term in *The Second Maiden's Tragedy*: in the earlier play, the Lady dies for her chastity, whereas Beatrice compromises her chastity by committing murder. By establishing her as 'the Lady', the play prepares us for the revelation that she is entirely unsuited to that title. Typical of the play's treatment of archetypal figures and situations, this deviation is at the core of *The Changeling*.

We should beware of seeing Beatrice, or the other characters, as simply generic figures, puppets animated by the requirements of the plot. The dramatists tread a narrow line between the universal and the particular. Beatrice is called 'lady', but also Joanna. Alsemero is a stock soldier-turned-lover, but he is also allergic to cherries. There is little sense of a location, of a specific castle in Alicante, but we learn a single, telling detail about Beatrice's family background: that she is a surviving twin sister, and therefore over-protected. She has general connotations which place her mythically, but she also has an individuality born of inner complexity. It is as an individual that she moves the plot along its familiar lines—not it her. With this in mind, we can now turn to one of those familiar lines, the assassin scenario.

Beatrice uses murder as her escape from an enforced marriage, but it is

[3] *OED* sb. 2c.
[4] A. Barton, *The Names of Comedy* (Oxford, 1990), 78–9.

important to realize that she has other options, which are clear if we view *The Changeling* in the light of what may have been Middleton's immediately preceding play, *Women Beware Women* (c.1621). Isabella, the heroine of that play's sub-plot, is compelled like Beatrice to wed a man she does not love; but she goes through with the marriage and cuckolds her husband. Besides adultery with Alsemero, moreover, Beatrice could elope with him, as Bianca does with Leantio in the other play. But instead she chooses to kill off her fiancé and, with her father's consent, marry Alsemero in his place.

Of course, she does not see the situation in such clear terms: she believes herself trapped, and seizes on murder as a way out when Alsemero proposes to fight a duel with his rival. The question is not why she chooses one from a set of clearly defined possibilities, but why the other possibilities never occur to her. In this respect, her initial vision of freedom is instructive:

> how well were I now
> If there were none such name known as Piracquo,
> Nor no such tie as the command of parents!   (II. ii. 18–20)

The subjunctive is despairing: such conditions do not obtain. But her identification of the two factors which restrict her is revealing. In listing Piracquo's existence as one, she has already taken a step towards securing his non-existence by murder. What sends her along this route is her acceptance of the command of parents as a tie. She is very consciously a child of her family: for example, she tells De Flores,

> Think but upon the distance that creation
> Set 'twixt thy blood and mine, and keep thee there,
>
> (III. iv. 130–1)

using her birth to assert her superiority over a mere household servant. In a patriarchal society, her will is therefore subject to her father's: she hopes to wind Alsemero 'Into my father's favour' (11), and must tolerate De Flores 'since he's a gentleman | In good respect with my father' (I. i. 134–5). Elopement and adultery are unthinkable to her because they would involve her defying patriarchal authority (in the latter case, transferred to her husband): 'the command of parents' defines the absolute limits within which she must work. We may observe a similar characteristic in Shakespeare's Juliet, who stages her own death rather than tell her father she has married a Montague. In Beatrice's case, however, it is another who dies, and in earnest.

Beatrice is blinkered to any other way out of her dilemma than murder, then. It remains to consider the casualness with which she undertakes this course: after all, it is one thing to want to be rid of an unloved fiancé, but quite another actively to wish him dead. Her motives in setting the deed in train are complicated by a second factor, however: her irrational aversion to

De Flores. In using him as an assassin, she says, she will kill two birds with one stone: he will have to flee the country, and

> I shall rid myself
> Of two inveterate loathings at one time,
> Piracquo, and his dog-face.   (ii. ii. 144–6)

Her use of the word 'inveterate' is revealing because, as far as Piracquo is concerned, it is not true: in the opening scene she makes remarks which indicate that she loved him, only to 'change [her] saint' (i. i. 155) on meeting Alsemero. This is not simply a case of love turning into intense hatred, however. It is true that Beatrice feels such emotions with an uncontrolled and unsubtle intensity; but we underestimate her capacity for indifference if we see nothing in between. But for her entanglement with him, it could be with indifference that she first speaks of Piracquo after changing her affections: 'what's Piracquo | My father spends his breath for?' (ii. i. 19–20) 'Nothing' is the answer she implies: there is no inveterate loathing here.

However, Piracquo is unfortunate in his herald: on his arrival, the doting De Flores gets himself sent to announce the fact to her. Presumably in the assumption that it will be welcome news, he playfully takes his time in the telling; his arch repetition of her supposed sweetheart's name produces obvious irritation in her. When finally given, the message causes an infuriated explosion:

> Vengeance strike the news!
> Thou thing most loath'd, what cause was there in this
> To bring thee to my sight?   (71–3)

It is notable that the news is an object of anger in itself, not just as the agent that has led De Flores into her presence. In the mouth of a man she finds 'ominous' (53), whose sight makes her 'think | Of some harm towards me' (89–90), Piracquo turns from an object of indifference to an object of hatred: the medium infects the message. In the metaphorical sense, she cuts him dead when they meet soon after; and it is not long before she has arranged for him to be cut dead more literally.

Beatrice's loathing for Piracquo is inveterate, then, because it antedates its object: it is the same loathing she feels for De Flores, transferred to a second person. This is why De Flores is so suitable a candidate to be Piracquo's murderer. Seizing on the idea, she alludes to medical practice:

> Why, men of art make much of poison,
> Keep one to expel another.   (ii. ii. 46–7)

The two men are understood to be of like quality, in so far as both are hateful, 'poison' to her. Neither, it seems, has any existence independent of her perception that might qualify this judgement; and it is a perception that misrepresents them. De Flores is regularly transformed into something sub-human—a thing, a serpent, a 'standing toad-pool' (II. i. 58). She recognizes that the two men are external in that they stimulate a certain kind of response in her, and are removable by murder; but she does not conceive of them as real people in the fullest sense of the term.

Her behaviour as she sets up the killing is ruthlessly calculating: she reasons that the murderer will be destroyed by the crime as surely as his victim, and she entraps De Flores by cynically playing up to his attraction to her. Critics often present her as the victim of De Flores, but at this point in the play the reverse is surely true.[5] Her attitude to him is encapsulated in her remark that 'the ugliest creature | Creation fram'd for some use' (II. ii. 43–4): the doctrine that everything has its purpose is twisted into utility, so that De Flores has not his own place in nature, but a function in the art of Beatrice. The realization of that function comes to her unexpectedly when she states that 'Blood-guiltiness becomes a fouler visage' (40) than Alse-mero's: the disfigured face of De Flores becomes a sign indicating the reason for his existence, to be a murderer for her.[6]

In using an assassin, she believes, she will not only delegate the business of killing but also the moral responsibility. The notion was not unique, despite the legal and ethical positions on procuring murder that were discussed in Chapter 1. 'I'de hire some shag-ragge or other for halfe a chickeene to cut's throat, only to save thy hands from doing it' (II. ii. 32–4), says a character in George Chapman's *May Day* (1602), proposing to save his cousin from a forced marriage. We find the same attitude in relation to the murder of Pompey in *The False One*: Achillas says he hired Septimius because the crime was not 'meritorious' (p. 315), and later Photinus claims reward from Caesar 'for keeping thy hands innocent' (p. 318).[7] Hands were often conceived as the instruments of murder in the seventeenth century: a common periphrasis for killing was to imbrue one's hands in blood, and in *Macbeth* Shakespeare uses the image of bloodstained hands as an objective correlative for moral responsibility. These hirers take the vehicle without the tenor: they conceive morality in wholly physical terms, and assume that the blood-guilt, like the blood, will remain on the assassin's hands. If blood-guiltiness is appropriate to a foul visage, thinks the fair Beatrice, it will not stain her.

Beatrice is utterly insensible to her own moral position. Because she does

---

[5] Cf. C. W. Crupi, *Neophilologus*, 68 (1984), 142–9.

[6] It is not made entirely clear what is wrong with De Flores's face. Some critics infer from a remark of his (II. ii. 76–7) that it is hairy and pimply; but Beatrice's statements, made deceivingly, that the deformity is caused by 'the heat of the liver' (80), and that, with a special preparation, it could be washed off, both suggest a livid red discoloration. If so, this would in turn suggest a murderer 'dipped in blood' (cf. III. iv. 126), making Beatrice's reasoning the clearer.

[7] The text is quoted from the Glover and Waller edition of Beaumont and Fletcher (1905–12).

not conceive the otherness and individual uniqueness of De Flores and Piracquo, she cannot understand the murder for what it is, the destruction of two human beings. All she can see are certain material consequences in relation to herself: the absence of two causes of vexation. In arranging for the crime, therefore, all she seeks to do is ensure that the right person becomes involved—De Flores and not Alsemero. Whether De Flores is arrested or goes into voluntary exile is immaterial to her: she is only concerned that he should be permanently out of her way. There is no imaginative engagement with the details of the crime or its consequences; she is intellectually aware of the guilt, and the 'horror ... blood and danger' (ii. ii. 119) involved, but has no sense of the unpleasant reality of a backstairs butchering. This is why the course of murder comes so easily to her: in the naïve moral consciousness of a sheltered adolescent, murder is a remote, nebulous sin that seems less real, and so more venial, than disobeying Daddy.

All this sets up a situation, murder by an assassin; the action then develops by playing on the paradigms of that situation. A woman wanting to have a former suitor murdered to make way for his rival has two options: she can hire an assassin, or she can set on her current lover to dispose of his predecessor. The authors could have known of the latter practice from English accounts of such Continental strumpets as Vittoria Corombona or the insatiate Countess of Cellant; it also occurred in a London setting in Marston's *The Dutch Courtesan* (1604). Beatrice makes a clear choice between these alternatives when she prevents Alsemero from fighting and engages De Flores instead. Unfortunately, and characteristically, she underestimates De Flores's responses.

She begins with the assumption that the servant will not work for someone who has rejected him: 'I ha' marr'd so good a market with my scorn' (42). Therefore she feigns a *volte face* and shows signs of attraction to him before giving him the job of murder. This is not a case of blindness or misconception so much as *under*-conception. Clearly she perceives the reason why De Flores has dogged her so obsessively—perhaps her aversion to him originates in that recognition. At any rate, she is unambiguous in simulating reciprocation: she says he appears 'lovely' (135) and 'amorously' (75) to her, and calls him 'my De Flores' (98). What she fails to consider is that this will have repercussions beyond winning him over; having secured his willingness to serve her, she believes she can keep their relationship on an economic footing. She has too limited a conception of him as an independent person to realize that, after her build-up, he may misunderstand her statement, 'Thy reward shall be precious' (130).

It becomes immediately clear after she has left that De Flores has indeed misunderstood, as his thoughts turn to that reward: 'Methinks I feel her in mine arms already' (147). Under the circumstances, it is a natural error to make: when he first entered in this scene, after having observed her meeting with Alsemero, he predicted that she would grow wanton, and hoped to benefit from the change; her behaviour towards him suggests that it has happened sooner than he expected. Moreover, confusion between the preciousness of wealth and of woman is a recurrent motif in Middleton's work: sexuality is portrayed in economic terms, husbands make their living at being cuckolds, and women are referred to as treasures that attract thieves. De Flores does not plan to double-cross Beatrice to obtain his pleasure, as many commentators believe; he makes a reasonable assumption about their relationship on the basis of the evidence to hand.

When hirer and assassin meet soon after the murder, the two versions of the contract are played off. The scene begins with suspense, as we wait for De Flores to realize that he will not be rewarded in the way he expected. Beatrice skates on thin ice when she gives him Piracquo's ring as his 'fees' (III. iv. 40): he looks 'offended' (52) and points out that it will not 'buy a capcase for one's conscience' (44); but she assures him that ''tis not given | In state of recompense' (49–50), and both are secure in their illusions again. Of course, there is never any question that it will be Beatrice who realizes that a misunderstanding has occurred. If she infers anything from De Flores's strong reaction to the offer of a three-hundred-ducat ring, it is that, as a professional killer, he finds a small fee insulting. Proffering a much larger sum in state of recompense only provokes a more explicit response: for three thousand florins he could have hired 'A journeyman in murder' (69) to do the job, and kept his own conscience clear; in offering 'salary' (63), she takes him for such a figure, 'in the rank of verminous fellows' who 'destroy things for wages' (64–5). But she cannot understand the implications even of so clear a statement as this:

BEATRICE
    I'll double the sum, sir.
DE FLORES   You take a course
    To double my vexation, that's the good you do.   (73–4)

Treating him as a hired assassin, she believes his vexation is inversely proportional to the size of the fee; but in fact it is the very offer of payment that offends him, so to up the ante as she does is to exacerbate the insult.

The balance of power changes soon afterwards: De Flores realizes that he has acted on false expectations, and turns to explicit demands. Now it is Beatrice who must learn the other side of the misunderstanding; but it is a slow process. She knows that she is trapped—'He speaks home' (87), she remarks when he explains the logic of the situation—but she tries hard to evade the realization. It is not that she cannot understand him: 'I dare not'

(101), she says when pressed. She does not want to conceive his meaning, even when he states it unambiguously:

> Would I had been bound
> Perpetually unto my living hate
> In that Piracquo, than to hear these words.   (127–9)

The offence lies in the words, and the act they portend is suppressed, an 'impossible' (120) wickedness that may go away if ignored. Only when she is certain there is no escape can she bring herself even to mention it:

> Was my creation in the womb so curs'd,
> It must engender with a viper first?   (165–6)

The rhetorical question is the last hopeless recoil from the future that, in the verb, she forces herself to see. It turns out that she has, after all, used her next lover to kill off her last.

It is often said that the play falls apart after the confrontation scene. One reason for this is that the authors have nothing more to offer in the psychological depiction of their characters: the only major turn, Beatrice's transference of her affections to De Flores, is simply a fulfilment of what he has been saying all along about wanton women—

> Thou'lt love anon
> What thou so fear'st and faint'st to venture on.   (170–1)

The play devolves into a sequence of dramatic devices—the virginity tests, the bed-trick, the ghost. In fact, the change is already under way in the confrontation scene, which shows us nothing new in the characters: Beatrice's inability to understand what is happening and De Flores's willingness to force his attentions on her develop from traits that have already been established in the preceding Acts. If we value the play solely for its psychological subtlety, then here is where it runs out of steam.

The power of the confrontation scene comes as much from situation as from character, however, and in particular from the manipulation of archetypes. In this respect the focus is on the device of the severed finger that De Flores brings back from the corpse, an element which the authors did not find in their source. Its introduction may have been influenced by the murder situation in *The Dutch Courtesan*, in which Franceschina, the courtesan of the title, asks her would-be lover Malheureux to kill his rival Freevill. This is, in effect, what De Flores believes Beatrice has asked him to do, and he acts true to type: Franceschina's request includes the stipulation that Malheureux return with proof of the murder in the form of a ring given to Freevill by his new love, Beatrice; De Flores acts without instructions to recover the ring his Beatrice has given Piracquo. Middleton and Rowley deviate from Marston, however, in making De Flores cut off the finger to get the ring; and in doing so they create an image of rich complexity.

De Flores presents Beatrice with the ring as a 'token' (26), a lover's gift, and regrets that he 'could not get the ring without the finger' (28). It seems to be the ring which interests him, but this only serves to facilitate the symbolic importance of the finger. In it, the authors play on two established paradigms. Like many assassins before him, De Flores is producing a part of the murdered body as evidence that the crime has been committed. The difference is that in previous cases the grisly proof is a fake, taken from an animal to cover up the fact that the killer has spared his victim: in *The Maid's Metamorphosis*, for instance, it is a goat kid's heart, not Eurymine's. In *The Changeling*, however, the finger does indeed belong to the corpse, and in that respect it is a truer token than the ring: De Flores has not expressed his love by procuring a ring, but by killing a man.

Of course, Beatrice does not understand the situation in these terms. Rather De Flores is a tormentor who presents her with a part of her former lover's body, as, for instance, Bosola did Antonio's hand to the Duchess of Malfi. De Flores does indeed torment her later in the scene, but in her case role and reality do not correspond. The Duchess is horrified by the hand because it tokens the death of her husband, whereas Beatrice no longer loves Piracquo, and is repelled by the simple gruesomeness of the finger. The juxtaposition of the paradigm with the facts of this case, then, serves to emphasize the falsity of Beatrice's pose: she may see herself as the victim of De Flores, but in fact she instigated his crime.

In exploiting these two paradigms, the authors establish the two functions of the finger. It is a metonymy for the physical fact of the murder, projecting out of the assassin's world into Beatrice's: 'What hast thou done?' (29), she asks when she sees this image of, to her, hitherto unimaginable violence; one might expect the procurer of the crime to know. And it is also a symbol of the moral responsibility from which, she assumed, De Flores would protect her. Instead, by bringing it, he begins the remorseless exposure of her moral naïvety that is the central concern of the scene:

> Why, are not you as guilty, in (I'm sure)
> As deep as I?   (83–4)

Beatrice is told that she need not literally have killed to be 'A woman dipp'd in blood' (126), and that 'fair murd'ress' (141) is not an oxymoron. The function of the scene is to correct the moral misapprehensions inherent in the character which the opening Acts established.

It is striking that the agent of this moral clarity should be De Flores, a murderer. The play stresses his lethal role: we are shown the killing in two otherwise inconsequential little scenes, and the use of the finger as proof, with the deviation from the usual paradigm, underlines the fact that the victim is dead. Indeed, that device reflects in little how the scene plays on the typical assassin situation of tragicomedy that was developed in *The Malcontent*: in both cases, the hirer plans to double-cross the killer, who turns the tables; but in *The Changeling* he has already gone through with the murder. De Flores can have no status whatsoever as a moral commentator. His behaviour is not characterized by ethical insight, but by the ability to argue a case. In some respects, indeed, he shares Beatrice's misconceptions: he thinks that his 'conscience might have slept at ease' (70) if he had used an assassin himself. Correcting Beatrice, though the purpose of the scene, is only the means to an end for him: he does not seek to make her virtuous, but to make her his.

In some respects the confrontation scene resembles films of the 'spoiled heiress' genre, such as *It Happened One Night* (1934), that was popular in America in the 1930s, in which upper-class girls are forced to rough it and are otherwise humiliated in order to teach them the realities of life. Such films enacted a lower-class revenge on the rich, extenuating it by inculcating moral development in the victimized heroine. There is no such development in Beatrice, however. She never comes to understand the enormity of homicide: in Act v, she is readier to confess to murder than adultery. She learns nothing about morality because De Flores has nothing to teach her. This makes her suffering at his hands pointless, however justifiable in strict moral terms. In the scene's severity, the authors are indulging in pure revenge on their creation: they expose her defects of character without showing her how to remedy them.

This is why the confrontation scene is almost entirely retrospective. If Beatrice became moral by becoming damned, as T. S. Eliot suggested, it would have initiated something for the last two Acts to develop.[8] In fact, De Flores shows her that she is at his moral level, and that is a level at which pragmatic concerns predominate—the satisfaction of bodily desires, and not getting caught. As a result, all that the scene bequeaths the rest of the play is mere plot: scenes of deception and detection. Their impoverishment reflects the impoverishment of the central characters that is enacted in the central scene.

II

There are only a few other substantial treatments of the assassin from the late Jacobean and Caroline period. Like *The Changeling*, they are primarily concerned with the situation, and play adroit games with the conventions involved. Philip Massinger's *The Duke of Milan* is a particularly clinical

---

[8] T. S. Eliot, *Selected Essays*, 3rd edn. (1951), 163.

example. The assassin scenario occurs at the start of the play: the title character, Ludovico Sforza, is concerned that his wife Marcelia should not survive him, and in Act I he hesitantly commissions his favourite, Francisco, to murder her in the event of his death; in Act II, Francisco double-crosses him by showing her the warrant.

We have met the situation many times before; but this play works to subvert it. At first, Sforza seems to be the leading villain: besides being murderous, he is named after a famous tyrant, though based on his son, Francesco Sforza. Admittedly he wants Marcelia dead for reasons of love, not lust or political ambition; and Francisco, 'of all Men the deerest' (I. iii. 293) to him, is an odd choice to perform the task. These are Massinger's loopholes. As the play goes on, we are shown a man with many good qualities whose extreme passion for his wife is his principal weakness. At the same time, Francisco emerges through a similar loophole, a minor character's remarks about Sforza's mistreatment of his vanished sister, as the villain: when he exposes the Duke to his wife, it is not for love of piety but in order to cuckold him; this failing, he pursues further practices against Sforza in the later Acts, all (it finally emerges) by way of revenge for his sister's lost honour. This is not simply a case, after *The Turk*, of a subsidiary villain becoming a leading one, or of the assassin becoming a revenger like Bosola. The play works by substitution, almost mathematical in its precision: the characters shed set roles in taking on others; and revenge supplants intrigue at the centre of the plot.

Part of the appeal of the play, then, lies in its changing one story into another, just as the masque scenery of Inigo Jones could transform its landscapes mechanically. Clearly Massinger is catering to a particularly sophisticated audience, one which responds to plays with its intellect as much as with its instincts—an audience, in short, of connoisseurs. Martin Butler has posited such an audience, pointing out that many Caroline plays expect recognition of allusions to earlier plays.[9] This was true not just of specific works but also of stock scenarios. Dramatists had a long tradition of 'what happens in plays' to draw on, including murder by a hired killer: several plays of the period, such as *The Custom of the Country*, *The Fatal Marriage* (1620s), and *The Sparagus Garden* (1635), have comic scenes which exploit the conventions of the assassin scenario to make characters believe, reasonably but erroneously, that they are being hired to commit murder. *The Changeling* and *The Duke of Milan* illustrate the serious applications of such cross-referencing, the one using it to powerful moral effect, the other in an exercise of authorial virtuosity. *'Tis Pity She's a Whore* (?1630), John Ford's tragedy of incest and intrigue, offers a further approach. To understand the play's use of its principal assassin, Vasques, we must

[9] M. Butler, *Theatre and Crisis* (Cambridge, 1984), 106–7.

first understand its two-part structure. Emrys Jones has made a case that the action breaks after Act III, as seems to have been usual in Shakespeare: he points out that, by a kind of 'structural rhyming', the Cardinal appears at the end of both halves.[10] This makes the play's turning-point the accidental murder of the foolish suitor Bergetto by his rival Grimaldi: it undermines the moral authority of Richardetto, who supplied the poison, and of the Cardinal, who protects the murderer—the two characters who stand up to condemn Giovanni and Annabella, the incestuous lovers, at the end of Act v. Jones is obviously right about the division of the play, but in choosing that division, Ford has defied the dictates of his story, which falls into a different two-part structure. The narrative would be much clearer in performance if the break were placed after, not before the first scene of Act IV: the first half of the play would then present the wooing of Annabella up to her marriage, and her incest up to her repentance, while her husband Soranzo's revenge would be the subject of the second. The case for this division is also strong: each part leads up to an abortive revenge plot at a social occasion (the wedding and birthday feasts) which involves all the main characters. It is with this division in mind that Vasques, the agent of both plots, is best understood.

The principal characteristic defining Vasques on his introduction is his absolute loyalty to his master, Soranzo: when Grimaldi impugns Soranzo's honour, it is Vasques who fights him for it, and the servant later speaks out, unprompted, in Soranzo's defence (I. ii. 57–9); the one charge he seems to fear is 'neglect of duty and service' (II. ii. 20–1). After Soranzo's confrontation with his ex-lover Hippolita, however, Vasques is openly critical of his master's behaviour: 'This part has been scurvily played.' (102) It is an unexpected turn of character, and Hippolita seizes on it. Telling him that he has been 'a too trusty servant to such a master' (129–30), she persuades him to help her poison Soranzo.

His involvement in Hippolita's plot is sinister because we are never privy to his motives: stage convention had thoroughly established a character's two options in such a situation, but Ford gives us obscure hints at both possibilities. It is made clear from the first that he is not naïvely convinced by Hippolita's offer of marriage: 'I have the wind of you' (146–7), he remarks aside. A later aside shows him concealing the plot from its victim, though: when Soranzo worries that Annabella's life is in danger, Vasques murmurs, 'and so is yours, if you knew all' (III. ii. 78).

He shows his hand as an *agent provocateur* only after he has poisoned Hippolita, with the result that his status as 'a trusty servant' (IV. i. 103) is confirmed. We now understand his criticisms of Soranzo as bait to make Hippolita reveal her plans to him. But his actions are still open to question:

[10] E. Jones, *Scenic Form in Shakespeare* (Oxford, 1971), 87–8.

instead of betraying her to Soranzo at once, he kept his own counsel and took it upon himself to counter her. This uncertainty is carried over into the second half of the story, in which he orchestrates Soranzo's revenge on Giovanni.

His involvement starts, once again, with a challenge to Soranzo's treatment of a woman, this time Annabella, in order to wind himself into her confidence. On this occasion, however, he makes his intentions clear: 'leave the scenting-out your wrongs to me' (iv. iii. 99–100), he tells Soranzo aside. Even so, he assumes a surprising dominance and independence: 'be ruled, as you respect your honour, or you mar all' (100–1). He takes the lead in the affair, efficiently winkling the truth out of Annabella's nurse Putana, hiring professional killers to take care of the violence, and repeatedly bolstering Soranzo's resolution, the one thing for which he cannot take responsibility. It is as if he is determined to go through with revenge whether his master wants it or not—as if, in fact, he had an ulterior motive.

That is the Cardinal's assumption when he learns of Vasques' role in the carnage:

> Speak, wretched villain, what incarnate fiend
> Hath led thee on to this? (v. vi. 113–14)

We have been set up for a surprising revelation of the servant's true motives; but the real surprise is that there is none. His actions, he replies, grew from his 'Honesty, and pity of my master's wrongs' (115). He is nothing more than what he was first presented as being, a loyal servant acting in Soranzo's best interests. We may contrast him with the other principal servant in the play, Poggio, who is effectively Bergetto's yes-man; Vasques, however, acts for his master's good rather than in accordance with his expressed wishes. The Cardinal clearly takes the point: first addressed as 'wretched villain' (113), Vasques is now upgraded to 'fellow' (122, 140); and whereas Putana is sentenced to death, he receives the mitigated penalty of banishment, 'since what thou didst was done | Not for thyself' (140–1).

Ford exploits his audience's connoisseurship in a variety of ways: he renders the lovers' incest disturbing by presenting it in terms of *Romeo and Juliet*; and by killing his comic character, the prototypical 'upper-class twit' Bergetto, he achieves an important moment of pathos.[11] In the case of Vasques, the intricate plotting works as an elaborate guessing-game: the audience knows the parameters in which stage assassins operate, and tries to work out which option Ford has taken. Whereas Elizabethan audiences watched the villain playing out his intrigues, Ford's is practised upon by the dramatist.

[11] On Ford's use of Shakespeare, see R. L. Smallwood, *Cahiers Élisabéthains*, 20 (Oct. 1981), 49–70.

In these plays, we are offered a peculiarly literary kind of pleasure, unrelated to human experience or ideological content. The dramatists seem uninterested in the assassin as anything other than an established stage type: they use him late in a tradition to which they have nothing to add. Even the major, if flawed, achievement of *The Changeling* has a quality of finality: the play sophisticates what has gone before; it does not initiate new developments. It is as if, well-worked as it had been over the preceding thirty-five years, the character has reached the limits of innovation.

III

The assassin did not simply fall into abeyance in these years, however: there was no shortage of minor plays using the character. The decline was rather an abatement of inventiveness: dramatists were largely content to re-use the characteristics and devices which their predecessors had developed, rarely adding anything of their own. Audiences evidently knew these features intimately: it was exactly the situation to produce Ford's smart, self-consciously playful treatments of the conventions in *'Tis Pity* and later, more feebly, *The Lady's Trial* (discussed in Chapter 7).

Let us consider, for example, the subsequent influence of the last innovator with the assassin, Webster. We should expect this to have been considerable: *The Duchess of Malfi* was successful enough with the King's Men to merit several revivals, and though *The White Devil* flopped at the Red Bull, it too had been 'divers times Acted' at the Phoenix by 1631.[12] Moreover, we should expect a particular pattern of influence, operating on two separate levels: external details and aesthetic sophistication. The former are always more detectable, because more easily imitable; sophistication requires talent; and, however influenced by Webster at a deep level, talented dramatists would probably wish to follow their own interests. In other words, we should find some plays scavenging scraps from Webster, while others, more individual in character, capitalize on his innovations.

A number of plays show indebtedness of the first kind. Webster's distinctive tone was imitated, for instance. Antipater, the bastard assassin-turned-hirer in *Herod and Antipater* (1621), has a smack of Flamineo in him as he dies:

> welcome Death;
> I, that have made thee as mine instrument,
> Will make thee my companion; and, I thus
> Ascend and come to meete thee.   (v. ii. 270–3)

---

12 Bentley, i. 132, 259.

Some dramatists recycled plot elements: like Flamineo, the villain of Lodowick Carlell's *The Deserving Favourite* (?1628), Jacomo, inveigles himself into a man's service as an assassin, proposing the murder himself, for his own purposes—

> For though great men for bloudy deeds
> Give money to a Knave;
> Yet if hee bee a witty one like mee,
> Hee'l make that Lord his Slave. (B4ᵛ)

Others turned to *The White Devil* for picturesque murder methods: the poisoned picture that kills Isabella in Webster's play was adopted by John Tatham in *The Distracted State* (1650), for example, and in James Shirley's *The Traitor* (1631), one of the mock charges made against Depazzi by his page is that he hired a groom to poison the Duke's saddle, one of Lodovico's favoured techniques for dispatching Bracciano.[13]

Most importantly, a number of plays recycled aspects of the characters of Webster's assassins. In *The Duke of Milan*, a play which Fredson Bowers thinks is 'linked in spirit' with *The White Devil*, Francisco knows, like Flamineo, that in a ducal court one must 'stoope to rise' (I. ii. 38); and the satirical tendencies of Castruchio, the killer in William Davenant's *The Cruel Brother* (1627), have been traced to Bosola.[14] There is an especially thorough imitation of Bosola in Dekker's 'comedy of disguises', *The Welsh Ambassador* (1623), in which the captain Voltimar is employed as a murderer. Like Bosola, his lethal work has begun before the start of the play, and when his services are re-engaged, he asks reluctantly, 'anie more throates to cutt?' (II. i. 154–5); but the new job turns out to be spying, not killing. He too has doubts about the murder because the victim was a virtuous man, and he too is delivered up to the law by his employer, though without the benefit of the pardon Ferdinand promises Bosola. Fortunately for him, he turns out, like so many characters before him, to have spared the victim.

All these are borrowings of the most superficial aspects of Webster's murderers: only a few plays take on any element of his empathy with these men. Dekker catches his former collaborator's sense of the peculiar precariousness of the assassin's position when he makes Voltimar say, 'A serving mans life ... walkes butt upon rotten crutches' (IV. ii. 15–16), but the remark is not made apropos of his own lot, nor, since the play is a tragicomedy and he not really a murderer, could Dekker develop it so. Thomas May suggests the same insecurity in a scene of his *Julia Agrippina* (1628) between Nero and his poisoner Locusta. Nero has had her administer

---

[13] J. Shirley, *The Traitor*, III. i. 106–7, from J. Webster, *The White Devil*, v. i. 69–70.

[14] F. T. Bowers, *Elizabethan Revenge Tragedy* (Princeton, NJ, 1940), 194; L. Potter (ed.), *The Revels History of Drama in English* iv. *1613–1660* (1981), 211.

to Britannicus 'a gentle poyson' (iv. 1002), which will take time to operate; but in that time, he has become paranoid about her fidelity. In the scene in question, he summons her, beats her, and then confronts her with the suggestion that she gave Britannicus 'an antidote' (999) instead of poison. Finally he instructs her to use a strong poison that will work instantly, assuring her that if Britannicus outlives the day, she will not. Locusta attracts a degree of sympathy despite her profession: we see her beaten and crying for mercy before she knows the reason, and when she learns it, it proves to be false. Like Bosola, she has carried out her orders faithfully, and falls a prey to the unstable moods of her master.[15]

Of the second type of Websterian influence, on the sophistication of later treatments of the assassin, there is virtually no sign. Webster's breakthrough had been to bring the assassin out of the shadow of the hirer, altering the traditional disposition of narrative that made him a functionary. This meant that he could go beyond stereotyping and portray hired murderers as tragic principals with the same complexity of characterization as we might find in, say, a Shakespearean tragic hero. Such complexity was never seen again. Even in *The Changeling*, the hirer predominates: it is not a play about De Flores so much as the use of De Flores by Beatrice; and, being deliberately unconventional, it draws most on more straightforward assassin scenarios than Webster's.

One play we should consider here is Fletcher and Massinger's *The False One*, which deals with Rome's relations with Egypt after Pharsalia. One of the more distinctive characters is Septimius, 'a revolted Roman Villain' (p.300) who is employed to butcher Pompey at the start of the play. He is a satirist known for 'scurrilous wit against authority' (p.304); occasionally there is acute social comment in his dialogue, such as his observation that, unless 'all the Gallants of the Court are Eunuchs', whores are safe from whipping until they are 'out of date' (p.305). It is his satire that makes him acceptable as a hanger-on of the great, including even his targets; but he retains a nagging sense that, as a Roman, he is an outsider in Egyptian society. His first action in the play is to inform the ambitious politician Photinus that he is available for employment, even if the job were

> A deed so dark, the Sun would blush to look on,
> For which Man-kind would curse me, and arm all
> The powers above, and those below against me.   (p. 306)

In the same conversation, he encourages Photinus to seek the crown, as he does in the second half of the play. The implication is that he is offering his services as a regicide. In fact, his commission proves to be for Pompey, not King Ptolemy, and the consequences are not what he expected:

---

[15] There is, however, no *prima-facie* evidence of Webster's direct influence on this play.

> I now perceive the great Thieves eat the less,
> And the huge Leviathans of Villany
> Sup up the merits, nay the men and all
> That do them service, and spowt 'em out again
> Into the air, as thin and unregarded
> As drops of Water that are lost i'th' Ocean.   (p. 322)

Instead of securing him a place in society, the murder has made him *persona non grata*.

The similarities with Bosola and especially Flamineo are too obvious to need listing. But the treatment of Septimius also partakes of the economic themes addressed through hired assassins. He is an atheist who attacks 'vertuous Morals, | And old religious principles, that fool us' (p. 304), and when Photinus pays him for the murder, belying his sense of betrayal, he says of the gold,

> This is the Lord I serve, the Power I worship,
> My Friends, Allies, and here lies my Allegiance.   (p. 323)

He believes that he can buy his way into society:

> This God creates new tongues, and new affections;
> And though I had kill'd my Father, give me Gold
> I'll make men swear I have done a pious Sacrifice.   (p. 323)

A later scene is devoted to disabusing him of this notion. Clad in fine new clothes as 'a span-new Gallant, | Fit for the choycest eyes' (p. 334), he finds that, in turn, the Roman officers, his ex-girlfriend, and three lame soldiers all reject his money and gifts when they learn who he is and what he has done:

> For mony, seldom they refuse a Leper:
> But sure I am more odious, more diseas'd too.   (p. 337)

When he next appears, he has 'given away his Gold to honest uses' (p. 352) and turned penitent.

Except for Caesar, Septimius is the only character in the play to develop in any significant way; and though, being both an assassin and a historical nonentity, he is not suited to a major role in the main plot, Fletcher and Massinger make his story the mainspring of a sub-plot, their principal departure from historical sources. He is also the title-character. Other figures, it is true, have some claim to be false ones: Ptolemy consents to the murder of his guardian, Pompey; Caesar knows his treason caused the civil war, and is temporarily unfaithful to Cleopatra out of avarice; and Photinus rebels against his King. But it is Septimius who is most entirely false, a deserter who murders his old commander, and whose allegiance changes from scene to scene; 'I in my nature | Was fashion'd to be false' (p. 362), he admits.

The Beaumont and Fletcher Folio of 1647 called *The False One* a tragedy, but Clifford Leech dissents, because 'all the main characters find in it a satisfactory ending'.[16] This is not true: Achillas and Photinus are beheaded, Ptolemy and the priest Achoreus are trampled to death, and Septimius is hanged on Caesar's orders when he tries to switch his loyalties back to Rome. Of these deaths, only the last has an element of tragedy: Ptolemy and Achoreus are killed by accident, and the other two villains have shown no potential for reformation—they are simply evil men coming to a bad end, so there is no sense of loss. In his scene of repentance, however, Septimius comes close to adopting a virtuous life, winning the admiration of the three soldiers who had earlier rejected him:

> If it be possible
> That an Arch-Villain may ever be recovered,
> This penitent Rascal will put hard.   (p. 352)

The events of this scene are the fulcrum of his tragedy. The first reverse comes when he asks Achoreus how he may atone for his sin of murder. The answer is severe and categorical:

> come not near the altar,
> Nor with thy reeking hands pollute the Sacrifice,
> Thou art markt for shame eternal.   (p. 354)

With hope of redemption blocked off like this, he can only fall again; and since Photinus has another use for him, as Caesar's murderer, fall he does. His resistance is neatly dramatized:

SEPTIMIUS
I am afraid you will once more—
PHOTINUS
Help to raise thee

.   .   .   .

SEPTIMIUS   I now feel
My self returning Rascal speedily.
O that I had the power—
ACHILLAS   Thou shalt have all:
And do all through thy power, men shall admire thee,
And the vices of *Septimius* shall turn vertues.
SEPTIMIUS
Off: off: thou must off: off my cowardize,
Puling repentance off.   (p. 356)

Each time the assassin struggles, the tempters interrupt him, deliberately misinterpreting his words and imposing their own opportunist system of values.

---

[16] C. Leech, *The John Fletcher Plays* (1962), 48.

With his collapse, Septimius is set on course for tragedy. He soon realizes that he has no future as a hired murderer:

> The Devil, *Photinus*,
> Employs me as a Property, and grown useless
> Will shake me off again ...
> ... Services done
> For such as only study their own ends,
> Too great to be rewarded, are return'd
> With deadly hate. (p. 362)

With his eye on the main chance, he offers to help Caesar turn the tables on the conspirators; but once again he has underestimated the virtue of others. Caesar rejects his proposal and, 'Nor true to Friend nor Enemy' (p. 364), he meets his ignoble end.

Baldwin Maxwell has made a case that Fletcher and Massinger developed the character of Septimius in order to exploit popular resentment against Sir Lewis Stukeley, who had been instrumental in the execution of Ralegh in 1618.[17] His argument is flawed in two respects. First, he takes Septimius to be a wholly depraved and contemptible character, ignoring his penitent scene. Though Achoreus, the play's most consistently moral figure, rejects him at this point, his is not the preferred viewpoint in the scene—it is the three soldiers who hold the stage, and their opinion is more humane and charitable. Achoreus, that is, condemns himself more effectively than Septimius here.

Secondly, Maxwell does not consider the fact that, as a hired murderer, Septimius is a character in a long tradition. Audiences would more likely see him in relation to other exemplars than to a real individual whose career had some vague similarities. We can best understand him, then, as a character created in the wake of Webster's assassins, a major tragic figure who has other elements of Flamineo and Bosola besides.

As an attempt to follow Webster's assassins, however, Septimius is not altogether successful: there is none of the earlier dramatist's subtlety, for the characterization generally works at the level of direct statement; and Websterian features coexist with older motifs, giving the whole a cobbled-together look. Though Fletcher and Massinger take advantage of the novel elements in Webster's work, the aim seems to be to cash in on their predecessor's success: *The False One* belongs with the more superficially imitative class of his dependants.

The pattern of Webster's influence, then, is not what we anticipated: some of his assassins' attributes were plundered to enrich the stereotype, but no playwright took up the challenge of portraying such figures as more than

[17] B. Maxwell, *Studies in Beaumont, Fletcher, and Massinger* (Chapel Hill, NC, 1939), 166–76.

stereotypes. We could hypothesize various explanations for this, but only one seems plausible. To suggest that there was a general falling-off of talent after Webster is untenable: Middleton, for example, continued writing until the 1620s, Webster himself did not end his career with *The Duchess of Malfi*, and after the work of Martin Butler, it would be unwise to write off Caroline drama either. Moreover, major writers did not ignore Webster altogether: Massinger and Shirley are among the authors responsible for the imitations detailed above. The obvious conclusion seems to be that these dramatists were simply not interested, as Webster had been, in exploring the character of the professional killer. To substantiate this hypothesis, we must first examine more extensively how the type was used in the years after *The Duchess*.

IV

The three decades leading up to the closure of the theatres were not, of course, a period during which theatrical fashion and taste marked time, but there are some general observations to be made about the use of the assassin during these years. Old plays continued in the repertory, and incidents in new ones are often derivative: Webster is a case in point. Another is *Macbeth*: we know little of its stage history during this period, but it was a frequent quarry for imitators. The murder plot of *Thorny Abbey* (c.1615) is founded upon it, with assassins imported from the Banquo scenes to kill the King; his grooms are also murdered, and, like Macbeth, the instigator of the regicide suggests that they were 'perhaps hired to doe it' (v. 73). The villain's arrangements in Henry Killigrew's *The Conspiracy* (1635) are also plainly modelled on Macbeth's provisions for the murder of Banquo: he sends his chosen killers written instructions, ordering that they 'receive this man the bearer into your company and councell' (B4ʳ). Elsewhere we find echoes of *The Malcontent*: Lodovick Sforza, for instance, contains a scene in which the assassin is 'killed' with his own poison, which turns out to be harmless.

There are also general similarities with the hired assassin of the 1580s and 1590s; plays of this era were still to be seen at the open-air theatres.[18] Advances since Kyd's inception of the character were not transformations but accretions: it is true that, as we saw in Chapter 5, the old question of tyrannical commands had lost its potency, but the relation of morality to economic activity remained a live issue. In *The False One*, pseudo-Websterian traits coexist with features that address that issue, and such features continued in use throughout Caroline times and beyond.

Occasionally there are finely conceived moments. In *The Bloody Banquet*

[18] See Butler, *Theatre and Crisis*, ch. 8.

(?1639), for example, the attendant Roxano chooses between the roles of pander and assassin by comparing the fee he has received for each: 'here's gold to bring *Tymethes*, and here's gold to kill *Tymethes*. I, let me see, which weighes heaviest; by my faith I thinke the killing gold will carry't: I shall like many a bad Lawyer, runne my Conscience upon the greatest fee; who gives most is like to fare best.' (927–31) The act of weighing bizarrely parodies the scales of justice, underlined by the explicit moral commentary; it is a neatly abbreviated portrayal of Roxano's decision. However, in most cases dramatists simply recycled ideas going back to the 1590s. The poisoner in Francis Quarles's *The Virgin Widow* (1641–2) is a worshipper of 'Almighty Gold' (F3ʳ): the pun introduces a religious frame of reference that marks him off from Christianity, as with the Messenger in *King Leir*. Ideologies are shown to be in conflict when the dumb-show murderers in Middleton's *Hengist, King of Kent* (1619–20) have the usual crisis of conscience:

> a while there fell a strife
> Of Pittye and furye, but the gold
> Made pittye faint, and furye bold.   (Chorus 3. 4–6)

Murder is 'the best thriving trade', and the professional is strikingly juxtaposed with the illicit: 'Men of our needfull profession, that deale in such commodities as mens lives, had need to looke about 'em 're they trafficke'.[19] The hired assassin has no allegiance to his employer, and will kill him as readily as the target if paid to do so; and the wages of murder proves to be death.[20]

Treatments were not entirely retrospective, however. From about the turn of the century, the assassin had been gravitating towards Mediterranean settings like Spain and Italy. In the 1580s and 1590s, the predominant setting was English, with other locations—north European, Mediterranean, classical, Ottoman, biblical—forming a large minority. By the 1630s, however, settings in Spain and Italy had become the norm, while an English or classical location for this kind of villainy had become exceptional. This need not be significant in itself, for there was a general tendency to geographical remoteness in Caroline drama. What is important is the change in the treatment of these foreign settings.

In the sixteenth century, Italy and Spain seem to have been generic Mediterranean locations: there is nothing especially Spanish about the Spain of *The Spanish Tragedy* or *Mucedorus*, any more than there is anything quintessentially Danish about Elsinore. It seems to have been in the early Jacobean drama that consciously 'Italianate' settings became popular, in plays like *The Malcontent*, *The Revenger's Tragedy*, and *The Turk*; and soon

---

[19] N. Richards, *Messalina*, l. 1286; T. Rawlins, *The Rebellion*, I2ᵛ.
[20] R. Gomersall, *Lodovick Sforza*, ll. 445–7; J. Tatham, *The Distracted State*, 91, 97.

afterwards, subjects were taken from actual Italian history, as in *The Devil's Charter* and, less luridly, *The White Devil*. By Caroline times, the Mediterranean countries were being portrayed more naturalistically, *loci* of vice and corruption rather than of wickedness *per se*. One effect of this new approach was a new type of hired assassin: the professional bravo.

The first bravo in extant English drama appeared about 1620 in one of Massinger's scenes of *The Custom of the Country*, set in Spain. The play is trashy, the incident pointless: the bravo is engaged to beat a man, and rapidly disengaged because he prefers to commit murder. Contributing nothing to the plot, the character is there solely to raise a wry laugh when he sets his fee for assault at twice the rate for murder—because, he reasons, 'should I beat or hurt him only, he may | Recover, and kill me' (p.352). Despite its faults the play was popular; the joke itself was imitated in *The Antiquary* (E4ʳ).[21] From the 1630s onwards assassins in Italian and Spanish settings were often identified as bravos.

Massinger's scene illustrates one important point about bravos: they did not confine their services to murder. Like the *bravi* in Italian drama of the sixteenth century, they are professional ruffians who offer lesser forms of violence too. In Thomas Killigrew's *The Princess* (1636) they help in a street-fight, for example, and in Shirley's *The Gentleman of Venice* (1639) they abduct and restrain people against their will; but in each case there are indications that they are also frequently employed as killers. In the bravo, then, the hiring of a murderer, a hitherto distinct activity, fuses with the hiring of a bully.

A corollary was that bravos would 'kill, or wound at severall prises'.[22] They had, that is, a fixed scale of charges according to the nature of the service provided. This could reflect other factors than the degree of violence involved: in *The Antiquary*, there are six rates for different classes of victim— lord, knight, gentleman, peasant, 'Stranger', and 'Native' (E3ᵛ). Obviously the appeal of this detail relates to the economic concerns still being addressed in the assassin type: it is a normal trade practice applied to the murder market.

Similarly, many bravos attempt to defend their calling on grounds of social usefulness: it is a 'needfull profession' according to the 'Brave' in *The Rebellion* (I2ᵛ), and the bravo in *The Antiquary* claims to be 'a kinde of lawlesse Justicer' (E4ᵛ). In *Imperiale*, Sir Ralph Freeman gives most of his characters the chance to justify their actions, and the killer Verdugo is no exception.[23] He argues at length that bravos promote civility by efficiently enacting revenge on wrongdoers, and that the trade is no worse than the soldier's;

[21] Bentley, iii. 327–8.
[22] Sir R. Freeman, *Imperiale* (1639), D4ʳ.
[23] C. C. Gumm, *Studies in English Drama*, 1st ser., ed. A. Gaw (New York, 1917), 122.

and at least, unlike usurers, they kill their victims swiftly.[24] Being practitioners in an established trade, these characters are claiming the corresponding established status; but morality is noticeably absent from their reasoning. In these respects, the stage bravo was not an innovation: when used as a murderer, he contributed a sharper edge to the convention of the assassin's professionalism; but in that he was simply a new bottle for old wine.

Attention to Continental institutions may also account for a more general trend. Earlier assassins had typically worked singly or in pairs, whereas Italians sometimes employed *bravi* in gangs. In the later Jacobean period, there is some recognition of this practice: in *The Duchess of Malfi*, the Cardinal offers Bosola 'some dozen of attendants' (v. ii. 313) to help him with the murder of Antonio, and in *Thierry and Theodoret* (1617), a character lies that there are 'Six villaines, | Sworne and in pay to kill mee' (II. iii. 28–9). Usually these are no more than references, though *'Tis Pity She's a Whore* requires an unspecified but apparently considerable number of banditti to perform the final massacre. *The Double Marriage* (1620) also has a group of four Switzers who are hired for a murder, but they are more important characters in disguise. In practice it may have been undesirable for a theatre company to expend actors in large numbers on such parts; but this seems to have occurred after the Restoration, with groups of four murderers in Thomas Otway's *Alcibiades* (1675), six in Thomas Southerne's *Sir Anthony Love* (1690), and eight in Dryden and Lee's *The Duke of Guise* (1682). Larger numbers made for more exciting stage action, and required no dialogue, and in consequence, characterization reached new degrees of minimalism in these plays: one of the bravos in *Sir Anthony Love* has a few unremarkable lines, but only when separated from his fellows; and in *The Duke of Guise*, the murderers are all non-speaking parts without intrinsic interest.

These Restoration dramatists had their reasons for underplaying the assassin like this: evidently the state of audience taste was such that, in these cases at least, action was more appealing than any of the effects that would be possible if the murderers were to be developed as characters. We can judge why from a more substantial treatment of the type, in a contemporary London setting, in Otway's comedy *The Soldier's Fortune* (1680). The plot concerns Beaugard's cuckolding Sir Davy Dunce by inducing Sir Davy to have him murdered, and then having his 'corpse' laid in Lady Dunce's room; the assassins are really Beaugard's French servant Fourbin, in disguise, and Bloody-Bones, who claims to be a professional cut-throat, born in Algier the son of 'a Ranegado *English* Man' and 'an Apostate *Greek*' (IV. 267–8), but who appears actually to be a servant of Beaugard's confederate Sir Jolly Jumble. In a long and entertaining hiring scene, Bloody-Bones explains that assassins have recently become common in England as a result of the insecurity engendered by the Popish Plot: 'In peaceable times a man may eat and drink comfortably upon't, a private Murder done handsomely is worth Money: but now that the Nation's unsettled, there are so many general undertakers, that 'tis grown almost a Monopoly, you may have a man Murder'd almost for little or nothing and no Body e'r know who did it neither.' (258–63) Market forces have operated to push down the price of blood, that is, and so it is harder to make a living as an assassin.

The characters have links with the stage bravo in economic concerns such as these: elsewhere, Bloody-Bones insists that he is a professional murderer, not a tradesman, because only 'Rascally Butchers make a trade on't' (244–5); and Fourbin sets the cost of a beating at half that of a murder (366–8). But these are literary motifs, and were perceived as such: before the end of the century, Gerard Langbaine pointed to the bravo in *The Antiquary* as Otway's source.[25] Indeed, the entire murder incident is self-consciously literary in character. When, for example, Sir Davy enters his wife's room to find Beaugard alive, he thinks he is seeing a ghost and utters familiar lines: 'who has done this? thou can'st not say I did it' (v. 377–8).[26] Shakespeare's words here only underline the triviality, and unreality, of the intrigue.

Accordingly, the primary appeal of Bloody-Bones lies in the extravagance of the character. His name is that of a nursery bugbear (as in 'raw-head and bloody-bones'), and at one point he even says, 'Fee, Fa, Fum' (IV. 403). Appropriately, he has cannibalistic tendencies which he shares with Fourbin, also larger than life in his role of Second Murderer: a human heart 'makes absolutely the best Raggoust in the World. I have eaten forty of 'em in my time without Bread' (297–9), says Fourbin; Bloody-Bones adds his preference for 'your well-grown Dutchmans Heart ... with Oyl and Pepper' (303–5). His career began with parricide and subsequently included military exploits in Malta, escape from prison, and selling his soul to the Devil. We learn some of this when Sir Davy demurs at paying £200 for the crime, and, by way of coercion, Bloody-Bones puts on a fit in which he speaks the only verse dialogue in the play:

> Have I for this dissolv'd Circean Charms?
> Broke Iron durance: whilst from these firm Legs
> The well fil'd useless Fetters dropt away,
> And left me Master of my native freedom?   (337–40)

In 1680, this rhetorical, huffing style, so unlike that of the rest of the play, was nearly a century old. Exaggerated, antiquated, and somewhat revolting, Bloody-Bones looks thoroughly out of place in his role of hired murderer. The assassin did not disappear altogether from Restoration drama: he was

---

[25] G. Langbaine, *An Account of the English Dramatick Poets* (Oxford, 1691), 399.
[26] Cf. W. Shakespeare, *Macbeth*, III. iv. 48–9.

too useful a minor character to do away with, but also too old-fashioned to be worth developing. When the plays of Shakespeare and his successors were adapted for Restoration audiences, then, the assassin's part was often reduced. There are exceptions, to be sure: the murderers of Duke Humphrey are greatly expanded into a comic double-act in John Crowne's recasting of *Henry VI, Part 2* (1681), and Nahum Tate's *King Lear* (1681) has a new scene in which Lear beats off Cordelia's murderers, stressing her survival in this version as well as giving the opportunity for a stage fight. But where such theatrical opportunities were not to be had, the tendency was to excision. Tate's revision of *Richard II, The Sicilian Usurper* (1680), removes the scene where Exton interprets Bolingbroke's words, and has Bolingbroke speak them on stage instead, at considerable cost to our sense of Exton's autonomy. In the anonymous *Piso's Conspiracy* (1675), an adaptation of *Nero* (?1618–19), Nero's murderous factotum Tigellinus loses the opportunity to explain his motives in soliloquy. When Thomas D'Urfey turned *Cymbeline* into *The Injured Princess* (1682), he made Pisanio a concerned friend, not a faithful servant, and so not strictly speaking an assassin at all. The murderers of Lady Macduff disappear altogether from William Davenant's *Macbeth* (1664), as do Clarence's from Colley Cibber's *Richard III* (1699). It is true that Cibber brings the princes' murderers Dighton and Forrest on stage and gives them a few lines, but this is primarily to frame the sequence in which Richard paces like a nervous expectant father outside the chamber where the murder is taking place, wishing it were over and done with: the focus, here as elsewhere, is on the central villain, at the expense of his instruments.

The creeping vitiation of the assassin in the course of the seventeenth century, and the shift towards the Mediterranean, become explicable in the light of the historical context: though the ideological content of the stereotype apparently remained the same, the other conditions no longer obtained that had originally produced an interest in the assassin in the later Elizabethan period. The perceived threat to the monarch had decreased markedly by the 1630s. The Gunpowder Plot of 1605 was the only major conspiracy to assassinate James I, and in England the last major stir over regicide before the very different circumstances of 1649 came in the aftermath of the murder of Henry IV in 1610: the comparisons that commentators liked to draw between the two cases reflect not only the perceived enormity of such crimes but also their relative infrequency.[27] Political assassinations continued sporadically throughout Europe (Ancre in 1617, Buckingham in 1628, Wallenstein in 1634), but with nothing like the frequency of the later sixteenth century; one biographer of Charles I notes with evident surprise that there were no attempts on his life during his personal rule, despite the unpopularity

---

[27] e.g. E. Skory, *An Extract ovt of the Historie of the last French King* (1610), D3^{r-v}.

of his government.[28] Assassination, according to one Interregnum writer, was 'a Villany scarce heard of in our Nation'.[29]

It is true that, even in the Restoration, such confidence was brittle: the fantasies of Titus Oates and his apes could not otherwise have produced the hysterical paranoia they did. Yet the very intensity of that hysteria may itself have been a reaction to the sense of security that had been growing for the best part of the century: just as the popular mind had consigned hired killers and international Catholic conspiracies to the Elizabethan past, they returned to threaten the nation's stability in 1678. Nonetheless, the Popish Plot did not institute a new age of assassination scares: it was an aberration in a century that saw the fear of regicide gradually edged out of mainstream English culture.

The same development seems to have occurred with the hired assassin. Obviously it is harder to generalize about cases. The Overbury murder, the single most celebrated use of paid killers in the seventeenth century, was committed in 1613 and came out two years later. According to Lawrence Stone, however, in the same decade it had become discreditable for aristocrats to keep bands of retainers to fight and kill for them, and the practice had fallen into abeyance: 'Though I keep men I fight not with their fingers,' says a gentleman in *The City Madam* (1632), eschewing upper-class vices.[30] Again, attention to the Popish Plot can distort the overall picture. It is true that the lies spun by William Bedloe and others around the unsolved murder of Sir Edmund Berry Godfrey in 1678 presented English Catholic hirelings as the culprits.[31] In general, however, the hired killer was seen after the Restoration as a villain most endemic on the Continent: there are references to 'the *Spanish-Bravo*', to 'the *A-la-mode*-Murderers, the *Poysoners in France*', and to being dogged by *bravi* in Rome.[32] English cases, when they occurred, took on a Continental cast: during the planning stages of the murder of Thomas Thynne in 1682, it was mooted to bring in an Italian assassin for the job; and though the three killers used hailed from Central and Eastern Europe, accounts of the crime emphasized that they were foreigners—'outlandish Villains' and 'base strangers'.[33] Assassins came to be regarded as simply un-English: in 1705, Daniel Defoe said that a recent murder case had 'something peculiar in it . . . for which it requires a most just Resentment from the English

---

[28] C. Carlton, *Charles I: The Personal Monarch* (1984), 157.

[29] *A True Account of the Late Bloody and Inhumane Conspiracy Against His Highness The Lord Protector* (1654), C4ᵛ.

[30] L. Stone, *The Crisis of the Aristocracy* (Oxford, 1965), 226; P. Massinger, *The City Madam*, I. ii. 38.   [31] J. P. Kenyon, *The Popish Plot* (1972), 94, 133.

[32] E. Hickeringill, *The Character of A Sham-Plotter or Man-Catcher* (1681), recto and verso; J. Addison, R. Steele, and others, *The Spectator*, ed. G. Smith, rev. edn. (1945), i. 411.

[33] H. Vizetelly, *Count Königsmark and 'Tom of Ten Thousand'* (1890), 82; *The Roxburghe Ballads*, ed. W. Chappell and J. W. Ebsworth (1871–97), v. 111; *Directions to Fame, About an Elegy On the Late Deceased Thomas Thynn, Esq* (1682), D4ʳ.

Nation; and that is the Practice of hiring Men to Beat and Murther their Enemy'.[34] Opinions like this were to continue in currency until the twentieth century.

It is in the context of this gradual exclusion of hired murderers that we can best understand the decline of the stage assassin in the 1620s and 1630s. The character was becoming a feature of alien, barbarous societies, appearing in English settings mostly in remote, pre-Conquest history. There was little place for murderous intrigue in the cultivated *beau monde* that was the England of Caroline drama. Without any relation to the contemporary understanding of real life, the assassin was not a figure to warrant major treatment in the manner of Webster. Instead he became, as a bravo, a piece of picturesque local colour, and in general, a literary fossil whose characterization came increasingly from simple repetition of the paradigms established in an earlier age.

[34] D. Defoe, *The Little Review*, 3 (13 June 1705), 10.

APPENDIX A

Chronological List of Plays

THIS Appendix lists sixteenth- and seventeenth-century plays written in English, or associated with English authors or performers, that include assassins among their on- or off-stage characters. In the definition of an assassin, I include characters who are identified as such but do not take on that role in the action of the play, and characters who are asked to act as assassins but do not comply; but I exclude characters who are identified as potential assassins but never asked, and related figures such as comic accomplices or sellers of poison. Also excluded are plays which contain general references to assassins or their employment, or historical or literary allusions to assassins. Revisions and adaptations are included where the assassin's part has undergone significant amendment or extension. The supplementary list gives non-extant plays in which there is reason (generally in the subject-matter) to suppose that an assassin may have appeared; but obviously we cannot be certain in such cases. I have not attempted to be comprehensive in the listing of plays which were not written for the professional London companies, or which were written after 1642.

Most of the dates given here are, of course, approximate; I have tried to indicate significant uncertainties. Alternative titles are given when they have a bearing on the identity of the play; assigned titles appear in square brackets. Plays in which an assassin features but does not appear on stage are marked with an asterisk.

Date	Play	Author	Company
c.1561	Cambises, King of Persia	Thomas Preston	Unknown
1562	Gorboduc*	Thomas Norton and Thomas Sackville	Gentlemen of the Inner Temple
1566	Jocasta*	Ludovico Dolce, tr. George Gascoigne and Francis Kinwelmershe	Gray's Inn
1566	Octavia	'Seneca', tr. Thomas Nuce	Unacted
1568	Gismond of Salerne	Robert Wilmot and others	Gentlemen of the Inner Temple
1580	Richardus Tertius, Part 3 (Latin)	Thomas Legge	St John's College, Cambridge
1582	Solymannidae tragoedia* (Latin)	Anonymous	Unknown
1582	Victoria (Latin)	Abraham Fraunce	St John's College, Cambridge

Date	Play	Author	Company
1583–4	*Fedele and Fortunio*	Anthony Munday	?Oxford's Boys
1587	*The Spanish Tragedy*	Thomas Kyd	Unknown (later Strange's, Admiral's)
c.1587	*David and Bethsabe*	George Peele	?Queen's
1588	*The Wounds of Civil War*	Thomas Lodge	Unknown (later Admiral's)
1588	*The Wars of Cyrus*	Anonymous	Chapel Boys
1588	*The Troublesome Reign of King John*	Anonymous	Queen's
1589	*The Battle of Alcazar*	George Peele	Unknown (later Admiral's)
1589	*King Leir and his Three Daughters*	Anonymous	Queen's
1590	*James IV*	Robert Greene	Unknown
1590	*Mucedorus*	Anonymous	Unknown
1590	*Arden of Faversham*	Anonymous	Unknown
1591	*Henry VI, Part 2*	William Shakespeare	?Pembroke's, ?Strange's
1591	*The True Tragedy of Richard III*	Anonymous	Queen's
c.1591 [or 1593]	*The Massacre at Paris*	Christopher Marlowe	Unknown (later Strange's)
1592	*Selimus, Emperor of the Turks*	Anonymous	Queen's
1592	*Edward II*	Christopher Marlowe	Pembroke's
1592	*Woodstock*	Anonymous	Unknown
1592–3	*Richard III*	William Shakespeare	?Pembroke's, ?Strange's
?1594	*Alphonsus, Emperor of Germany*	Anonymous	Unknown
1594–5	*Two Lamentable Tragedies*	Robert Yarington	Unknown
1595	*Caesar's Revenge*[1]	Anonymous	?Admiral's
1595	*Richard II*	William Shakespeare	Chamberlain's
1595–6	*Romeo and Juliet**	William Shakespeare	Chamberlain's
1596	*Mustapha*	Fulke Greville	Unacted
1596	*King John*	William Shakespeare	Chamberlain's
1598	*The Death of Robert, Earl of Huntingdon*	Henry Chettle and Anthony Munday	Admiral's
1598	*Much Ado About Nothing*	William Shakespeare	Chamberlain's

[1] ? a.k.a. *Caesar and Pompey, Part 2.*

Date	Play	Author	Company
1598–9	Henry V	William Shakespeare	Chamberlain's
1599	Edward IV, Part 2	Thomas Heywood	Derby's
1599	Look About You	Anonymous	Admiral's
1600	As You Like It	William Shakespeare	Chamberlain's
1600	The Weakest Goeth to the Wall	Anonymous	Oxford's
1600	Alaham	Fulke Greville	Unacted
1600	The Maid's Metamorphosis	Anonymous	Paul's Boys
1600	Jack Drum's Entertainment	John Marston	Paul's Boys
1600	The Devil and his Dame[2]	William Haughton	Admiral's
1600	The Blind Beggar of Bethnal Green, Part 1	Henry Chettle and John Day	Admiral's
?1600	The First Part of Hieronimo	Anonymous	?Chapel Boys
1602	The Gentleman Usher	George Chapman	?Chapel Boys, ?Paul's Boys
1603	Sejanus' Fall*	Ben Jonson	Chamberlain's
1603	The Malcontent	John Marston	Chapel Boys (later King's)
1603	Nero (Latin)	Matthew Gwinne	Unacted[3]
?c.1603	Der bestrafte brudermord	Anonymous	?English Players in Germany
1603–4	The Phoenix	Thomas Middleton	Paul's Boys
1603–4	Othello, the Moor of Venice	William Shakespeare	King's
1604	Bussy D'Ambois	George Chapman	Paul's Boys
1604	The Fair Maid of Bristol	Anonymous	?King's
1604	The Honest Whore, Part 1	Thomas Dekker and Thomas Middleton	Prince's
1604	Croesus	William Alexander	Unacted
1604	Charlemagne	Anonymous	Unknown
1604	Antipoe	Francis Verney	?Trinity College, Oxford
?1605	Nobody and Somebody	Anonymous	Queen's
1605	Caesar and Pompey	George Chapman	Unknown
1605	If You Know Not Me,	Thomas Heywood	Queen's

[2] a.k.a. Grim, the Collier of Croydon. [3] Rejected by St John's College, Oxford.

Date	Play	Author	Company
	You Know Nobody, Part 2		
1605	Sophonisba	John Marston	Queen's Revels Boys
?1605	Claudius Tiberius Nero	Anonymous	?Prince's
1605–6	King Lear	William Shakespeare	King's
1605–6	Volpone	Ben Jonson	King's
1606	The Revenger's Tragedy	Thomas Middleton	King's
1606	Macbeth	William Shakespeare	King's
1606	Antony and Cleopatra	William Shakespeare	King's
1606	The Devil's Charter	Barnabe Barnes	King's
1606	The Whore of Babylon	Thomas Dekker	Prince's
1607	The Turk	John Mason	King's Revels Boys
1607	Pericles, Prince of Tyre	?George Wilkins and William Shakespeare	King's
1607	The Alexandrian Tragedy*	William Alexander	Unacted
1608	Humour out of Breath	John Day	King's Revels Boys
1608	Cupid's Revenge	Francis Beaumont and John Fletcher	Queen's Revels Boys
1608	Periander	?John Sansbury	St John's College, Oxford
1609	The Atheist's Tragedy	Cyril Tourneur	?King's
1609	Cymbeline, King of Britain	William Shakespeare	King's
1609	A Woman is a Weathercock	Nathan Field	Queen's Revels Boys
1610	The Golden Age*	Thomas Heywood	Queen's
1610	The Winter's Tale	William Shakespeare	King's
1611	Catiline's Conspiracy	Ben Jonson	King's
1611 [?or 1621]	Match Me in London	Thomas Dekker	Queen's
1612	The White Devil	John Webster	Queen's
1613	The Honest Man's Fortune	John Fletcher and Nathan Field	Lady Elizabeth's
1614	Valentinian	John Fletcher	King's
1614	The Duchess of Malfi	John Webster	King's
1614	The Hector of Germany	Wentworth Smith	Tradesmen at the Red Bull
c.1615	Thorny Abbey	Anonymous	Unknown
1617	Thierry and Theodoret	John Fletcher and Philip Massinger	King's
1617	Rollo, Duke of	John Fletcher, Philip	?King's

Date	Play	Author	Company
	Normandy	Massinger, and others	
1618	*The Raging Turk*	Thomas Goffe	Christ Church, Oxford
1618	*Andronicus Comnenus* (Latin)	Samuel Bernard	Magdalen College, Oxford
?1618–19	*Nero*	Anonymous	Unknown (?King's)
1619	*Fraus honesta* (Latin)	Edmund Stubbe	Trinity College, Cambridge
1619–20	*Hengist, King of Kent*	Thomas Middleton	Unknown (later King's)
1620	*The Custom of the Country*	John Fletcher and Philip Massinger	King's
1620	*The Heir*	Thomas May	Red Bull
1620	*The False One*	John Fletcher and Philip Massinger	King's
1620	*The Virgin Martyr*	Thomas Dekker and Philip Massinger	Red Bull
1620	*The Double Marriage*	John Fletcher and Philip Massinger	King's
1621	*The Island Princess*	John Fletcher	King's
1621	*Herod and Antipater*	Gervase Markham and William Sampson	Red Bull
1621	*The Pilgrim*	John Fletcher	King's
1621	*The Duke of Milan*	Philip Massinger	King's
1622	*Beggar's Bush*	John Fletcher and Philip Massinger	King's
1622	*The Two Noble Ladies and the Converted Conjurer*	Anonymous	Red Bull
1622	*The Noble Spanish Soldier*	Thomas Dekker	Unknown
1622	*The Changeling*	Thomas Middleton and William Rowley	Lady Elizabeth's
1622	*The Prophetess*	John Fletcher and Philip Massinger	King's
1623	*The Welsh Ambassador*	Thomas Dekker	?Lady Elizabeth's
1624	*A Wife for a Month*	John Fletcher	King's
1624	*Theoctistus* (Latin)	Joseph Simons, SJ	St Omers
c.1625	*The Partial Law*	Anonymous	Unacted
1625–6	*The Valiant Scot*	'J.W.'	Unknown (later Red Bull)

Date	Play	Author	Company
1626	*The Maid's Revenge*	James Shirley	Queen's
?1626	*The Jews' Tragedy*	William Heminges	Unknown
1626–7	*Pseudomagia* (Latin)	William Mewe	Emmanuel College, Cambridge
1627	*The Cruel Brother*	William Davenant	King's
?1628	*The Deserving Favourite*	Lodowick Carlell	King's
1628	*Lodovick Sforza*	Robert Gomersall	?Unacted
1628	*Julia Agrippina, Empress of Rome*	Thomas May	Unknown
1628	*The Witty Fair One*	James Shirley	Queen's
1628	*King John and Matilda*	Robert Davenport	Queen's
1629	*The Just Italian*	William Davenant	King's
1630	*The Inconstant Lady*	Arthur Wilson	King's
?1630	*'Tis Pity She's a Whore*	John Ford	Queen's
?1630	*The Telltale*	Anonymous	Unknown
1631	*The Emperor of the East*	Philip Massinger	King's
1631	*Rhodon and Iris*	Ralph Knevet	Society of Florists, Norwich
1631	*The Traitor*	James Shirley	Queen's
1631	*Believe as You List*	Philip Massinger	King's
1631	*The Humorous Courtier*	James Shirley	Queen's
1631	*Love's Cruelty*	James Shirley	Queen's
?1631	*The Queen's Exchange*	Richard Brome	?King's
1632	*The Jealous Lovers*	Thomas Randolph	Trinity College, Cambridge
1634	*Albertus Wallenstein*	Henry Glapthorne	King's
1635	*Adrasta*	John Jones	Unacted[4]
1635	*The Conspiracy*	Henry Killigrew	Unknown (later King's)
1635	*The Prisoners*	Thomas Killigrew	Queen's
1635	*The Antiquary*	Shakerley Marmion	Queen's
1635	*Messalina the Roman Empress*	Nathaniel Richards	King's Revels
1635	*The Lady Mother*	Henry Glapthorne	King's Revels
1635	*The Platonic Lovers**	William Davenant	King's
1635	*The Queen and Concubine*	Richard Brome	King's Revels
1636	*The Duke's Mistress*	James Shirley	Queen's
1636	*The Rebellion*	Thomas Rawlins	King's Revels

[4] Rejected by players.

Date	Play	Author	Company
1636	*Arviragus and Philicia, Part 1*	Lodowick Carlell	King's
1636	*The Floating Island*	William Strode	Students of Christ Church, Oxford
1636	*The Princess*	Thomas Killigrew	?King's
?1637	*Mortimer's Fall*[5]*	Ben Jonson	Unacted
1637	*The Royal Master**	James Shirley	Ogilby's, Dublin, and Queen's
1637–8	*The Lost Lady**	William Berkeley	King's
1638	*The Passionate Lovers, Part 2*	Lodowick Carlell	King's
1638	*The Lady's Trial*	John Ford	Beeston's Boys
1638	*The Bride*	Thomas Nabbes	Beeston's Boys
?1639	*The Bloody Banquet*	?Thomas Drue	Beeston's Boys
1639	*Imperiale*	Sir Ralph Freeman	?Unacted
1639	*The Gentleman of Venice*	James Shirley	?Ogilby's, Dublin, and Queen's
?1639	*The Politician*	James Shirley	Queen's
?1640	*Thibaldus* (Latin)	Thomas Snelling	St John's College, Oxford
c.1640	*Revenge for Honour*	Henry Glapthorne	Unknown
1640	*Sicily and Naples*	Samuel Harding	Unacted
1640	*The Imposture*	James Shirley	King's
1641–2	*The Virgin Widow*	Francis Quarles	'Young Gentlemen' of Chelsea
?1642–3	*Andromana*	'J.S.'	?Unacted
1642–3	*Andronicus: Impiety's Long Success*	?Thomas Fuller	?Oxford
1650	*The Distracted State*	John Tatham	?Unacted
1650	*Cicilia and Clorinda, Part 2*	Thomas Killigrew	Unacted
1651	*Marcus Tullius Cicero*	Anonymous	?Unacted
1652	*The Bastard*	Anonymous	Unknown
c.1655	*Innocentia Purpurata* (Latin)	?Francis Clarke, SJ	St Omers
1655	*Mirza*	Robert Baron	Unacted
1658	*Love's Victory*	William Chamberlayne	Unacted
1658	*Orgula*	Leonard Willan	?Unacted
1662	*The Surprisal*	Sir Robert Howard	King's
1663	*Pompey*	Pierre Cornielle (tr. Katherine Philips)	Ogilby's, Dublin
1663	*The Unfortunate Usurper*	Anonymous	Unacted

[5] Left incomplete; relevant Act planned but unwritten.

Date	Play	Author	Company
1663	The Stepmother	Sir Robert Stapleton	Duke's
1663–4	Pompey the Great	Pierre Corneille (tr. Sir Edward Filmer, Sir Charles Sedley, and others)	Duke's
1664	The Comical Revenge	George Etherege	Duke's
1664	Andronicus Comnenius	John Wilson	Unacted
1665	Mustapha	Roger Boyle	Duke's
1666	The English Princess	John Caryl	Duke's
1667	The Spiteful Sister	Abraham Bailey	Unacted
1669	Marcelia	Frances Boothby	King's
1671	Cambyses, King of Persia	Elkanah Settle	Duke's
c.1672	Herod the Great	Roger Boyle	Unacted
1672	Henry III of France, Stabbed by a Friar	Thomas Shipman	King's
1673	The Empress of Morocco	Elkanah Settle	Duke's
1674	Nero, Emperor of Rome	Nathaniel Lee	Duke's
1674	Love and Revenge	Elkanah Settle	Duke's
1675	The Conquest of China by the Tartars	Elkanah Settle	Duke's
1675	Alcibiades	Thomas Otway	Duke's
1676	Abdelazer	Aphra Behn	Duke's
1677	Antony and Cleopatra	Sir Charles Sedley	Duke's
1677	Scaramouch a Philosopher	Edward Ravenscroft	King's
1677	Belphegor	John Wilson	Smock Alley, Dublin
1679	Caesar Borgia	Nathaniel Lee	Duke's
1679	The Young King	Aphra Behn	Duke's
1679	Caius Marius	Thomas Otway	Duke's
1680	The Soldier's Fortune	Thomas Otway	Duke's
1681	King Lear	Nahum Tate (after Shakespeare)	Duke's
1681	Henry VI, Part 1	John Crowne (after Shakespeare)	Duke's
1682	The Duke of Guise	John Dryden and Nathaniel Lee	United
1684	The Island Queens	John Banks	Unacted
1689	The Massacre of Paris	Nathaniel Lee	United
1689	The Successful Strangers	William Mountfort	United

Date	Play	Author	Company
1690	*The Bloody Duke*	Anonymous	Unacted
1690	*King Edward III*	?William Mountfort	United
1690	*Sir Anthony Love*	Thomas Southerne	United
1694	*The Fatal Marriage*	Thomas Southerne	United
1695	*The Rival Sisters*	Robert Gould	Patent
1696	*The Royal Mischief*	Mary Delarivière Manley	Betterton's
1697	*The Italian Husband*	Edward Ravenscroft	Betterton's
1698	*Beauty in Distress*	Peter Motteux	Betterton's
1698	*Queen Catharine*	Mary Pix	Betterton's
1699	*Massaniello, Part 1*	Thomas D'Urfey	Patent
1699	*Richard III*	Colley Cibber (after Shakespeare)	Patent
1700	*The Generous Choice*	Francis Manning	Betterton's
Unknown	*Perfidus Hetruscus* (Latin)	Anonymous	Unknown

SUPPLEMENTARY LIST: LOST PLAYS

Date	Play	Author	Company
*c.*1580	[*Tancred and Gismunda*][6]	?Richard Farrant	Chapel Boys
1586	*Tancredo* (?Latin)	Henry Wotton	The Queen's College, Oxford
1589	*Hamlet*	?Thomas Kyd	Unknown (later Chamberlain's, Admiral's)
*c.*1590	Unknown play[7]	Anonymous	Unknown
?1590	*Valentine and Orson*	Anonymous	Queen's
1596	*Vortigern*	Anonymous	Admiral's
1597–8	*Astiages* (?Latin)	Anonymous	St John's College, Oxford
1598	*Pierce of Exton*	Thomas Dekker, Henry Chettle, Michael Drayton, Robert Wilson	Admiral's
1598	*Valentine and Orson*	Richard Hathway and Anthony Munday	Admiral's
1599	*Page of Plymouth*	Thomas Dekker and Ben Jonson	Admiral's
1602	*Richard Crookback*	Ben Jonson	Admiral's
?1615	*Guise*	John Webster	Unknown

[6] Song survives: G. E. P. Arkwright, *N&Q* 10th ser., 5 (1906), 341.
[7] Quoted in 1601: Dekker, *Satiromastix*, IV. iii. 130–1.

Date	Play	Author	Company
1617	[*The Marquesse d'Ancre*]	Anonymous	Unknown
1623	*Richard III*	Samuel Rowley	Palsgrave's
?1623	*The Duke of Guise*	Henry Shirley	Unknown
?1628	[*Philander, King of Thrace*][8]	Anonymous	Unknown
Unknown	*Lusiuncula*[9] (Latin)	Anonymous	Unknown

[8] Author-plot survives: see J. Q. Adams, *The Library*, 4th ser., 26 (1945–6), 17–27.
[9] Allegedly based on *Macbeth*: Bentley, v. 1369.

APPENDIX B

Assassins in Non-Dramatic Works

THIS is a selective list of non-dramatic narratives involving assassins, both fictional and non-fictional, written in or translated into English between 1500 and 1642. In the case of printed texts, the date given is that of first publication (new style, and, where the work survives only in later editions, conjectural), and of composition in the case of manuscript works. Later editions are listed when they add relevant new material. For collections (e.g. of *novelle*), I have specified the individual items concerned; for ballads, I have given in footnotes the location of the text in *The Roxburghe Ballads (RB)*, ed. W. Chappell and J. W. Ebsworth (1871–97).

*c.*1504	Henry Watson (tr.), *Valentine and Orson*
1512	*The Knight of the Swan*
*c.*1513	Thomas More, *The History of King Richard III*
1518	*Frederick of Jennen*
1542	Edward Hall, *The Union of the Two Noble and Illustre Families, York and Lancaster*
1557	Nicholas à Moffa, 'The Horrible and Cruel Murder of Sultan Solyman ... done upon his Eldest Son Mustapha'; tr. William Painter[1]
1559	William Baldwin and others, *The Mirror for Magistrates*: 5, 8, 10, 15
1563	John Foxe, *Acts and Monuments*
1566	William Painter, *The Palace of Pleasure*, Tome I: 16, 42, 55
1567	Geoffrey Fenton, *Certain Tragical Discourses of Bandello*: 9
1567	William Painter, *The Palace of Pleasure*, Tome II: 23
1570	Robert Sempill, *The Poisoned Shot*[2]
1574	Barnaby Rich, *Mercury and an English Soldier*
?1576	Laurence Twine, *The Pattern of Painful Adventures*[3]
1576	George Pettie, *A Petite Palace of Pettie's Pleasure*: 1
1576	Thomas Achelley, *A Most Lamentable and Tragical History*
1576	George Whetstone, *The Rock of Regard*: 'Rinaldo and Giletta'
1577	Robert Smythe, *Strange, Lamentable, and Tragical Histories*: 3
1577	Raphael Holinshed, *The Chronicles of England, Scotland, and Ireland*
1578	Thomas Blenerhasset, *The Second Part of The Mirror for Magistrates*: 4, 11
1583	Brian Melbancke, *Philotimus*
1584	'R.F.', [*Letter to his Friend*]
1585	Robert Greene, *Planetomachia*: 'Venus' Tragedy'
?1585	'W.C.', *The Adventures of Lady Egeria*

[1] Later incorporated into *The Palace of Pleasure* (II. 34).
[2] *RB*, viii. 366–70.
[3] Earliest extant edition, ?1594.

1586	William Warner, *Albion's England*
1587	John Polemon, *The Second Part of the Book of Battles*
1587	George Turberville, *Tragical Tales translated by Turberville*: 2
1587	Thomas Higgins and others, *The Mirror for Magistrates*: 39, 40
?c.1587	*The Famous History of Friar Bacon*[4]
1588	Robert Greene, *Pandosto*
1589	William Warner, *The Second Part of Albion's England*
1590	Sir Philip Sidney, *Arcadia*
1590	Thomas Lodge, *Rosalynde*
1591	*Sundry Strange and Inhuman Murders, Lately Committed*
1594	Michael Drayton, *Matilda*
1595	Samuel Daniel, *The Civil Wars*, Book III
1595	*The Norfolk Gentleman's Last Will and Testament*[5]
?1595	Emanuel Forde, *Ornatus and Artesia*
1596	Edmund Spenser, *The Faerie Queene*, Book VI
1596	Michael Drayton, *Mortimeriados*
1597	Thomas Beard, *The Theatre of God's Judgements*
1597	Marguerite of Navarre, *The Queen of Navarre's Tales*: 1; tr. 'A.B.'
1598	Emanuel Forde, *Parismus*
1599	*A True Discourse of a Cruel Fact Committed by a Gentlewoman*
1599	*The Spanish Tragedy*[6]
?1599	Richard Johnson, *Tom o' Lincoln*[7]
1602	Thomas Deloney, *Strange Histories*: 6–8
c.1603	Thomas Rogers, *Leicester's Ghost*
1603	Michael Drayton, *The Barons' Wars*
1603	Richard Knolles, *The General History of the Turks*
1604	Gilbert Dugdale, *A True Discourse of the Practices of Elizabeth Caldwell*
1605	Michael Drayton, *The Legend of Matilda*, revised version
1608	George Wilkins, *The Painful Adventures of Pericles, Prince of Tyre*
1612	Thomas Beard, *The Theatre of God's Judgements*, 2nd edn.
1614	Christopher Brooke, *The Ghost of Richard III*
1619	Sir George Buc, *The History of King Richard III*
1620	Giovanni Boccaccio, *The Decameron*: II. 9
1621	John Reynolds, *The Triumphs of God's Revenge*, Book I: 1–3
1622	Gonzalo de Céspedes y Meneses, *Gerardo, the Unfortunate Spaniard*; tr. Leonard Digges
1622	John Reynolds, *The Triumphs of God's Revenge*, Book II: 6, 7, 9
1622	*The Strangling and Death of the Great Turk*
1623	John Reynolds, *The Triumphs of God's Revenge*, Book III: 11–13
1628	Sir Francis Hubert, *The Deplorable Life and Death of Edward II*
1632	Giovanni Francesco Biondi, *Eromena*; tr. James Hayward
1633	*The Complaint and Lamentation of Mistress Arden of Faversham*[8]

[4] Earliest extant edition, 1627.
[5] *RB*, ii. 216–21; a.k.a. *The Children in the Wood*.
[6] Earliest extant edition, 1631.
[7] Ballad version of the play; *RB*, ii. 454–9.

1635   John Reynolds, *The Triumphs of God's Revenge*, Books IV–VI: IV. 17–19,
        V. 21, 24.
1638   Nicholas Caussin, *The Unfortunate Politique*; tr. 'G.P.'
1639   Jean Pierre Camus, *Admirable Events*: I. 9; tr. S. du Verger.

[8] *RB*, viii. 49–53.

BIBLIOGRAPHY

PRIMARY SOURCES

1. Manuscripts

F., R., [Letter to his Friend], London: Public Record Office, SP 15/28, no. 113.

PERCY, WILLIAM, A Forrest Tragaedye in Vacunium or Loues Sacrifice, Alnwick Castle (Northumberland): MS 509.

Perfidus Hetruscus, Oxford: Bodleian Library, MS Rawlinson C. 787.

Solymannidae tragoedia, London: British Library, MS Lansdowne 723.

VERNEY, FRANCIS, The tragedye of Antipoe with othere poeticall verses, Oxford: Bodleian Library, MS Eng. poet. e.5.

WILMOT, ROBERT, and others, Gismond of Salerne, London: British Library, MS Hargrave 205.

2. Printed Books

ACHELLEY, THOMAS, A most lamentable and Tragicall historie (1576).

ADAMS, JOSEPH QUINCY (ed.), Chief Pre-Shakespearean Dramas ([1924]).

—— (ed.), 'The Author-Plot of an Early Seventeenth Century Play', The Library, 4th ser., 26 (1945–6), 17–27.

ADDISON, JOSEPH, STEELE, RICHARD, and others, The Spectator, ed. G. Smith, 4 vols., rev. edn. (1945).

ALEXANDER, SIR WILLIAM, The Poetical Works of Sir William Alexander Earl of Stirling, ed. L. E. Kastner and H. B. Charlton, Scottish Text Society, 2 vols. (1921–9).

ALLEN, WILLIAM, A Trve Sincere and Modest Defence of English Catholiqves that Svffer for their Faith both at home and abrode (Ingolstadt, 1584).

Alphonsus, Emperor of Germany, in The Plays and Poems of George Chapman: The Tragedies, ed. T. M. Parrott (1910).

ALTON, R. E., 'The Academic Drama in Oxford: Extracts from the Records of Four Colleges', Malone Society Collections, 5 (1959 [= 1960]), 29–95.

APPIAN, An Avncient Historie and exquisite Chronicle of the Romanes warres, both Ciuile and Foren (1578).

ARBER, EDWARD (ed.), A Transcript of the Registers of the Company of Stationers of London, 1554–1640 A.D., 5 vols. (1875–94).

Arden of Faversham, see The Tragedy of Master Arden of Faversham.

ARISTOTLE, The Politics, tr. T. A. Sinclair (Harmondsworth, 1962).

ARMIN, ROBERT, The History of the Two Maids of More-Clacke, ed. A. S. Liddie (1979).

ARNAULD, ANTOINE, The Arrainement of the whole societie of Iesuites in Fraunce (1594).

ASCHAM, ROGER, English Works, ed. W. A. Wright (Cambridge, 1904).

BACON, SIR FRANCIS, The Advancement of Learning and New Atlantis, ed. A. Johnston (Oxford, 1974).

BAILEY, ABRAHAM, The Spightful Sister (1667).

BAILLIE, WILLIAM M. (ed.), *A Choice Ternary of English Plays: Gratiae Theatrales (1662)*, Medieval Renaissance Texts and Studies 26 (Binghamton, NY, 1984).

BALDWIN, WILLIAM, and others, *The Mirror for Magistrates*, ed. L. B. Campbell (Cambridge, 1938).

BALE, JOHN, *Select Works of John Bale, D.D.*, ed. H. Christmas, Parker Society (Cambridge, 1849).

BANDELLO, MATTEO, *The Novels of Matteo Bandello, Bishop of Agen*, tr. J. Payne, 6 vols. (1890).

BANKS, JOHN, *The Island Queens: Or, The Death of Mary, Queen of Scotland* (1684).

BARNES, BARNABE, *The Devil's Charter*, ed. J. C. Pogue (1980).

BARON, ROBERT, *Mirza* ([1655]).

The Bastard (1652).

BEARD, THOMAS, *The Theatre of Gods Iudgements* (1597).

—— *The Theatre of Gods Ivdgements*, 2nd edn. (1612).

BEAUMONT, FRANCIS, and FLETCHER, JOHN, *The Works of Francis Beaumont and John Fletcher*, ed. A. Glover and A. R. Waller, 10 vols. (Cambridge, 1905–12).

—— *The Dramatic Works in the Beaumont and Fletcher Canon*, gen. ed. F. T. Bowers, 7 vols., ongoing (Cambridge, 1966–).

BECON, THOMAS, *The Early Works of Thomas Becon, S.T.P.*, ed. J. Ayre, Parker Society (Cambridge, 1843).

—— *The Catechism of Thomas Becon, S.T.P.*, ed. J. Ayre, Parker Society (Cambridge, 1844).

BEHN, APHRA, *The Works of Aphra Behn*, ed. M. Summers, 6 vols. (1915).

BELLEFOREST, FRANÇOIS and BOAISTUAU, PIERRE, *Premier et second thome des histoires tragiqves, contenans xxxvi. livres*, 2 vols. (Paris, 1568).

BERKELEY, SIR WILLIAM, *The Lost Lady*, ed. D. F. Rowan and G. R. Proudfoot, Malone Society (Oxford, 1987 [= 1989]).

BERNARD, SAMUEL, *Andronicus Comnenus*, ed. J. L. Klause, Renaissance Latin Drama in England, 1st ser., 6 (Hildesheim and New York, 1986).

BERNERS, JOHN BOURCHIER, LORD, *The Boke of Duke Huon of Burdeux*, ed. S. L. Lee, 2 vols., Early English Text Society (1882–3).

Der bestrafte brudermord, in BULLOUGH, vol. vii.

The Bible, see *The Holy Bible*.

BIONDI, GIOVANNI FRANCESCO, *Eromena, Or, Love and Revenge*, tr. J. Hayward (1632).

The Bloody Duke: or, The Adventures for a Crown (1690).

BOCCACCIO, GIOVANNI, *The Decameron*, The Tudor Translations 41–4, 4 vols. (1909).

—— *The Decameron*, tr. G. H. McWilliam (Harmondsworth, 1972).

A Booke of Proclamations, 2nd edn. (1613).

BOOTHBY, FRANCES, *Marcelia: or The Treacherous Friend* (1670).

BOYLE, ROGER, *The Dramatic Works of Roger Boyle, Earl of Orrery*, ed. W. S. Clark II, 2 vols. (Cambridge, Mass., 1937).

BRATHWAIT, RICHARD, *Natvres Embassie: Or, The Wilde-Mans Measvres* (1621).

BROOKE, ARTHUR, *Romeus and Juliet*, in BULLOUGH, vol. i.

BROOKE, C. F. TUCKER (ed.), *The Shakespeare Apocrypha* (Oxford, 1908).

BROOKE, CHRISTOPHER, *The Ghost of Richard the Third*, ed. J. P. Collier, Shakespeare Society (1844).

BROME, RICHARD, *The Dramatic Works of Richard Brome*, 3 vols. (1873).

BUC, SIR GEORGE, *The History of King Richard the Third*, ed. A. N. Kincaid (Gloucester, 1979).

BUCHANAN, GEORGE, *Ane Detectiovn of the duinges of Marie Quene of Scottes, touchand the murder of hir husband* ([?Edinburgh, ?1572]).

—— *De jure regni apud Scotos. Or A Dialogue, concerning the due Priviledge of Government in the Kingdom of Scotland, Betwixt George Buchanan And Thomas Maitland*, tr. Philaletes (n.pl., 1680).

BULLINGER, HEINRICH, *The Decades of Henry Bullinger*, tr. H.I., ed. T. Harding, Parker Society, 4 vols. (Cambridge, 1849–52).

BULLOUGH, GEOFFREY (ed.), *Narrative and Dramatic Sources of Shakespeare*, 8 vols. (1957–75).

BURGHLEY, WILLIAM CECIL, LORD, *The Execution of Iustice in England* (1583).

BURTON, ROBERT, *The Anatomy of Melancholy*, ed. F. Dell and P. Jordan-Smith (New York, 1948).

C., W., *The Adventures of Ladie Egeria* ([?1585]).

Caesar's Revenge, see *The Tragedy of Caesar's Revenge*.

Calendar of State Papers, Domestic Series, of the Reigns of Edward VI., Mary, Elizabeth 1547–1580, ed. R. Lemon (1856).

Calendar of State Papers, Domestic Series, of the Reign of Elizabeth, 1591–1594, ed. M. A. E. Green (1867).

Calendar of State Papers, Foreign Series, of the Reign of Elizabeth, 1563, ed. J. Stevenson (1869).

CAMMELLI, ANTONIO, *Filostrato e Panfila*, published as *Tragedia di Antonio da Pistoia nuouamente Impressa* ([Florence, c.1520]).

CAMUS, JEAN PIERRE, *Admirable Events: Selected ovt of Fovre Bookes*, tr. S. du Verger (1639).

CARLELL, LODOWICK, *The Deseruing Fauorite* (1629).

—— *Arviragvs and Philicia* (1639).

—— *The Passionate Lovers* (1655).

CARLETTI, ANGELO, *Summa Angelica* (Chivasso, 1486).

CARTWRIGHT, WILLIAM, *The Plays and Poems of William Cartwright*, ed. G. B. Evans (Madison, 1951).

CARYL, JOHN, *The English Princess, or, The Death of Richard III* (1667).

CASTIGLIONE, BALDASSARE, *The Book of the Courtier*, tr. Sir T. Hoby (1974).

CAUSSIN, NICHOLAS, *The Unfortunate Politique*, tr. G.P. (Oxford, 1638).

CAWDREY, ROBERT, *A Treasvrie or Store-Hovse of Similies* (1600).

CÉSPEDES Y MENESES, GONZALO DE, *Gerardo the Vnfortvnate Spaniard. Or A Patterne for Lascíviovs Lovers*, tr. L. Digges (1622).

CHAMBERLAIN, JOHN, *Letters written by John Chamberlain during the Reign of Queen Elizabeth*, ed. S. Williams, Camden Society (1861).

CHAMBERLAYNE, WILLIAM, *Loves Victory* (1658).

CHAPMAN, GEORGE, *Bussy D'Ambois*, ed. N. Brooke, The Revels Plays (1964).

—— *The Plays of George Chapman: The Comedies*, gen. eds. A. Holaday and M. Kiernan (1970).

—— *The Plays of George Chapman: The Tragedies with 'Sir Gyles Goosecappe'*, gen. ed. A. Holaday (Cambridge, 1987).

Charlemagne, or The Distracted Emperor, ed. J. H. Walter, Malone Society (Oxford, 1937 [= 1938]).

CHAUCER, GEOFFREY, *The Works of Geoffrey Chaucer*, ed. F. N. Robinson, 2nd edn. (1957).

The Chester Mystery Cycle, ed. R. M. Lumiansky and D. Mills, Early English Text Society, 2 vols. (Oxford, 1974–86).

CHETTLE, HENRY, *The Tragedy of Hoffman*, ed. H. Jenkins, Malone Society (Oxford, 1950 [= 1951]).

—— and DAY, JOHN, *The Blind-beggar of Bednal-Green, VVith The merry humor of Tom Strowd the Norfolk Yeoman* (1659).

CIBBER, COLLEY, *The Tragical History of King Richard III*, in *Five Restoration Adaptations of Shakespeare*, ed. C. Spencer (Urbana, Ill., 1965).

CLARKE, FRANCIS, SJ, *Innocentia Purpurata*, in C. Houlihan [Sister Winefride] (ed.), 'Three Jesuit Plays: An Edition from Manuscripts and Translation of *Britanniae Primitiae*, *S. Eduardus, Confessor* and *Innocentia Purpurata*', Ph.D. thesis (Birmingham, 1967).

Claudius Tiberius Nero, see *The Tragedy of Tiberius*.

CLAY, WILLIAM KEATINGE (ed.), *Liturgical Services: Liturgies and Occasional Forms of Prayer set forth in the Reign of Queen Elizabeth*, Parker Society (Cambridge, 1847).

COKE, SIR EDWARD, *The Reports of Sir Edward Coke, Knt.*, 6 vols. (1826).

CONGREVE, WILLIAM, *The Comedies of William Congreve*, ed. A. G. Henderson (Cambridge, 1982).

Constance of Cleveland, in *The Roxburghe Ballads*, vi. 572–5.

CORNEILLE, PIERRE, *Pompey*, tr. K. Philips (Dublin, 1663).

—— *Pompey the Great*, [tr. Sir E. Filmer, S. Godolphin, C. Sackville, Sir C. Sedley, and E. Waller] (1664).

CORYATE, THOMAS, *Coryat's Crudities*, 2 vols. (Glasgow, 1905).

Coventry Plays, see *Two Coventry Corpus Christi Plays*.

CRASHAW, WILLIAM (tr.), *A Discovrse to the Lords of the Parliament. As Tovching the Murther committed vppon the person of Henrie the Great, King of Fraunce* (1611).

CROWNE, JOHN, *Henry the Sixth, The First Part. With the Murder of Humphrey Duke of Glocester* (1681).

CUNLIFFE, J. W., (ed.), *Early English Classical Tragedies* (Oxford, 1912).

DABORNE, ROBERT, *A Christian turn'd Turke*, ed. A. E. H. Swaen, *Anglia*, 20 (1897–8), 188–256.

DANIEL, SAMUEL, *The Complete Works in Verse and Prose of Samuel Daniel*, ed. A. B. Grosart, 5 vols. (1885–96).

DAUNCE, EDWARD, *A Briefe Discovrse Dialogvevvise* (1590).

DAVENANT, SIR WILLIAM, *The Dramatic Works of Sir William D'Avenant*, ed. J. Maidment and W. H. Logan, 5 vols. (1872–4).

DAVENPORT, ROBERT, *King Iohn and Matilda* (1655).

DAY, JOHN, *Humour out of breath* (1608).

—— *Law Tricks*, ed. J. Crow, Malone Society (Oxford, 1949 [= 1950]).

DEFOE, DANIEL, *Defoe's Review*, ed. A. W. Secord, 22 vols. (New York, 1938).

DEKKER, THOMAS, *The Dramatic Works of Thomas Dekker*, ed. F. Bowers, 4 vols. (Cambridge, 1953–61).

—— *Selected Prose Writings*, ed. E. D. Pendry, Stratford-upon-Avon Library 4 (1967).

DELONEY, THOMAS, *The Works of Thomas Deloney*, ed. F. O. Mann (Oxford, 1912).

The Digby Plays, With an Incomplete 'Morality' of Wisdom, who is Christ, ed. F. J. Furnivall, Early English Text Society (1896).

Directions to Fame, About an Elegy On the Late Deceased Thomas Thynn, Esq (1682).

DOLCE, LUDOVICO, *Jocasta*, tr. G. Gascoigne and F. Kinwelmershe, in CUNLIFFE.

ĐORĐEVIĆ, BARTOLOMEJ, *The ofspring of the house of Ottomanno, and officers pertaining to the greate Turkes Court*, tr. H. Goughe ([1570]).

DRAYTON, MICHAEL, *The Works of Michael Drayton*, ed. J. W. Hebel, 5 vols., corr. edn. (Oxford, 1961).

DRUE, THOMAS, *The Bloody Banquet*, ed. S. Schoenbaum, Malone Society (Oxford, 1961 [= 1962]).

DRYDEN, JOHN, *The Dramatic Works*, ed. M. Summers, 6 vols. (1931–2).

—— *The Poems of John Dryden*, ed. J. Kinsley, 4 vols. (Oxford, 1958).

DUGDALE, GILBERT, *A True Discourse Of the practises of Elizabeth Caldwell* (1604).

D'URFEY, THOMAS, *The Injured Princess, Or The Fatal UUager* (1682).

—— *The Famous History of the Rise and Fall of Massaniello* (1700).

ESTIENNE, HENRI, *L'Introdvction av traité de la conformité des merueilles anciennes auec les modernes* (Geneva, 1566).

ETHEREGE, SIR GEORGE, *The Plays of Sir George Etherege*, ed. M. Cordner (Cambridge, 1982).

FABYAN, ROBERT, *The Chronicle of Fabian, whiche he nameth the concordaunce of histories* (1559).

The Faire Maide of Bristovv (1605).

The Famous Historie of Fryer Bacon (1627).

The Fatal Marriage, ed. S. B. Younghughes and H. Jenkins, Malone Society (Oxford, 1958 [= 1959]).

FENTON, GEOFFREY, *Certain Tragical Discourses of Bandello*, The Tudor Translations 19–20, 2 vols. (1898).

FIELD, NATHAN, *The Plays of Nathan Field*, ed. W. Peery (Austin, Texas, 1950).

The First Part of Hieronimo and KYD, THOMAS, *The Spanish Tragedy*, ed. A. S. Cairncross, Regents Renaissance Drama [edition attributes both plays to Kyd] (1967).

FLETCHER, JOHN, see under BEAUMONT and FLETCHER.

—— MASSINGER, PHILIP, and others, *Rollo, Duke of Normandy or The Bloody Brother*, ed. J. D. Jump (Liverpool, 1948).

FORD, JOHN, *John Fordes Dramatische Werke*, ed. W. Bang and H. de Vocht, 2 vols., Materialen zur Kunde des älteren englischen Dramas 23 and NS 1 (Louvain, 1908–27).

—— *'Tis Pity She's a Whore*, ed. D. Roper, The Revels Plays (1975).

FORDE, EMANUEL, *The Most Pleasant Historie of Ornatus and Artesia* ([?1595]).

—— *Parismus, The Renovmed Prince of Bohemia* (1598).

FOXE, JOHN, *The Acts and Monuments of John Foxe*, 4th edn., ed. J. Pratt, 8 vols. ([1877]).

FRAUNCE, ABRAHAM, *Victoria*, ed. G. C. Moore Smith, Materialen zur Kunde des älteren englischen Dramas 14 (Louvain, 1906).

Frederick of Jennen, in BULLOUGH, vol. viii.

FREEMAN, SIR RALPH, *Imperiale* (1639).

FULBECKE, WILLIAM, *A Parallel or Conference of the Civill Law, the Canon Law, and the Common Law of this Realme of England* (1601).

FULLER, THOMAS, *Andronicus: A Tragedy, Impieties Long Successe, or Heavens Late Revenge* (1661).

GENTILLET, INNOCENT, *A Discovrse vpon the Meanes of VVel Governing and Maintaining in Good Peace, a Kingdome, or Other Principalitie*, tr. S. Patericke (1602).

Gesta Grayorum, ed. W. W. Greg, Malone Society (Oxford, 1914 [= 1915]).

GIOVIO, PAULO, *A shorte treatise vpon the Turkes Chronicles*, tr. P. Ashton (1546).

GLAPTHORNE, HENRY, *The Plays and Poems of Henry Glapthorne*, 2 vols. (1874).

—— *Revenge for Honour*, in *The Plays and Poems of George Chapman: The Tragedies*, ed. T. M. Parrott (1910).

—— *The Lady Mother*, ed. A. Brown, Malone Society (Oxford, 1958 [= 1959]).

GOFFE, THOMAS, *The Raging Turke* and *The Couragious Turke*, ed. D. Carnegie, Malone Society (Oxford, 1968 [= 1974]).

GOLDSMID, EDMUND (ed.), *The Trial of Francis Ravaillac for the Murder of King Henry the Great* (Edinburgh, 1885).

GOMERSALL, ROBERT, *The Tragedie of Lodovick Sforza Duke of Milan*, ed. B. R. Pearn, Materials for the Study of the Old English Drama NS 8 (Louvain, 1933).

GOULD, ROBERT, *The Rival Sisters: Or, The Violence of Love* (1696).

GREENE, ROBERT, *The Life and Complete Works in Prose and Verse of Robert Greene, M.A., Cambridge and Oxford*, ed. A. B. Grosart, 15 vols. (1881–6).

—— *The Scottish History of James the Fourth*, ed. J. A. Lavin, The New Mermaids (1967).

—— *The Scottish History of James the Fourth*, ed. N. Sanders, The Revels Plays (1970).

—— and PEELE, GEORGE, *The Dramatic and Poetical Works of Robert Greene and George Peele*, ed. A. Dyce (1861).

GREG, W. W. (ed.), *Two Elizabethan Stage Abridgements: The Battle of Alcazar & Orlando Furioso*, Malone Society (Oxford, 1922 [= 1923]).

GREVILLE, FULKE, *Poems and Dramas of Fulke Greville, First Lord Brooke*, ed. G. Bullough, 2 vols. ([1938]).

GUEVARA, ANTONIO DE, *The Diall of Princes*, tr. T. North (1557).

GWINNE, MATTHEW, *Nero*, ed. H.-D. Leidig, Renaissance Latin Drama in England, 1st ser., 13 (Hildesheim and New York, 1983).

HALL, EDWARD, *Hall's Chronicle* (1809).

HARDING, SAMUEL, *Sicily and Naples. Or, The Fatall Union*, ed. J. W. Roberts, The Renaissance Imagination 15 (1986).

HARRISON, WILLIAM, *The Description of England*, ed. G. Edelen (Ithaca, NY, 1968).

HAUGHTON, WILLIAM, *The Devil and his Dame*, published as *Grim, the Collier of Croydon*, in BAILLIE.

HAYWARD, JOHN, *The First Part of The Life and raigne of King Henrie the IIII* (1599).

HEMINGES, WILLIAM, *The Jewes Tragedy*, ed. H. A. Cohn, Materialen zur Kunde des älteren englischen Dramas 40 (Louvain, 1913).

HENSLOWE, PHILIP, *Henslowe's Diary*, ed. R. A. Foakes and R. T. Rickert (Cambridge, 1961).

HEYWOOD, THOMAS, *The Dramatic Works of Thomas Heywood*, ed. ?R. H. Shepherd, 6 vols. (1874).

—— *If You Know Not Me You Know Nobody Part II*, ed. M. Doran, Malone Society (Oxford, 1934 [= 1935]).

HICKERINGILL, EDMUND, *The Character of A Sham-Plotter or Man-Catcher* (1681).

HIGGINS, JOHN, and BLENERHASSET, THOMAS, *Parts Added to The Mirror for Magistrates*, ed. L. B. Campbell (Cambridge, 1946).

The History of King Leir, ed. W. W. Greg, Malone Society (Oxford, 1907 [= 1908]).

HOLINSHED, RAPHAEL, *Holinshed's Chronicles of England, Scotland, and Ireland*, 6 vols. (1807–8).

The Holy Bible, Authorized Version (1957).

HOOPER, JOHN, *Early Writings of John Hooper, D.D.*, ed. S. Carr, Parker Society (Cambridge, 1843).

HOWARD, SIR ROBERT, *The Surprisal* (1665).

HOWELL, T. B. (ed.), *A Complete Collection of State Trials*, 34 vols. (1816–28).

HUBERT, SIR FRANCIS, *The Poems of Sir Francis Hubert*, ed. B. Mellor (Hong Kong, 1961).

HUGHES, PAUL L. and LARKIN, JAMES F. (eds.), *Tudor Royal Proclamations*, 3 vols. (1964–9).

Hymenaeus, ed. G. C. Moore Smith (Cambridge, 1908).

JOHNSON, RICHARD, *The Most Pleasant History of Tom a Lincolne*, ed. R. S. M. Hirsch (Columbia, 1978).

JONES, JOHN, *Adrasta: Or, The Womans Spleene, And Loves Conqvest* (1635).

JONSON, BEN, *Ben Jonson*, ed. C. H. Herford, P. and E. Simpson, 11 vols. (Oxford, 1925–52).

—— *Volpone, or The Fox*, ed. J. W. Creaser (1978).

JOURDAN, ATHANASE JEAN LÉGER, DECRUSY, and ISAMBERT, FRANÇOIS ANDRÉ (eds.), *Recueil général des anciennes lois Françaises*, 29 vols. (Paris, [1822–33]).

JUDGES, A. V. (ed.), *The Elizabethan Underworld* (1930).

KILLIGREW, HENRY, *The Conspiracy* (1638).

KILLIGREW, THOMAS, *Comedies, and Tragedies* (1664).

King Leir, see *The History of King Leir*.

KLARWILL, VICTOR VON (ed.), *The Fugger News-Letters*, tr. P. de Chary (1924).

KNEVET, RALPH, *Rhodon and Iris* (1631).

The Knight of the Swanne ([?1550]).

KNOLLES, RICHARD, *The Generall Historie of the Turkes* (1603).

KNOX, JOHN, *The History of the Reformation of Religion within the Realm of Scotland*, ed. C. J. Guthrie (1898).

KYD, THOMAS, *The Works of Thomas Kyd*, ed. F. S. Boas (Oxford, 1901).

—— *The Spanish Tragedy*, ed. P. Edwards, The Revels Plays (1959).

—— see also *The First Part of Hieronimo*.

LANGBAINE, GERARD, *An Account of the English Dramatick Poets* (Oxford, 1691).

LEE, NATHANIEL, *The Works of Nathaniel Lee*, ed. T. B. Stroup and A. L. Cooke, 2 vols. (New Brunswick, NJ, 1954–5).

LEEUWEN, SIMON VAN, *Commentaries on Roman-Dutch Law*, ed. C. W. Decker, tr. J. G. Kotzé, 2nd edn., 2 vols. (1921–3).

LEGGE, THOMAS, *Richardus Tertius*, ed. R. J. Lordi (1979).

LODGE, THOMAS, *Rosalynde*, in BULLOUGH, vol. ii.

—— *The Wounds of Civil War*, ed. J. W. Houppert, Regents Renaissance Drama (1970).

Look About You, ed. W. W. Greg, Malone Society (Oxford, 1913).

Ludus Coventriae or The Plaie called Corpus Christi, ed. K. S. Block, Early English Text Society (1922).

LUPTON, THOMAS, *A Moral and Pitiefvl Comedie, Intituled, All for Money* (1578).

MACHIAVELLI, NICCOLÒ, *The Discourses,* tr. L. J. Walker, rev. B. Richardson, ed. B. Crick, corr. edn. (Harmondsworth, 1974).

—— *The Prince,* tr. G. Bull, rev. edn. (Harmondsworth, 1981).

The Maid's Metamorphosis, in *The Complete Works of John Lyly,* ed. R. W. Bond, 3 vols. (Oxford, 1902).

MANLEY, MARY DELARIVIÈRE, *The Royal Mischief* (1696).

MANNING, FRANCIS, *The Generous Choice* (1700).

MANNINGHAM, JOHN, *The Diary of John Manningham of the Middle Temple 1602–1603,* ed. R. P. Sorlien (Hanover, NH, 1976).

Marcus Tullius Cicero, see *The Tragedy of that Famovs Roman Oratovr Marcus Tullius Cicero.*

MARGUERITE, QUEEN OF NAVARRE, *The Queene of Nauarres Tales,* tr. A. B. (1597).

MARKHAM, GERVASE, and SAMPSON, WILLIAM, *The True Tragedy of Herod and Antipater,* ed. G. N. Ross (1979).

MARLOWE, CHRISTOPHER, *Edward the Second,* ed. W. M. Merchant, The New Mermaids (1967).

—— *Edward II,* ed. R. Gill (Oxford, 1967).

—— *Dido Queen of Carthage* and *The Massacre at Paris,* ed. H. J. Oliver, The Revels Plays (1968).

—— *The Jew of Malta,* ed. N. W. Bawcutt, The Revels Plays (Manchester, 1978).

—— *Tamburlaine the Great,* ed. J. S. Cunningham, The Revels Plays (Manchester and Baltimore, 1981).

MARMION, SHAKERLEY, *The Antiquary* (1641).

MARSTON, JOHN, *The Plays of John Marston,* ed. H. H. Wood, 3 vols. (1934–9).

—— *The Malcontent,* ed. G. K. Hunter, The Revels Plays (1975).

—— *Antonio's Revenge,* ed. W. R. Gair, The Revels Plays (Manchester and Baltimore, 1978).

—— *The Selected Plays of John Marston,* ed. MacD. P. Jackson and M. Neill (Cambridge, 1986).

MASON, JOHN, *The Turke,* ed. J. Q. Adams, jun., Materialen zur Kunde des älteren englischen Dramas 37 (Louvain, 1913).

MASSINGER, PHILIP, *The Plays and Poems of Philip Massinger,* ed. P. Edwards and C. Gibson, 5 vols. (Oxford, 1976).

MAY, THOMAS, *The Heire* (1622).

—— *Julia Agrippina Empresse of Rome,* ed. F. E. Schmid, Materialen zur Kunde des älteren englischen Dramas 43 (Louvain, 1914).

MELBANCKE, BRIAN, *Philotimus. The Warre betwixt Nature and Fortune* (1583).

MEWE, WILLIAM, *Pseudomagia,* ed. J. C. Coldewey and B. P. Copenhaver, Bibliotheca Humanistica & Reformatorica 28 (Nieuwkoop, 1979).

MIDDLETON, THOMAS, *The Works of Thomas Middleton,* ed. A. H. Bullen, 8 vols. (1885–6).

—— *The Puritan,* in C. F. T. BROOKE.

—— *Hengist, King of Kent; or The Mayor of Queenborough*, ed. R. C. Bald (1938).

—— *A Game at Chess*, ed. J. W. Harper, The New Mermaids (1966).

—— *The Revenger's Tragedy*, ed. R. A. Foakes, The Revels Plays [edition attributes to Tourneur] (1966).

—— *The Second Maiden's Tragedy*, ed. A. Lancashire, The Revels Plays [edition makes no attribution] (Manchester, 1978).

—— and ROWLEY, WILLIAM, *The Changeling* (1653).

—— and ROWLEY, WILLIAM, *The Changeling*, ed. N. W. Bawcutt, The Revels Plays (1958).

MORE, THOMAS, *The History of King Richard III*, ed. R. S. Sylvester, in *The Complete Works of St. Thomas More*, vol. ii (1963).

MORYSON, FYNES, *An Itinerary*, 4 vols. (Glasgow, 1907–8).

MOTTEUX, PETER, *Beauty in Distress* (1698).

MOUNTFORT, WILLIAM, *The Successfull Straingers* (1690).

—— *King Edward the Third, with the Fall of Mortimer Earl of March* (1691).

Mucedorus, in C. F. T. BROOKE.

MUNDAY, ANTHONY, *A VVatch-vvoord to Englande To beware of traytours and tretcherous practises* (1584 [? = 1585]).

—— *Fedele and Fortunio*, ed. R. Hosley (1981).

—— and CHETTLE, HENRY, *The Death of Robert Earl of Huntingdon*, ed. J. C. Meagher, Malone Society (Oxford, 1965 [= 1967]).

—— and others, *Sir Thomas More*, ed. V. Gabrieli and G. Melchiori, The Revels Plays (Manchester and New York, 1990).

NABBES, THOMAS, *The Works of Thomas Nabbes*, ed. A. H. Bullen, Old English Plays NS 1–2, 2 vols. (1887).

NASHE, THOMAS, *The Works of Thomas Nashe*, ed. R. B. McKerrow, 5 vols., 2nd edn., rev. F. P. Wilson (Oxford, 1958).

Nero, see *The Tragedy of Nero*.

Nobody and Somebody, ed. D. L. Hay (1980).

Octavia, in SENECA.

OTWAY, THOMAS, *The Works of Thomas Otway. Plays, Poems, and Love-letters*, ed. J. C. Ghosh, 2 vols. (Oxford, 1932).

P., G., *The Trve Report of the Lamentable Death, of VVilliam of Nassawe Prince of Orange* (Middleborough, 1584).

PAINTER, WILLIAM, *The Palace of Pleasure*, ed. J. Jacobs, 3 vols. (1890).

PARSONS, ROBERT, *The Copie of a Leter, vvryten by a Master of Arte of Cambrige, to his friend in London* ([?Antwerp], 1584).

The Partiall Law, ed. B. Dobell (1908).

PASQUALIGO, LUIGI, *Il Fedele Comedia* (Venice, 1576).

Pathomachia: or, The Battell of Affections (1630).

PEELE, GEORGE, *The Battle of Alcazar*, ed. W. W. Greg, Malone Society (Chiswick, 1907).

—— *The Life and Works of George Peele*, gen. ed. C. T. Prouty, 3 vols. (New Haven, Conn., 1952–70).

—— see also under GREENE and PEELE.

PETTIE, GEORGE, *A Petite Pallace of Pettie his Pleasure*, ed. H. Hartman (Oxford, 1938).

[*Philander, King of Thrace*], see ADAMS (1945–6).

PILKINGTON, JAMES, *The Works of James Pilkington, B.D.*, ed. J. Scholefield, Parker Society (Cambridge, 1842).

Piso's Conspiracy (1676).

PIX, MARY, *Queen Catharine or, The Ruines of Love* (1698).

PLANTIN, CHRISTOFFEL (tr.), *A Trve Discovrse of the Assavlt Committed vpon the Person of the most noble Prince, William Prince of Orange* (1582).

PLUTARCH, *Moralia*, ed. F. C. Babbitt and others, 15 vols. in 16, Loeb Classical Library (1927–69).

POLEMON, JOHN, *The Second part of the booke of Battailes, fought in our age* (1587).

POLO, MARCO, *The Travels of Marco Polo*, tr. R. Latham (Harmondsworth, 1958).

PRESTON, THOMAS, *Cambises*, in ADAMS (1924).

QUARLES, FRANCIS, *The Virgin Widow* (1649).

RANDOLPH, THOMAS, *Poetical and Dramatic Works of Thomas Randolph*, ed. W. C. Hazlitt, 2 vols. (1875).

RASTELL, JOHN, *The Expositions of the Termes of the Lawes of Englande* (1572).

RAVENSCROFT, EDWARD, *Scaramouch a Philosopher, Harlequin A School-Boy, Bravo, Merchant, and Magician* (1677).

—— *The Italian Husband* (1698).

RAWLINS, THOMAS, *The Rebellion* (1640).

REYNOLDS, JOHN, *The Triumphs of Gods Revenge Against The Crying and Execrable Sinne of (Willfull and Premeditated) Murther* (1635).

RICH, BARNABY, *A Right Exelent and pleasaunt Dialogue, betwene Mercvry and an English Souldier* (1574).

RICHARDS, NATHANIEL, *Messallina The Roman Emperesse*, ed. A. R. Skemp, Materialen zur Kunde des älteren englischen Dramas 30 (Louvain, 1910).

ROBBINS, ROSSELL HOPE (ed.), 'A Dramatic Fragment from a Caesar Augustus Play', *Anglia*, 72 (1954–5), 31–4.

ROCHESTER, JOHN WILMOT, EARL OF, *The Complete Poems of John Wilmot, Earl of Rochester*, ed. D. M. Vieth (1968).

—— *The Letters of John Wilmot, Earl of Rochester*, ed. J. Treglown (Oxford, 1980).

ROGERS, THOMAS, *Leicester's Ghost*, ed. F. B. Williams, jun. (Chicago, 1972).

ROLLINS, HYDER E. (ed.), *Old English Ballads 1553–1625 Chiefly from Manuscripts* (Cambridge, 1920).

ROWLEY, SAMUEL, *When You See Me, You Know Me*, ed. F. P. Wilson, Malone Society (Oxford, 1952).

The Roxburghe Ballads, ed. W. Chappell and J. W. Ebsworth, 9 vols. (1871–97).

S., J., *Andromana: Or the Merchant's Wife* (1660).

S., S., *The Honest Lavvyer* (1616).

SACKVILLE, THOMAS, and NORTON, THOMAS, *Gorboduc or Ferrex and Porrex*, ed. I. B. Cauthen, Regents Renaissance Drama (1970).

SAINT GERMAN, CHRISTOPHER, *The Secunde Dyalogue in Englysshe wyth New Addycyons* (1531).

SANSBURY, JOHN, *Periander*, in *The Christmas Prince*, ed. F. S. Boas, Malone Society (Oxford, 1922 [= 1923]).

SCOTT, S. P. (ed.), *The Civil Law*, 17 vols. in 7 (Cincinnati, 1932).

The Second Maiden's Tragedy, see under MIDDLETON, THOMAS.

SEDLEY, SIR CHARLES, *Antony and Cleopatra* (1677).

Selimus, see *The Tragical Reign of Selimus*.

SENECA, *Seneca his Tenne Tragedies*, ed. T. Newton, The Tudor Translations, 2nd ser., 11–12, 2 vols. (1927).

SETTLE, ELKANAH, *Cambyses King of Persia* (1671).

—— *The Empress of Morocco* (1673).

—— *Love and Revenge* (1675).

—— *The Conquest of China, By the Tartars* (1676).

SHAKESPEARE, WILLIAM, *The Complete Works*, gen. eds. S. Wells and G. Taylor (Oxford, 1986).

—— and collaborator, *Pericles*, ed. F. D. Hoeniger, New Arden Shakespeare (1963).

SHARPHAM, EDWARD, *The Fleire*, ed. H. Nibbe, Materialen zur Kunde des älteren englischen Dramas 36 (Louvain, 1912).

SHIPMAN, THOMAS, *Henry the Third of France, Stabb'd by a Fryer. With the Fall of the Guise* (1678).

SHIRLEY, JAMES, *The Dramatic Works and Poems of James Shirley*, ed. W. Gifford and A. Dyce, 6 vols. (1833).

—— *The Traitor*, ed. J. S. Carter, Regents Renaissance Drama (1965).

SIDNEY, SIR PHILIP, *The Countess of Pembroke's Arcadia*, ed. M. Evans (Harmondsworth, 1977).

SIMONS, JOSEPH, SJ, *Tragoediae quinque* (Liège, 1656).

SKORY, EDMUND, *An Extract ovt of the Historie of the last French King Henry the fourth of famous memorie* (1610).

SMITH, WENTWORTH, *The Hector of Germany. Or The Palsgraue, Prime Elector* (1615).

SMYTHE, ROBERT, *Stravnge, Lamentable, and Tragicall Hystories* (1577).

SNELLING, THOMAS, *Thibaldus sive vindictae ingenium*, ed. L. Cerny, Renaissance Latin Drama in England, 1st ser., 12 (Hildesheim and New York, 1982).

Soliman and Perseda, in KYD (1901).

SOUTHERNE, THOMAS, *The Works of Thomas Southerne*, ed. R. Jordan and H. Love, 2 vols. (Oxford, 1988).

SPENSER, EDMUND, *The Faerie Qveene*, ed. A. C. Hamilton (1977).

STAPLETON, SIR ROBERT, *The Step-Mother* (1664).

The Statutes of the Realm, 10 vols. in 11 (1810–24).

STOW, JOHN, *The Annales of England* (1601).

The Strangling and Death of the Great Tvrke, and his Two Sonnes (1622).

STRODE, WILLIAM, *The Floating Island* (1655).

STRYPE, JOHN, *Annals of the Reformation*, new edn., 4 vols. in 7 (Oxford, 1824).

STUBBE, EDMUND, *Fraus honesta*, ed. T. W. Best, Renaissance Latin Drama in England, 2nd ser., 2 (Hildesheim, Zurich, and New York, 1987).

STUBBES, PHILIP, *The Intended Treason, of Doctor Parrie* ([1585]).

Sundrye strange and inhumaine Murthers, lately committed (1591).

TATE, NAHUM, *The History of King Richard The Second, Acted at the Theatre Royal, Under the Name of the Sicilian Usurper* (1681).

—— *The History of King Lear*, ed. J. Black, Regents Restoration Drama (1976).

TATHAM, JOHN, *The Dramatic Works of John Tatham*, ed. J. Maidment and W. H. Logan (1879).

TAVERNER, RICHARD, *The second booke of the Garden of wysedome, wherin are conteyned wytty, pleasaunt, and nette sayenges of renowmed personages* (1539).

—— *Prouerbes or Adagies, gathered out of the Chiliades of Erasmus* (1569).

The Telltale, ed. R. A. Foakes and J. C. Gibson, Malone Society (Oxford, 1959 [= 1960]).

Thorny Abbey, in BAILLIE.

TOURNEUR, CYRIL, *The Atheist's Tragedy, or, The Honest Man's Revenge*, ed. I. Ribner, The Revels Plays (1964).

—— see also MIDDLETON, THOMAS, *The Revenger's Tragedy*.

The Towneley Plays, ed. G. England, Early English Text Society (1897).

The Tragedy of Caesar's Revenge, ed. F. S. Boas, Malone Society (Oxford, 1911).

The Tragedy of Master Arden of Faversham, ed. M. L. Wine, The Revels Plays (1973).

The Tragedy of Nero, ed. E. M. Hill (1979).

The Tragedy of that Famovs Roman Oratovr Marcus Tullius Cicero (1651).

The Tragedy of Tiberius, ed. W. W. Greg, Malone Society (Oxford, 1914 [= 1915]).

The Tragical Reign of Selimus, ed. W. Bang, Malone Society (Chiswick, 1908 [= 1909]).

The Troublesome Raigne of John, King of England, ed. J. W. Sider (1979).

A True Account of the Late Bloody and Inhumane Conspiracy Against His Highness The Lord Protector, and this Commonwealth (1654).

A Trve and plaine declaration of the horrible Treasons, practised by William Parry the Traitor, against the Queenes Maiestie (1584 [= 1585]).

A Trve Discovrse of A cruell fact committed by a Gentlewoman towardes her Husband, her Father, her Sister and two of her Nephewes (1599).

A Trve Report of Svndry Horrible Conspiracies of late time detected to haue (by Barbarous murders) taken away the life of the Queenes most excellent Maiestie (1594).

The True Tragedy of Richard the Third, ed. W. W. Greg, Malone Society (Oxford, 1929).

TURBERVILLE, GEORGE, *Tragicall Tales translated by Tvrbervile* (1587).

TURNÈBE, ADRIEN, *Adversariorvm libri triginta*, 3 vols. (Paris, 1580).

TWINE, LAURENCE, *The Pattern of Painful Adventures*, in BULLOUGH, vol. vi.

Two Coventry Corpus Christi Plays, ed. H. Craig, Early English Text Society, 2nd edn. (1957).

The Two Noble Ladies, ed. R. G. Rhoads, Malone Society (Oxford, 1930).

The Unfortunate Usurper (1663).

W., J., *The Valiant Scot*, ed. G. F. Byers (1980).

W., R., *Martine Mar-Sixtvs* (1591).

WAGER, W., *The Longer Thou Livest* and *Enough is as Good as a Feast*, ed. R. M. Benbow, Regents Renaissance Drama (1968).

WARNER, WILLIAM, *The First and Second parts of Albions England* (1589).

The Wars of Cyrus, ed. J. P. Brawner, Illinois Studies in Language and Literature 28. 3–4 (Urbana, Ill., 1942).

WATSON, HENRY (tr.), *Valentine and Orson*, ed. A. Dickson, Early English Text Society (1937).

The Weakest Goeth to the Wall, ed. W. W. Greg, Malone Society (Oxford, 1912 [= 1913]).

WEBSTER, JOHN, *The White Devil*, ed. J. R. Brown, The Revels Plays (1960).

—— *The Duchess of Malfi*, ed. J. R. Brown, The Revels Plays (1964).

—— *The Devil's Law-Case*, ed. E. M. Brennan, The New Mermaids (1975).

WHETSTONE, GEORGE, *The Rocke of Regard, diuided into foure parts* (1576).

WILKINS, GEORGE, *The Painful Adventures of Pericles, Prince of Tyre*, in BULLOUGH, vol. vi.

WILLAN, LEONARD, *Orgula: or The Fatall Error* (1658).

WILMOT, ROBERT, *The Tragedy of Tancred and Gismund*, ed. W. W. Greg, Malone Society (Oxford, 1914 [= 1915]).

—— and others, *Gismond of Salerne*, in CUNLIFFE.

WILSON, ARTHUR, *The Inconstant Lady*, ed. L. V. Itzoe (1980).

WILSON, JOHN, *The Dramatic Works of John Wilson*, ed. J. Maidment and W. H. Logan (1874).

Woodstock: A Moral History, ed. A. P. Rossiter (1946).

WRIGHT, HERBERT G. (ed.), *Early English Versions of the Tales of Guiscardo and Ghismonda and Titus and Gisippus from the Decameron*, Early English Text Society (1937).

YARINGTON, ROBERT, *Two Lamentable Tragedies* (1601).

The York Plays, ed. R. Beadle (1982).

SECONDARY SOURCES

AKRIGG, G. P. V., 'A Phrase in Webster', *N&Q* 193 (1948), 454.

ALEXANDER, NIGEL, 'Intelligence in *The Duchess of Malfi*', in MORRIS, 95–112.

ALLEN, DON CAMERON, 'A Source for *Cambises*', *MLN* 49 (1934), 384–7.

APPLEBY, ANDREW B., *Famine in Tudor and Stuart England* (Liverpool, 1978).

ARDOLINO, FRANK, 'The Hangman's Noose and the Empty Box: Kyd's Use of Dramatic and Mythological Sources in *The Spanish Tragedy* (III. iv–vii)', *Renaissance Quarterly*, 30 (1977), 334–40.

ARKWRIGHT, G. E. P., 'The Death Songs of Pyramus and Thisbe', *N&Q* 10th ser., 5 (1906), 341–3, 401–3.

ARMSTRONG, W. A., 'The Elizabethan Conception of the Tyrant', *RES* 22 (1946), 161–81.

—— 'The Influence of Seneca and Machiavelli on the Elizabethan Tyrant', *RES* 24 (1948), 19–35.

BABB, LAWRENCE, *The Elizabethan Malady, A Study of Melancholia in English Literature from 1580 to 1642* (East Lansing, Mich., 1951).

BAIRD, HENRY MARTYN, *History of the Rise of the Huguenots*, 2 vols. (1880).

BALDWIN, T. W., *On the Literary Genetics of Shakspere's Plays 1592–1594* (Urbana, Ill., 1959).

BARKER, RICHARD HINDRY, *Thomas Middleton* (New York, 1958).

BARTON, ANNE, *Ben Jonson, Dramatist* (Cambridge, 1984).

—— *The Names of Comedy* (Oxford, 1990).

BAWCUTT, N. W., '"Policy", Machiavellianism, and the Earlier Tudor Drama', *English Literary Renaissance*, 1 (1971), 195–209.

BAX, CLIFFORD, *The Life of the White Devil* (1940).

BEIER, A. L., 'Vagrants and the Social Order in Elizabethan England', *Past and Present*, 64 (1974), 3–29.

BENJAMIN, EDWIN B., 'Patterns of Morality in *The White Devil'*, *English Studies*, 46 (1965), 1–15.

BENTLEY, GERALD EADES, *The Jacobean and Caroline Stage*, 7 vols. (Oxford, 1941–68).

BERLIN, NORMAND, 'Thomas Dekker: A Partial Reappraisal', *SEL* 6 (1966), 263–77.

BEVINGTON, DAVID M., *From 'Mankind' to Marlowe: Growth of Structure in the Popular Drama of Tudor England* (Cambridge, Mass., 1962).

BLAYNEY, GLENN H., 'Field's Parody of a Murder Play', *N&Q* 200 (1955), 19–20.

BLISS, LEE, *The World's Perspective: John Webster and the Jacobean Drama* (Brighton, 1983).

BOAS, FREDERICK S., *An Introduction to Stuart Drama* (Oxford, 1946).

BOKLUND, GUNNAR, *The Sources of 'The White Devil'*, Essays and Studies on English Language and Literature 17 (Uppsala, 1957).

—— *The Duchess of Malfi: Sources, Themes, Characters* (Cambridge, Mass., 1962).

BOUGHNER, DANIEL C., *The Braggart in Renaissance Comedy. A Study in Comparative Drama from Aristophanes to Shakespeare* (Minneapolis,1954).

BOWERS, FREDSON THAYER, 'Kyd's Pedringano: Sources and Parallels', *Harvard Studies and Notes in Philology and Literature*, 13 (1931), 241–9.

—— 'The Audience and the Poisoners of Elizabethan Tragedy', *Journal of English and Germanic Philology*, 36 (1937), 491–504.

—— *Elizabethan Revenge Tragedy 1587–1642* (Princeton, NJ, 1940).

BOYER, CLARENCE VALENTINE, *The Villain as Hero in Elizabethan Tragedy* (1914).

BRADBROOK, M. C., *Themes and Conventions of Elizabethan Tragedy*, 2nd edn. (Cambridge, 1952).

—— *The Growth and Structure of Elizabethan Comedy*, new edn. (Cambridge, 1973).

—— *John Webster: Citizen and Dramatist* (1980).

—— *The Artist and Society in Shakespeare's England: The Collected Papers of Muriel Bradbrook Volume I* (Brighton and Totowa, NJ, 1982).

BRADLEY, A. C., *Shakespearean Tragedy*, 2nd edn. (1905).

BRAY, ALAN, *Homosexuality in Renaissance England* (1982).

BRIGGS, WILLIAM DINSMORE, 'On the Meaning of the Word "Lake" in Marlowe's *Edward II'*, *MLN* 39 (1924), 437–8.

BROOKE, NICHOLAS, 'Marlowe the Dramatist', in J. R. Brown and B. Harris (eds.), *Elizabethan Theatre*, Stratford-upon-Avon Studies 9 (1966), 87–105.

—— *Horrid Laughter in Jacobean Tragedy* (1979).

BROWN, JOHN RUSSELL, 'On the Dating of Webster's *The White Devil* and *The Duchess of Malfi'*, *Philological Quarterly*, 31 (1952), 353–62.

BURMAN, EDWARD, *The Assassins* ([Wellingborough,] 1987).

BUTLER, MARTIN, *Theatre and Crisis, 1632–1642* (Cambridge, 1984).

CALDERWOOD, JAMES L., 'Commodity and Honour in *King John'*, *University of Toronto Quarterly*, 29 (1959–60), 341–56.

CARLTON, CHARLES, *Charles I: The Personal Monarch* (1984).

CARR, VIRGINIA MASON, *The Drama as Propaganda: A Study of 'The Troublesome Reign of King John'*, Salzburg Studies in English Literature: Elizabethan and Jacobean Studies 28 (Salzburg, 1974).

CHAMBERS, E. K., *The Elizabethan Stage*, 4 vols. (Oxford, 1923).

CHAMPION, LARRY S., 'Ford's *'Tis Pity She's a Whore* and the Jacobean Tragic Perspective', *PMLA* 90 (1975), 78–87.

CHAPMAN, RAYMOND, 'Arden of Faversham: Its Interest Today', English, 11 (1956–7), 15–17.

CHARNEY, MAURICE, 'The Persuasiveness of Violence in Elizabethan Plays', RenD NS 2 (1969), 59–70.

CHESTER, ALLAN GRIFFITH., Thomas May: Man of Letters 1595–1650 (Philadelphia, 1932).

CLEMEN, WOLFGANG, A Commentary on Shakespeare's 'Richard III', tr. J. Bonheim (1968).

COLE, DOUGLAS, 'The Comic Accomplice in Elizabethan Revenge Tragedy', RenD 9 (1966), 125–39.

COLLEY, SCOTT, 'Richard III and Herod', Shakespeare Quarterly, 37 (1986), 451–8.

CRAIK, T. W., 'Violence in the English Miracle Plays', in M. Bradbury, D. Palmer, and N. Denny (eds.), Medieval Drama, Stratford-upon-Avon Studies 16 (1973), 173–95.

CRUPI, CHARLES W., 'The Transformation of De Flores in The Changeling', Neophilologus, 68 (1984), 142–9.

CUNLIFFE, JOHN W., 'Gismond of Salerne', PMLA 21 (1906), 435–61.

CURTIS, MARK H., 'The Alienated Intellectuals of Early Stuart England', Past and Present, 23 (1962), 25–43.

DENT, R. W., John Webster's Borrowing (Berkeley and Los Angeles, 1960).

DESSEN, ALAN C., Elizabethan Stage Conventions and Modern Interpreters (Cambridge, 1984).

DIEHL, HUSTON, 'The Iconography of Violence in English Renaissance Tragedy', RenD NS 11 (1980), 27–44.

DORAN, MADELEINE, Endeavors of Art: A Study of Form in Elizabethan Drama (1954).

DUDRAP, CLAUDE, 'La Tragédie Espagnole face à la critique Élisabéthaine et Jacobéenne' in J. Jacquot (ed.), Dramaturgie et société (Paris, 1968), ii. 607–31.

DUTHIE, GEORGE IAN, The 'Bad' Quarto of 'Hamlet': A Critical Study (Cambridge, 1941).

ELIOT, T. S., Selected Essays, 3rd edn. (1951).

ELLIS-FERMOR, UNA, The Jacobean Drama: An Interpretation (1936).

EMMISON, F. G., Elizabethan Life: Disorder (Chelmsford, 1970).

FINK, Z. S., 'Jaques and the Malcontent Traveler', Philological Quarterly 14 (1935), 237–52.

FISHMAN, BURTON J., 'Pride and Ire: Theatrical Iconography in Preston's Cambises', SEL 16 (1976), 201–11.

FORSTER, E. M., Aspects of the Novel, ed. O. Stallybrass (Harmondsworth, 1976).

FORSYTHE, ROBERT S., 'Notes on The Spanish Tragedy', Philological Quarterly, 5 (1926), 78–84.

FREEMAN, ARTHUR, Thomas Kyd: Facts and Problems (Oxford, 1967).

GASPER, JULIA, The Dragon and the Dove: The Plays of Thomas Dekker (Oxford, 1990).

GAW, ALLISON, 'John Sincklo as One of Shakespeare's Actors', Anglia, 49 (1925–6), 289–303.

GRICE, DERMOT BERTRAND, 'The Bosola Context', Ph.D. thesis (Toronto, 1975). [Abstract in Dissertation Abstracts, 37 (1977), 6495A–6496A.]

GUMM, CHARLES CLAYTON, 'Sir Ralph Freeman's Imperiale', Studies in English Drama, 1st ser., ed. A. Gaw (New York, 1917), 105–29.

GUNBY, D. C., 'The Duchess of Malfi: A Theological Approach', in MORRIS, 181–204.

—— The White Devil, Studies in English Literature 45 (1971).

Gurr, Andrew, *Playgoing in Shakespeare's London* (Cambridge, 1987).

Hallett, Charles A. and Hallett, Elaine S., *The Revenger's Madness: A Study of Revenge Tragedy Motifs* (1980).

Hamel, Guy, 'King John and The Troublesome Reign: A Reexamination', in D. T. Curren-Aquino (ed.), 'King John': New Perspectives (1989), 41–61.

Harbage, Alfred, 'Intrigue in Elizabethan Tragedy', in R. Hosley (ed.), *Essays on Shakespeare and Elizabethan Drama in Honour of Hardin Craig* (1963), 37–44.

—— and Schoenbaum, Samuel, *Annals of English Drama 975–1700*, 2nd edn. (1964).

Harrison, Thomas P., jun., 'The Literary Background of Renaissance Poisons', *Texas University Studies in English*, 27 (1948), 35–67.

Hartwig, Joan, 'Macbeth, the Murderers, and the Diminishing Parallel', *Yearbook of English Studies*, 3 (1973), 39–43.

Heinemann, Margot, *Puritanism and Theatre: Thomas Middleton and Opposition Drama under the Early Stuarts* (Cambridge, 1980).

Hirst, David L., *Tragicomedy*, The Critical Idiom 43 (1984).

Holdsworth, Sir William, *A History of English Law*, 4th edn., 17 vols. (1927–72).

Hunter, G. K., *Dramatic Identities and Cultural Traditions. Studies in Shakespeare and His Contemporaries* (Liverpool, 1978).

Imbs, Paul (ed.), *Trésor de la langue Française: Dictionnaire de la langue du XIXe et du XXe siècle (1789–1960)*, 13 vols., ongoing (Paris, 1971–).

Ives, George, *A History of Penal Methods. Criminals, Witches, Lunatics* (1914).

Jackson, J. E., 'Charles, Lord Stourton, and the Murder of the Hartgills', *The Wiltshire Archaeological and Natural History Magazine*, 8 (1864), 242–341.

Jones, Emrys, *Scenic Form in Shakespeare* (Oxford, 1971).

—— *The Origins of Shakespeare* (Oxford, 1977).

Jordan, Robert, 'Myth and Psychology in *The Changeling*', *RenD* ns 3 (1970), 157–65.

Kenyon, J. P., *The Popish Plot* (1972).

Law, Robert Adger, 'Yarington's *Two Lamentable Tragedies*', *Modern Language Review*, 5 (1910), 167–77.

—— 'Richard the Third, Act i Scene 4', *PMLA* 27 (1912), 117–41.

—— 'Further Notes on *Two Lamentable Tragedies*' *N&Q* 153 (1927), 93–4.

—— 'Richard the Third: A Study in Shakespeare's Composition', *PMLA* 60 (1945), 689–96.

Layman, B. J., 'The Equilibrium of Opposites in *The White Devil*: A Reinterpretation', *PMLA* 74 (1959), 336–47.

Leech, Clifford, *The John Fletcher Plays* (1962).

—— *The Duchess of Malfi*, Studies in English Literature 8 (1963).

Leggatt, Alexander, '*Arden of Faversham*', *Shakespeare Survey*, 36 (1983), 121–33.

Lekhal, Catherine, 'The Historical Background of Robert Greene's *The Scottish History of James IV*, or *Cross the Foe Before He Have Betrayed You* (iii. 3. 29)', *Cahiers Élisabéthains*, 35 (April, 1989), 27–45.

Lever, J. W., *The Tragedy of State: A Study in Jacobean Drama* (1971).

Levin, Harry, *Christopher Marlowe: The Overreacher* (1961).

Lewis, C. S., *English Literature in the Sixteenth Century Excluding Drama*, Oxford History of English Literature 3 (Oxford, 1954).

LINDVALL, LARS, 'Être l'assassin de sa dame', *Studia Neophilologica*, 46 (1974), 32–52.

LIPSCOMB, GEORGE, *The History and Antiquities of the County of Buckingham*, 4 vols. (1847).

LUECKE, JANE MARIE, 'The Duchess of Malfi: Comic and Satiric Confusion in a Tragedy', *SEL* 4 (1964), 275–90.

LUISI, DAVID, 'The Function of Bosola in *The Duchess of Malfi*', *English Studies*, 53 (1972), 509–13.

MCALINDON, T., *English Renaissance Tragedy* (1986).

MCELWEE, WILLIAM, *The Murder of Sir Thomas Overbury* (1952).

MAHOOD, M. M., *Shakespeare's Wordplay* (1957).

MARAÑON, GREGORIO, *Antonio Pérez, 'Spanish Traitor'*, tr. C. D. Ley (1954).

MAXWELL, BALDWIN, *Studies in Beaumont, Fletcher, and Massinger* (Chapel Hill, NC, 1939).

—— 'Middleton's *The Phoenix*', in J. G. McManaway, G. E. Dawson, and E. E. Willoughby (eds.), *Joseph Quincy Adams Memorial Studies* (Washington, DC, 1948), 743–53.

MEYER, EDWARD, *Machiavelli and the Elizabethan Drama* (Weimar, 1897).

MOLMENTI, POMPEO, *Venice: Its Individual Growth from the Earliest Beginnings to the Fall of the Republic*, tr. H. F. Brown, Part III: *The Decadence*, 2 vols. (1908).

MORRIS, BRIAN (ed.), *John Webster*, Mermaid Critical Commentaries (1970).

MUIR, KENNETH, *The Sources of Shakespeare's Plays* (1977).

MULRYNE, J. R., '*The White Devil* and *The Duchess of Malfi*', in J. R. Brown and B. Harris (eds.), *Jacobean Theatre*, Stratford-upon-Avon Studies 1 (1960), 201–25.

MUSGROVE, S., 'The Nomenclature of *King Lear*', *RES* NS 7 (1956), 294–8.

NEALE, J. E., *The Age of Catherine de Medici* and *Essays in Elizabethan History* (1963).

—— *Elizabeth I and her Parliaments*, 2 vols. (1965).

NOHL, JOHANNES, *The Black Death: A Chronicle of the Plague*, tr. C. H. Clarke (1926).

ORAS, ANTS, 'Fulke Greville's *Mustapha* and Robert Wilmot's *Tancred and Gismund*', *N&Q* 205 (1960), 24–5.

ORNSTEIN, ROBERT, *The Moral Vision of Jacobean Tragedy* (Madison and Milwaukee, 1960).

OUSBY, IAN, and OUSBY, HEATHER DUBROW, 'Art and Language in *Arden of Faversham*', *Durham University Journal*, 68 (1975–6), 47–54.

Oxford English Dictionary, 2nd edn., ed. J. A. Simpson and E. S. C. Weiner, 20 vols. (Oxford, 1989).

PATON, ALLAN PARK, 'Was Macbeth Himself the Third Murderer at Banquo's Death?', *N&Q* 4th ser., 4 (1869), 211.

PEARSON, JACQUELINE, *Tragedy and Tragicomedy in the Plays of John Webster* (Manchester, 1980).

PENDLETON, THOMAS A., 'Shakespeare's Disguised Duke Play: Middleton, Marston, and the Sources of *Measure for Measure*', in J. W. Mahon and T. A. Pendleton (eds.), *'Fanned and Winnowed Opinions': Shakespearean Essays Presented to Harold Jenkins* (1987), 79–98.

PHELPS, WILLIAM LYON, 'A Plea for Charles the Wrestler', in I. Gollancz (ed.), *A Book of Homage to Shakespeare* (Oxford, 1916), 362–3.

PICOT, GEORGES, *Histoire des États Généraux*, 4 vols. (Paris, 1872).

PINCISS, G. M., *Literary Creations: Conventional Characters in the Drama of Shakespeare and his Contemporaries* (Wolfeboro and Woodbridge, 1988).

POTTER, LOIS (ed.), *The Revels History of Drama in English* iv. *1613–1660* (1981).

PRAZ, MARIO, 'Machiavelli and the Elizabethans', *Proceedings of the British Academy*, 14 (1928), 49–97.

PROSSER, ELEANOR, *Hamlet and Revenge*, 2nd edn. (Stanford, 1971).

RAAB, FELIX, *The English Face of Machiavelli. A Changing Interpretation 1500–1700* (1965).

REIBETANZ, JOHN, 'Hieronimo in Decimosexto: A Private-Theater Burlesque', *RenD* NS 5 (1972), 89–121.

RIBNER, IRVING, *Jacobean Tragedy: The Quest for Moral Order* (1962).

—— *The English History Play in the Age of Shakespeare*, 2nd edn. (1965).

ROBERTS, CLAYTON, *The Growth of Responsible Government in Stuart England* (Cambridge, 1966).

ROSENBERG, MARVIN, *The Masks of Macbeth* (Berkeley, Ca., 1978).

SALGĀDO, GĀMINI, *The Elizabethan Underworld* (1977).

SAMAHA, JOEL, *Law and Order in Historical Perspective. The Case of Elizabethan Essex* (1974).

SANDERS, WILBUR, *The Dramatist and the Received Idea. Studies in the Plays of Marlowe and Shakespeare* (Cambridge, 1968).

SAUNDERS, CLAIRE, '"Dead in his Bed": Shakespeare's Staging of the Death of the Duke of Gloucester in *2 Henry VI*', *RES* NS 36 (1985), 19–34.

SCOTT, MARGARET, 'Machiavelli and the Machiavel', *RenD* NS 15 (1984), 147–74.

SEDGWICK, HENRY DWIGHT, *The House of Guise* (1938).

SKINNER, QUENTIN, *The Foundations of Modern Political Thought*, 2 vols. (Cambridge, 1978).

SMALLWOOD, R. L., '*'Tis Pity She's a Whore* and *Romeo and Juliet*', *Cahiers Élisabéthains*, 20 (October, 1981), 49–70.

SMITH, A. J., 'The Power of *The White Devil*', in MORRIS, 71–91.

SMITH, FRED MANNING, 'The Relation of *Macbeth* to *Richard the Third*', *PMLA* 60 (1945), 1003–20.

SMITH, G. C. MOORE, 'Edwardum Occidere Nolite Timere Bonum Est', *Times Literary Supplement*, 9 Aug. 1928, 581.

SMITH, LACEY BALDWIN, *Treason in Tudor England: Politics and Paranoia* (1986).

SMITH, ROBERT M., 'A Good Word for Oswald', in A. Williams (ed.), *A Tribute to George Coffin Taylor* (Chapel Hill, NC, 1952), 62–6.

SPARGO, JOHN WEBSTER, 'Clarence in the Malmsey-Butt', *MLN* 51 (1936), 166–73.

SPENCER, THEODORE, 'The Elizabethan Malcontent', in J. G. McManaway, G. E. Dawson, and E. E. Willoughby (eds.), *Joseph Quincy Adams Memorial Studies* (Washington, DC, 1948), 523–35.

SPIVACK, BERNARD, *Shakespeare and the Allegory of Evil: The History of a Metaphor in Relation to His Major Villains* (1958).

STOLL, ELMER EDGAR, *John Webster: The Periods of his Work as Determined by his Relations to the Drama of his Day* (Boston, 1905).

STONE, LAWRENCE, *The Crisis of the Aristocracy, 1558–1641* (Oxford, 1965).

STROUP, THOMAS B., 'Flamineo and the "Comfortable Words"', *Renaissance Papers, 1964* (Durham, NC, 1965), 12–16.

SULLIVAN, S. W., 'The Tendency to Rationalize in *The White Devil* and *The Duchess of Malfi*', *Yearbook of English Studies*, 4 (1974), 77–84.

TAWNEY, R. H., *Religion and the Rise of Capitalism: A Historical Study* (Harmondsworth, 1938).

THAYER, C. G., 'The Ambiguity of Bosola', *Studies in Philology*, 54 (1957), 162–71.

THOMPSON, STITH, *Motif-Index of Folk Literature*, rev. edn., 6 vols. (Copenhagen, 1955–8).

TILLEY, MORRIS PALMER, 'Shakespeare and his Ridicule of *Cambyses*', *MLN* 24 (1909), 244–7.

—— *A Dictionary of The Proverbs in England in the Sixteenth and Seventeenth Centuries* (Ann Arbor, Mich., 1950).

TWEEDCROFT, DIGGORY, *The Eng. Lit. Kit* (Hampton, 1982).

VIZETELLY, HENRY, *Count Königsmark and 'Tom of Ten Thousand'* (1890).

WAITH, EUGENE M., 'The Death of Pompey: English Style, French Style', in W. R. Elton and W. B. Long (eds.), *Shakespeare and Dramatic Tradition. Essays in Honor of S. F. Johnson*, (Newark, 1989), 276–85.

WEINSTOCK, HORST, 'Loyal Service in Shakespeare's Mature Plays', *Studia Neophilologica*, 43 (1971), 446–73.

WHARTON, T. F., '*The Malcontent* and "Dreams, Visions, Fantasies"', *Essays in Criticism*, 24 (1974), 261–74.

WIGGINS, MARTIN, '*Macbeth* and Premeditation', in A. Marwick (ed.), *The Arts, Literature, and Society* (1990), 23–47.

WILLIAMS, GEORGE WALTON, 'The Third Murderer in *Macbeth*', *Shakespeare Quarterly*, 23 (1972), 261.

WILSON, J. DOVER, 'The Composition of the Clarence Scenes in *Richard III*', *Modern Language Review*, 53 (1958), 211–14.

YACHNIN, PAUL, 'The Significance of Two Allusions in Middleton's *Phoenix*', *N&Q* 231 (1986), 375–7.

YOUNGBLOOD, SARAH, 'Theme and Imagery in *Arden of Feversham*', *SEL* 3 (1963), 207–18.

INDEX